Research on Group Treatment Methods

Research on Group Treatment Methods

A Selectively Annotated Bibliography

Bernard Lubin
C. Dwayne Wilson
Suzanne Petren
Alicia Polk

Foreword by George M. Gazda

**Published in cooperation with NTL Institute
for Applied Behavioral Science**

Bibliographies and Indexes in Psychology, Number 9

Greenwood Press
Westport, Connecticut • London

Library of Congress Cataloging-in-Publication Data

Research on group treatment methods : a selectively annotated
  bibliography / Bernard Lubin . . . [et al.]. ; foreword by George M.
  Gazda.
        p.   cm.—(Bibliographies and indexes in psychology, ISSN
  0742–681X   ; no. 9
      Includes index.
      ISBN 0–313–28339–7 (alk. paper)
      1. Group counseling—Bibliography.   2. Group guidance in
  education—Bibliography.   3. Group counseling for children—
  Bibliography.   4. Group counseling for teenagers—Bibliography.
  5. Group psychotherapy—Bibliography.   6. Group psychotherapy for
  children—Bibliography.   7. Group psychotherapy for teenagers—
  Bibliography.   I. Wilson, C. Dwayne.   II. Petren, Suzanne.
  III. Polk, Alicia.   IV. Title.   V. Series.
  Z7204.A6L83   1996
  [BF637.C6]
  016.61689′152—dc20   96–23114

British Library Cataloguing in Publication Data is available.

Library of Congress Catalog Card Number: 96–23114
ISBN: 0–313–28339–7
ISSN: 0742–681X

First published in 1996

Greenwood Press, 88 Post Road West, Westport, CT 06881
An imprint of Greenwood Publishing Group, Inc.

Printed in the United States of America

The paper used in this book complies with the
Permanent Paper Standard issued by the National
Information Standards Organization (Z39.48–1984).

10 9 8 7 6 5 4 3 2 1

NTL Institute is a community of members and staff whose purposes are to
advance the field of Applied Behavioral Science, eliminate oppression and
foster our core values by: Training in the theory and practice of group
dynamics, organizational change and societal change; Learning from these
experiences; Sharing the results of the learning; and, Engaging in inquiry,
knowledge building and the publication of findings.

Contents

Foreword

The great increase in research in group methods of treatment during the past three decades makes a selectively annotated bibliography on the subject both timely and useful. As senior editor of this work, Bernard Lubin continues his productive interest in this area. Previously, he compiled a comprehensive index to the group therapy literature that contained more than 14,000 items from 1906 through 1980. He also produced two book chapters on group therapy and several research based articles on group treatment.

Based on a selection of books and articles on group therapy, group psychotherapy, group counseling, and psychodrama, this bibliography emphasizes underlying commonalities among the methods. One of the things that we have learned from three decades of research is that no theoretical perspective, and no categorization (group therapy, group psychotherapy, group counseling, psychodrama), has a monopoly on conceptualization or research method. Thus, sampling from each of these areas should promote dissemination of findings and improved quality of research.

The majority of group interventions reported in the included citations are group psychotherapy and group counseling. Often these basic interventions are further defined by a prefacing descriptor of the specific theoretical model of group counseling or group psychotherapy employed, such as "Adlerian" group counseling or "rational-emotive" group psychotherapy. Interestingly, on occasion the descriptor might be used interchangeably, such as behavioral group counseling or behavioral group therapy.

The Preface indicates that the number of citations by age category represents the approximate ratio that exists in the research literature. I was interested in tallying the number of articles by age category that were described as group counseling or group psychotherapy/therapy. The ratios by groups are Children, 3 counseling/2 psychotherapy/therapy; Adolescents, 2.5 counseling/2 psychotherapy/therapy; College Students, 3 counseling/2 psychotherapy/therapy; Adults, 3 psychotherapy/therapy/1 counseling; and the Elderly, 4 psychotherapy/therapy/1 counseling.

Division 49 of the American Psychological Association, the Division of Group Psychology and Group Psychotherapy, applauds this work as an invaluable resource for group practitioners, educators, and researchers. It presents a gold mine of information. For example, meta-analyses can be computed on any number of research questions pertaining to therapeutic group interventions. Each age category can be analyzed for any number of issues that group specialists may wish to answer. For example, what are the most effective interventions by age category? An almost unlimited number of related questions can be studied within and *across* age categories.

This resource, therefore, should be in every major university library and in the library of every group educator, practitioner and researcher. The availability of this resource should significantly enhance the practice and research of group interventions. It should be the starting point for all group specialists who are studying, practicing, or researching group phenomena, especially as related to therapeutic/clinical interventions.

George M. Gazda
Professor Emeritus, The University of Georgia

Preface

As the title of this selectively annotated bibliography indicates, we have attempted to cast our search as broadly as possible, to sample from all domains of research articles and books having to do with group methods used to understand, change, ameliorate, or heal a broad range of human concerns. Shortly after beginning this project we became convinced that in many cases the terms "group therapy," "group psychotherapy," and "group counseling" are used without clear referents and frequently are used interchangeably, sometimes within the same article. We decided, therefore, to survey the research in all three of these areas.

The decision was made to err on the side of over-inclusion of types of research represented (outcome, process, predictive, instrument development, etc.). Although most of the studies included in this bibliography involve group comparisons utilizing sufficiently large numbers of subjects, we have included a few case studies because they contained instruments, methods, hypotheses, etc., that seemed to be worth noting for future more rigorous study.

Psychlit, Medline, and *Social Science Citation Index* were searched for the period 1970 through 1995. The annual number of items over this period included in the bibliography ranges from a low of 1 in 1971 to a high of 126 in 1992. Eight hundred eighty-four (49%) of the overall total of 1,793 items presented in the bibliography are annotated. In addition, 44 books are annotated. Only English-language items from journals and books that are available in university and large public libraries are included. In the case of prolific authors, we only present a few of their writings.

Of the several ways that the items could have been organized, we decided that an age categorization (children, adolescents, college students, adults, and the elderly) would involve the fewest preconceptions and would permit the broadest potential cross-fertilization across theoretical orientations, group and therapeutic techniques, work settings, etc. The Elderly is the smallest category in the bibliography and the largest is Adults. These are also the smallest and largest categories respectively to be found in the literatures.

Citations and annotations are indexed by key words. The following categories, because they have been receiving a considerable amount of attention in the group treatment literature, are indexed in more detail: alcoholism, anxiety, depression, long- and short-term treatment, outcome research, self-help groups, and stress and relaxation.

There have been many developments in theory, technique, training, research, etc., during the nine decades since the birth of the modern version of group therapy. Our major purpose has been to present a sampling of the research in group treatment during the past quarter century. Great strides have been made during the past 25 years in raising the quality of research in group treatment. Few would deny, however, that a great deal of work remains to be done in this complex and exciting area.

B.L.
D.W.
S.P.
A.P.

Research on Group Treatment Methods

1

Children

1. Abrahams, G. (1984). Treating the family-school interface: Multiple family group therapy with high risk children. *Dissertation Abstracts International, 44*(09), 2711.
    Hypothesized that multiple family group therapy treatment would lead to changes from extreme levels, either high or low, to more moderate levels in the following dimensions: family cohesion, expressiveness and conflict, and organization and control. Results indicate that the treatment group made significant changes in the desired direction in the family cohesion and control dimensions. The expressiveness, conflict and organization subscales produced equivocal results. Descriptive feedback from the experimental group suggests that over 90% of the participants experienced subjective growth in at least one of the hypothesized dimensions. Addresses implications for school psychologists.

2. Abramovitch, R., Konstantareas, M. M., & Sloman, L. (1980). An observational assessment of change in two groups of behaviorally disturbed boys. *Journal of Child Psychology and Psychiatry and Allied Disciplines, 21,* 133-141.
    Describes the usefulness of observational techniques in assessing the effectiveness of group therapy with five- to seven-year-old behaviorally disturbed males. The ratio of prosocial to aggressive behavior increased, but imitative behavior rate remained stable.

3. Adams, B. C. (1982). A comparison of the effects of two structured group counseling programs on the self-concept of fourth-grade students. *Dissertation Abstracts International, 43*(05), 1423A. (University Microfilm No. AAC82-24257)
    Studied the effects of two structured group counseling/guidance programs on fourth graders' self-concept: the DUSO program (Dinkmeyer, 1973), and the TA for Kids programs (Freed & Freed, 1979). Found no significant differences among the four groups—two group counseling programs, placebo group activities, or no group meetings—in improving self-concept.

4. Adams, K. (1993). Understanding speech-impaired children through the activity of group psychotherapy. *Masters Abstracts International, 31*(02), 919.

Examined the use of group therapy with four speech-impaired five- to seven-year-olds to better understand the child's subjective experience.

5.   Allen, J. M. (1991). Reality therapy with at-risk elementary students to enhance self-esteem and improve grades and attendance. *Dissertation Abstracts International, 51*(12), 4020. (University Microfilms No. AAC91-14834)
Divided 90 at- risk elementary school children into three groups: reality therapy group, study skills group and control group. Found no significant group differences in general self-esteem, academic grades and attendance rates. Found significant differences on teacher ratings of self-esteem between the reality therapy group and the study skills group, indicating the study skills group gained more control of their academic environment.

6.   Altman, H. A., & Scollon, J. (1973). The influence of process variables on self-esteem. *Psychology, 10,* 37-43.
Compared a group role-playing approach with a group discussion approach in the treatment of forty 4th-grade students exhibiting low self-esteem. Neither treatment group showed significant improvement relative to control subjects.

7.   Altmann, H. A., & Firnesz, K. M. (1973). A role-playing approach to influencing behavioral change and self-esteem. *Elementary School Guidance and Counseling, 7,* 276-281.
Assigned subjects with low scores on a behavioral rating form either to counseling groups using role-playing, or to control discussion groups. Found differences in the behavior ratings between the two groups.

8.   Amerikaner, M., & Summerlin, M. L. (1982). Group counseling with learning disabled children: Effects of social skills and relaxation training on self-concept and classroom behavior. *Journal of Learning Disabilities, 15,* 340-343.
Compared the effectiveness of a social skills treatment (SST) and a relaxation training treatment (RTT) with 46 first- and second-grade learning disabled children. RTT participants were less distractable and exhibited less acting out behavior while those in SST had higher self-concept scores.

9.   Amplo, J. E. (1981). Relative effects of group play therapy and Adlerian teacher training upon social maturity and school adjustment of primary grade students. *Dissertation Abstracts International, 41*(07), 3001. (University Microfilm No. AAC80-28220)

10.   Anderson, R. F., Kinney, J., & Gerler, E. R. (1984). The effects of divorce groups on children's classroom behavior and attitudes towards divorce. *Elementary School Guidance and Counseling, 19,* 70-76.
Compared third- to sixth-grade students with divorced parents who participated in group therapy with those who did not. The treatment group improved significantly in attitudes toward divorce and in classroom conduct.

11.   Arnold, T. J., & Simpson, R. L. (1975). The effects of a TA group on emotionally disturbed school-age boys. *Transactional Analysis Journal, 5,* 238-241.
Examined the effectiveness of a transactional analysis (TA) group experience with eight 10- to 16-year-old emotionally disturbed males. Subjects showed no

improvement in classroom behaviors of fighting, name calling, arguing, talking back or destroying property.

12.   Barke-Stein, J. A. (1976). A study of self-concept in the elementary school using different methods of group counseling. *Dissertation Abstracts International, 37*(02), 798. (University Microfilm No. AAC76-18321)

13.   Barnes, L. W. (1978). The effects of group counseling on the self-concept and achievement of primary grade Mexican American pupils. *Dissertation Abstracts International, 38*(10), 5920.

14.   Basso, R. (1991). A structured-fantasy group experience in a children's diabetic education program. *Patient Education and Counseling, 18,* 243-251.
       Describes the benefits of a group education and counseling program for children from 3 to 15 years old with insulin-dependent diabetes. Benefits include increased communications and enhanced ability to express emotions.

15.   Bellucci, M. T. (1975). Treatment of latency-age adopted children and parents. *Social Casework, 56*(5), 297-301.
       Describes group therapy designed to enable 9- to 13-year-old newly adopted children to share their angry and confused feelings.

16.   Ben-Aaron, M., & Jarus, A. (1978). Remarks on the communication of psychotic children as seen in group therapy. *Mental Health and Society, 5,* 224-230.

17.   Berry, K., Turone, R. J., & Hardt, P. (1980). Comparison of group therapy and behavioral modification with children. *Psychological Reports, 46,* 975-978.
       Compared self-concept (SC) psychotherapy with behavior modification (BM) therapy for 24 six- to nine-year-olds exhibiting disruptive classroom behaviors. Self-esteem scores did not change significantly for either group; the SC group showed greater changes on behavioral measures of improvement.

18.   Betts, E. L. (1976). Effects of behavioral group counseling on community college students. *Dissertation Abstracts International, 37*(02), 799A. (University Microfilm No. AAC76-19012)

19.   Bigbee, K. A. (1990). A group guidance approach to alter self-concept in elementary children. *Dissertation Abstracts International, 50*(07), 1942. (University Microfilm No. AAC89-25710)
       Examined the relative effectiveness of a structured and a non-structured group guidance and counseling approach in increasing self-concept in 70 fifth- and sixth-grade children. Neither approach effectively increases self-concept.

20.   Bingham, M. D. (1978). The effects of Adlerian group counseling on goal-oriented behavior and adjustment of children in a Parochial high school. *Dissertation Abstracts International, 38*(10), 5920. (University Microfilm No. AAC78-02885)

21.   Bishop, I. H. (1978). Comparative effects of cognitive and affective group counseling on self-esteem of second-grade children. *Dissertation Abstracts International, 38*(07), 3948. (University Microfilm No. AAC77-28036)

22.   Bland, M., Melang, P., & Miller, D. (1986). The effect of small group counseling on underachievers. *Elementary School Guidance and Counseling, 20,* 303-305.
       Examined the effectiveness of small group counseling with 47 underachieving fourth graders. The only significant difference between treatment and control subjects was on the Elementary Guidance Behavior Rating Scale for Teachers.

23.   Bleck, R. T. (1978). Developmental group counseling using structured play with elementary school disruptive children. *Dissertation Abstracts International, 38*(07), 3949.

24.   Blohm, A. L. A. (1978). Group counseling with moderately mentally retarded and learning disabled elementary school children. *Dissertation Abstracts International, 39*(06), 3362. (University Microfilms No. AAC78-24128)

25.   Bly, L. N. (1988). Self-help and child-abuse: Victims, victimizers, and the development of self-control. Groves conference on marriage and the family. *Contemporary Family Therapy, an International Journal, 10*(4), 243-255.

26.   Boren, R. (1983). The therapeutic effects of a school-based intervention program for children of the divorced. *Dissertation Abstracts International, 43*(12), 3811. (University Microfilm No. AAC83-09834)
       Discusses the use of a school-based group counseling program in treating third and fourth-grade children experiencing parental separation or divorce. No statistically significant differences were found for the experimental and control groups in outcome measures.

27.   Bozigar, J. A., & Hansen, R. A. (1984). Group treatment of elective mute children. *Social Work, 29,* 478-480.
       Examined the success of a group therapy program which used behavior modification and desensitization techniques to eliminate elective mutism in four 6 to 9 year old subjects.

28.   Brennan, D. J. (1989). Effects of group counseling and interactive bibliotherapy on children's adjustment to separation and divorce. *Dissertation Abstracts International, 51*(01), 413. (University Microfilm No. AAC90-15429)

29.   Buccolo, M. A. (1983). The effects of therapist intervention content style and work style on group psychotherapy process. *Dissertation Abstracts International, 44*(06), 1952. (University Microfilm No. AAC83-22757)

30.   Bullock, M. D. (1988). The effects of elementary school counseling on self-esteem, behavior and locus-of-control of elementary school children. *Dissertation Abstracts International, 49*(02), 200. (University Microfilm No. AAC88-04447)

31.   Bunting, K. P. (1985). The use and effect of puppetry and bibliotherapy in group counseling with children of divorced parents. *Dissertation Abstracts International, 45*(10), 3094. (University Microfilm No. AAC84-28466)

32.   Callanan, L. H. (1992). Group counseling for latency aged children of separation/divorce: A school based program to facilitate psychological and classroom adjustment. *Dissertation Abstracts International, 53*(11), 6004. (University Microfilm No. AAC93-08214)
       Investigated the effectiveness of a short-term group counseling program for elementary school children experiencing the divorce of their parents. Post-test measures showed no differences between the experimental and control groups in anxiety level and classroom adjustment.

33.   Campbell, C. B. (1983). An exploratory study of a group counseling program for early latency aged children of divorced parents in an elementary school in Southeastern Pennsylvania. *Dissertation Abstracts International, 44*(05), 1336.

34.   Carns, A. W. (1979). The effectiveness of parent group counseling as compared to individual parent consultation in changing parent attitudes and child behavior. *Dissertation Abstracts International, 40*(03), 1272. (University Microfilm No. AAC79-19717)

35.   Carpenter, P. (1984). "Green Stamp Therapy" revisited: The evolution of 12 years of behavior modification and psychoeducational techniques with young delinquent boys. *Psychological Reports, 54,* 99-111.
       Describes the improvement in empathy and feeling sensitivity in 10 to 13 year old delinquent boys after moving from a loosely structured format to a highly structured format.

36.   Carty, L. (1993). Group counseling and the promotion of mental health. *Journal for Specialists in Group Work, 18,* 29-39.
       Describes the success of a health promotion program conducted during group counseling in improving coping and social support among high school students.

37.   Chandler, E. S. (1978). Videotape feedback in group counseling: Improving self-concepts of children. *Dissertation Abstracts International, 38*(10), 5921. (University Microfilm No. AAC78-03664)

38.   Charlton, T., & Terrell, C. (1987). Enhancing internal locus of control beliefs through group counseling: Effects upon children's reading performance. *Psychological Reports, 60,* 928-930.

39.   Chase, J. L. (1991). Inpatient adolescent and latency-age children's perspectives on the curative factors in group psychotherapy. Special Issue: Child and Adolescent group psychotherapy. *Group, 15,* 95-108.
       Examined which factors were deemed most curative by group therapy members, who were 33 adolescent and 11 child psychiatric inpatients. Level of functioning and age had a minimal effect on perceptions, and members valued hope, cohesiveness, and universality.

40. Chen, C. (1984). Group therapy with Chinese schoolchildren. *International Journal of Group Psychotherapy, 34,* 485-501.
Examined a group therapy treatment for third- to fifth -grade Taiwanese students who were exhibiting behavior problems. Students participating in therapy showed significant improvement in behavior compared to the control group.

41. Chester, P. V. (1988). The efficacy of a specific adolescent group therapy. *Masters Abstracts International, 27*(03), 347. (University Microfilm No. AAC13-34957)
Describes a group therapy approach aimed at increasing internal locus of control and decreasing depression in six troubled adolescents. Therapy concentrated on problem-solving, role-playing, communication skills, self-control and anger management.

42. Clarkson, P. J. (1979). Effects of parent training and group counseling on children's functioning in elementary school. *Dissertation Abstracts International, 39*(08), 4726. (University Microfilm No. AAC79-01985)

43. Clement, P. W., Roberts, P. V., & Lantz, C. E. (1976). Mothers and peers as child behavior therapists. *International Journal of Group Psychotherapy, 26,* 335-359.

44. Coltrane, R. D. (1975). An investigation of unstructured play media and structured discussion group counseling techniques with preschool children. *Dissertation Abstracts International, 35*(07), 4154. (University Microfilm No. AAC75-00507)

45. Cordell, A. S., & Bergman-Meador, B. (1991). The use of drawings in group intervention for children of divorce. *Journal of Divorce and Remarriage, 17,* 139-155.

46. Costantino, G., Malgady, R. G., & Rogler, L. H. (1984). Cuentos folkloricos as a therapeutic modality with Puerto Rican children. *Hispanic Journal of Behavioral Sciences, 6,* 169-178.
Compared the effectiveness of Puerto Rican and Americanized folktale therapies with traditional group therapy for 208 Puerto Rican children in kindergarten through the third grade. Found that folktale therapies reduced trait anxiety of first graders, and raised comprehension scores on the WISC-R for all grades.

47. Culbertson, F. M. (1974). An effective, low-cost approach to the treatment of disruptive school children. *Psychology in the Schools, 11,* 183-187.
Examined an integrated approach using behavior modification and relationship therapy to help six highly disruptive kindergartners. By the end of the school year, the children developed positive attitudes toward school.

48. Davis-Susser, S. A. (1991). Group therapy for latency-age children of alcoholics: A treatment outcome study. *Dissertation Abstracts International, 51*(10), 5024. (University Microfilm No. AAC91-04105)

49. Deluca, A. V. (1980). The impact of a parent effectiveness training program on parents and the behavior of their problem school children. *Dissertation Abstracts International, 41*(01), 103A.

50. DeLucia, J. L., & Bowman, V. E. (1991). Internal consistency and factor structure of the Group Counselor Behavior Rating Form. *Journal for Specialists in Group Work, 16*(2), 109-114.
     Analysis of data from 104 graduate students indicated a high reliability and internal consistency for the 30 item instrument, which assesses group leadership behavior and skills. Four factors were indicated by factor analysis: interventions, applications of theory, facilitative conditions, and professionalism.

51. Denkowski, K. M., & Denkowski, G. C. (1984). Is group progressive relaxation training as effective with hyperactive children as individual EMG biofeedback treatment? *Biofeedback and Self-Regulation, 9,* 353-364.
     Compared group progressive relaxation (PR) and individual EMG biofeedback training in their utility for improving academic achievement and self-control in 45 hyperactive grade school students. The PR subjects reported significantly more internality in locus of control than did the EMG biofeedback subjects.

52. Dies, R. R., & Riester, A. E. (1986). Research on child group therapy: Present status and future directions. In A. E. Riester & I. A. Kraft (Eds.), *Child group psychotherapy: Future Tense* (pp. 173-220). Madison, CT: International Universities Press.
     Presents a summary of 18 impressionistic reports and 22 empirical studies of research on group therapy with children. The critique of the latter group of studies finds many deficiencies in design and execution, making a number of the stated positive findings unwarranted.

53. Dishion, T. J., Patterson, G. R., & Kavanagh, K. A. (1992). An experimental test of the coercion model: Linking theory, measurement, and intervention. In J. McCord & R. E. Tremblay (Eds.), *Preventing antisocial behavior: Interventions from birth through adolescence* (pp. 253-282). New York: Guilford Press.
     Shows the linkage of the measurement model to coercion theory development in a sample of 119 at-risk families who participated in the field experiment.

54. Donaldson-Williams, M. B. (1988). Children of divorce: A model for group counseling in the church. *Dissertation Abstracts International, 49*(08), 3499. (University Microfilm No. AAC88-20024)
     Describes the effectiveness of a church program designed to help children during and after their parents' divorce. Participants' self-esteem measures increased significantly.

55. Downing, C. J. (1977). Teaching children behavior change techniques. *Elementary School Guidance and Counseling, 11,* 277-283.
     Describes the effectiveness of a group counseling program designed to change the behavior of 37 classroom-disruptive elementary school children. The experimental group made greater academic achievement gains, was absent less frequently from school and made greater improvements in classroom behavior than did the control group.

56.   Drago, A. L. (1987). The effects of Experiential Developmental and Cognitive Multimodal Group Counseling on children of divorce. *Dissertation Abstracts International, 48*(04), 834. (University Microfilm No. AAC87-14664)

57.   Eaker, H. A., Allen, S. S., Gray, J., & Heckel, R. V. (1982). A factor-analytic study of a group therapy screening scale for children and adolescents. *Journal of Clinical Psychology, 38,* 742-743.
       Describes the usefulness of factor analysis in evaluating a group prediction scale administered to 200 delinquent youths.

58.   Edleson, J. L., & Rosen, S. D. (1981). Investigations into the efficacy of short-term group social skills training for socially isolated children. *Child Behavior Therapy, 3,* 1-16.
       Describes two studies in which 81 socially withdrawn fourth to sixth-grade subjects participated in short-term group social-skills training.   Found no significant effects for the treatment groups relative to a control group.

59.   Ellison, R. J. (1985). Ego-Analytic Small Group Counseling with children of divorce. *Dissertation Abstracts International, 45*(12), 3548. (University Microfilm No. AAC84-29169)

60.   Feldman, G. M. (1984). An evaluation of an intensive group therapy program for behaviorally disruptive and academically underachieving upper elementary Black school children in an urban public school. *Dissertation Abstracts International, 46*(05) 1709. (University Microfilm No. AAC85-09363)

61.   Ferrante, R. J. (1986). An evaluation of a school-based group counseling program for fourth-, fifth- and sixth-grade children of divorce. *Dissertation Abstracts International, 47*(02), 772. (University Microfilm No. AAC86-09879) Examined the effects of a school based group counseling program for 22 fourth to sixth-graders of divorce, designed to address concerns about separation, divorce, and living with a stepparent. The program included guided discussion, problem-solving, bibliography, role-playing, and brainstorming. There were no differences between the experimental and control groups in locus of control or problem solving, but communication between children and their parents increased in the experimental group.

62.   Feuquay, D. A. (1980). The effects of structured group counseling and parent counseling-consultation on the reported self-concepts and observed behaviors of children diagnosed as learning disabled. *Dissertation Abstracts International, 40*(08), 4409. (University Microfilm No. AAC80-03569)

63.   Fong-Toy, A. (1986). The effects of a psychological guidance program on the self-esteem of children from divorced and intact families. *Dissertation Abstracts International, 46*(09), 2565. (University Microfilm No. AAC85-24720)

64.   Forrer, S. L. (1986). Divorce discussion groups for elementary-age children: A curriculum plan. *Dissertation Abstracts International, 46*(11), 3252. (University Microfilm No. AAC86-00741)

65.   Frankel, A. J. (1992). Groupwork with recovering families in concurrent parent
        and children's group. *Alcoholism Treatment Quarterly, 9*(3-4), 23-37.
        Presents a concurrent parent training-children's groupwork model (PTCGM) that
        improved parenting skills, opened up communication in recovering families,
        gave more support for the expression of feelings, and helped families gain
        insight into the effects of prior addictions on children. Results suggest that there
        was value in conducting parallel parent training and children's groups for
        recovering families. Most parents demonstrated the ability to apply effectively
        the parent training skills they learned in group with their children at home.

66.   Gamble, R. E. (1984). The effects of short-term group counseling on custodial
        parents and their minor children experiencing a family separation/divorce.
        Dissertation Abstracts International, 45(05), 1298A.
        Offered short-term, structured group counseling to custodial parents and their
        minor children immediately after the parents' separation; a matched control
        group was provided no treatment. Results demonstrated that subjects from both
        groups were functioning within the "average" or normal ranges established by
        specific tests. The lowest functional area (non-clinical) was income management
        for adults. The experimental groups improved significantly over the control
        groups in only one area for adults and one area for children, physical symptoms
        and dependency, respectively. In all other clinical areas, the experimental and
        control groups showed no significant between group differences.

67.   Garvin, V., Leber, D., & Kalter, N. (1991). Children of divorce: Predictors of
        change following preventive intervention. *American Journal of Orthopsychiatry,
        61,* 438-447.
        Examined the effectiveness of a preventive intervention program with 53 fourth
        and fifth-grade children of divorce. Program participants showed improvement
        in adjustment.

68.   Gaulden, G. L. (1975). Developmental-play group counseling with early primary
        grade students exhibiting behavioral problems. *Dissertation Abstracts
        International, 36*(05), 2628. (University Microfilm No. AAC75-24150)

69.   Gauldin, K. B. (1982). A study of the relationships among the self-concept,
        group counseling, and family structure of fourth-grade boys. *Masters Abstracts
        International, 20*(01), 25. (University Microfilm No. AAC13-17119)

70.   George, D. A. (1993). Impact of structured group therapy on problematic
        sexualized and non-sexualized behaviors in victims of child sexual abuse.
        Dissertation Abstracts International, 54(06), 3339. (University Microfilm No.
        AAC93-24337)
        Examined the use of a Parallel Group Treatment Program with 25 Latino and
        36 Caucasian victims of childhood sexual abuse, ranging from 4 to 16 years old.
        Discusses cultural impact on participation in group therapy.

71.   Gerler, E. R., Kinney, J., & Anderson, R. F. (1985). The effects of counseling
        on classroom performance. *Special Issue: Multimodal approaches. Journal of
        Humanistic Education and Development, 23,* 155-165.

Multimodal group and individual treatment methods with 41 underachieving third and fourth-grade students showed positive changes in grades and in perceptions of classroom behavior.

72.   Giacobbe, G. A., & Traynelis-Yurek, E. (1992). Attitudinal changes as measured by the Jesness Behavior Checklist in a residential peer group program. *International Journal of Adolescence and Youth, 3,* 345-351.
Describes the usefulness of a residential peer group therapy program in treating 130 adolescents in rehabilitative treatment. The greatest change was between pre- and post-test measurements of obtrusiveness, conformity and rapport.

73.   Gifford, C. A. (1994). Changes in self-concept and mothers' perceptions of change in self-concept in latency-age children in group treatment. *Dissertation Abstracts International, 54*(12), 6460. (University Microfilm No. AAC94-08183)

74.   Ginsberg, B. G., Stutman, S. S., & Hummel, J. (1978). Group filial therapy. *Social Work, 23,* 154-156.
Reports on a group program in which parents conduct play therapy with their withdrawn or acting-out first-grade children. After six months, four of the six children showed improvement in behavior.

75.   Greene, R. L. (1976). The effects of group counseling and consultation on the classroom behaviors and attitudes of selected elementary school children. *Dissertation Abstracts International, 37*(01), 144. (University Microfilm No. AAC76-14688)

76.   Griesinger, W. S. (1978). Short-term group counseling of parents of handicapped children. *Dissertation Abstracts International, 39*(02), 675A.

77.   Grossman, F., & Retish, P. M. (1976). Classroom counseling: An approach to improve student self-concept. *Counseling and Values, 21,* 64-66.
Describes the success of a program designed to improve the self-concept of 500 Black sixth graders. The program used a group counseling format in which students were encouraged to discuss problems and issues.

78.   Gumaer, J., & Myrick, R. D. (1974). Behavioral group counseling with disruptive children. *School Counselor, 21,* 313-317.
Discusses a study implementing client centered and behavior modification techniques in group counseling, with 24 disruptive children. Subjects reduced disruptive behaviors.

79.   Guttman, K. A. (1994). Evaluating the effect of an elementary small group counseling program on various components of self-esteem and related behaviors. *Dissertation Abstracts International, 54*(07), 2466. (University Microfilm No. AAC93-33251)

80.   Gwynn, C. A., & Brantley, H. T. (1987). Effect of a divorce group intervention for elementary school children. *Psychology in Schools, 24,* 161-164.
Reports the success of a primary prevention educational support group for 60 nine to eleven year old children of divorce. Intervention resulted in decreases

in anxiety, depression, and negative feelings about divorce, and in increases in information about divorce.

81.   Hall-Marley, S. E., & Damon, L. (1993). Impact of structured group therapy on young victims of sexual abuse. Special Issue: Group treatment after child and adolescent sexual abuse. *Journal of Child and Adolescent Group Therapy, 3,* 41-48.
Describes the effectiveness of the parallel group model of L. Damon and J. Waterman (1986) in caring for 13 victims of sexual abuse, aged four to seven years. Findings suggest that the model is effective in decreasing problematic behaviors.

82.   Hamburger, D. B. (1977). Group counseling as a means of effecting change in reported self-concepts of children. *Masters Abstracts International, 15*(01), 13. (University Microfilm No. AAC13-09054)

83.   Hankins, E. G. (1977). The comparative effectiveness of Adlerian group counseling with homework and Adlerian group counseling without homework in the elementary school. *Dissertation Abstracts International, 37*(08), 4864. (University Microfilms No. AAC77-01546)

84.   Hargrave, G. E., & Hargrave, M. C. (1979). A peer group socialization therapy program in the school: An outcome investigation. *Psychology in the Schools, 16,* 546-550.

85.   Hartsfield, L. D. (1990). A study to compare the play media model to the Carkhuff model in relation to self-concept, school attendance, and teacher perception in an elementary school setting. *Dissertation Abstracts International, 51*(05), 1509. (University Microfilm No. AAC90-20331)

86.   Hayes, E. J., Cunningham, G. K., & Robinson, J. B. (1977). Counseling focus: Are parents necessary? *Elementary School Guidance and Counseling, 12,* 8-14. Compared direct versus indirect group counseling with the parents of 92 fifth- and sixth-grade students exhibiting behavior problems. There were no differences between the types of counseling in student motivation, self-esteem and anxiety; both counseling groups scored higher than the no-treatment control on all measures.

87.   Heckel, R. V., Hursh, L., & Hiers, J. M. (1977). Analysis of process data from token groups in a summer camp. *Journal of Clinical Psychology, 33,* 241-244. Forty-two 8- to 15-year-olds attending summer camp for disturbed children were treated with group therapy combined with a token economy, using peer judgements as the basis for token awards. After treatment, irrelevant responses and leader-directed responses declined, while group responses and decision-making increased.

88.   Henthorn, J. W. (1980). An experimental study of a group counseling approach to improve the perceived self-concept and cognitive skills of Title I primary school children. *Dissertation Abstracts International, 41*(04), 1404. (University Microfilm No. AAC80-21169)

89.   Hett, G. G., & Rose, C. D. (1991). Counselling children of divorce: A divorce lifeline program. *Canadian Journal of Counselling, 25,* 38-49.
       Reports on the effectiveness of a group counseling program for 6- to 12-year-old children of divorce. Found no differences between the counseling group and a control group in locus of control and problem behaviors, but found significant differences in other areas.

90.   Hiebert-Murphy, D., de- Luca, R. V., & Runtz, M. (1992). Group treatment for sexually abused girls: Evaluating outcome. *Families in Society, 73,* 205-213.
       Reports on an evaluation of a group therapy program used with five sexually abused girls from seven to nine years old. The girls improved on internalizing symptoms, externalizing behaviors, and sexual behavior problems.

91.   Hill, S. G. (1983). The effects of a program of structured group counseling on the self-concept and leadership skills of disadvantaged gifted elementary school students. *Dissertation Abstracts International, 43*(11), 3510. (University Microfilm No. AAC83-07094)

92.   Hinton, P. O. (1984). The impact of the Hammond Group Counseling Model with fourth- and fifth-grade children of divorce. *Dissertation Abstracts International, 45*(05), 1298. (University Microfilm No. AAC84-19061)

93.   Hoare, P., & Kerley, S. (1992). Helping parents and children with epilepsy cope successfully: The outcome of a group programme for patients. *Journal of Psychosomatic Research, 36,* 759-767.

94.   Jacobsen, L. K., Sweeney, C. G., & Racusin, G. R. (1993). Group psychotherapy for children of fathers with PTSD: Evidence of psychopathology emerging in the group process. *Journal of Child and Adolescent Group Therapy, 3,* 103-120.
       Examines a psychotherapy group conducted with children of Vietnam veterans experiencing post-traumatic stress disorder (PTSD). Describes changes in the group, noting that significant levels of psychopathology were identified in many group members.

95.   Johnson, J. H., Rasbuy, W. C., & Siegel, L. J. (1986). *Approaches to child treatment: Introduction to theory, research, and practice.* New York: Pergamon Press.
       Reviews 20 years of outcome research in group therapy with children. Included are findings of research from the psychoanalytic, client centered, behavioral, and eclectic approaches.

96.   Jupp, J. J., & Purcell, I. P. (1992). A school-based group programme to uncover and change the problematic beliefs of children from divorced families. *School Psychology International, 13,* 17-29.
       Discusses use of a group intervention (GI) with 11- to 13-year-olds whose parents had been divorced for less than three years. GI reduced feelings of shame, increased acceptance of changed family circumstances and awareness of common problems faced by children of divorce.

97.   Keat, D., Metzgar, K. L., Raykovitz, D., & McDonald, J. (1985). Multimodal counseling: Motivating children to attend school through friendship groups. Special Issue: Multimodal approaches. *Journal of Humanistic Education and Development, 23,* 166-175.

98.   Kendall, P. C. (1982). Individual versus group control cognitive-behavioral self-control training: 1-year follow-up. *Behavior Therapy, 13,* 241-247.
       Describes the differing benefits of individual and group therapy for nine-year-olds with behavior problems. All subjects showed improvements but in different areas: Those in group therapy improved in self-control while those in individual therapy improved in recall of the ideas learned.

99.   Kendall, P. C., & Zupan, B. A. (1981). Individual versus group application of cognitive behavioral self-control procedures with children. *Behavior Therapy, 12,* 344-359.
       Describes cognitive behavioral self-control individual and group training with third- to fifth-grade children. The therapy succeeded in improving self-control.

100.   Kern, R. M., & Hankins, G. (1977). Adlerian group counseling with contracted homework. *Elementary School Guidance and Counseling, 11,* 284-290.

101.   Kidd, N. V. (1977). The effect of group counseling and mini courses on women in a community college. *Dissertation Abstracts International, 38*(02), 633A. (University Microfilm No. AAC77-17702)

102.   Kilmann, P. R., Henry, S. E., Scarbro, H., & Laughlin, J. E. (1979). The impact of affective education on elementary school underachievers. *Psychology in the Schools, 16,* 217-223.
       Compared 63 underachieving fourth- to sixth- grade participants in counseling groups with 77 underachievers receiving no treatment. Group counseling participants showed greater increase in reading skills and described themselves as more emotionally stable, vigorous, venturesome, and warmhearted than did the controls.

103.   Klein, R. W. (1990). Social skills training and parent intervention with learning-disabled children. *Dissertation Abstracts International, 51*(06), 1911. (University Microfilm No. AAC90-21870)

104.   Knudsen, W. W. (1985). Psychopuppetry, non-directive group play therapy using puppets as the intermediary objects: A comparison with traditional non-directive group counseling or no counseling in the treatment of emotionally handicapped elementary school children. *Dissertation Abstracts International, 45*(08), 2452. (University Microfilm No. AAC84-25281)

105.   Kolko, D. J., Watson, S., & Faust, J. (1991). Fire safety/prevention skills training to reduce involvement with fire in young psychiatric inpatients: Preliminary findings. *Behavior Therapy, 22,* 269-284.
       Compared the effectiveness of a fire safety prevention/skills training condition (FSST) with an individual fire assessment awareness condition (FAA) on the fire setting behaviors of 24 4- to 8-year-old psychiatric inpatients. FSST subjects exhibited a significant improvement in fire safety knowledge and a reduction in

contact with fire-related toys. At six month follow-up, FSST subjects were also reported to have less contact with fire than FAA subjects.

106.   Lang, F. A. (1975). Effects of maternal group counseling on the academic achievement of high risk first-grade children. *Dissertation Abstracts International, 36*(03), 1309. (University Microfilms No. AAC75-20925)

107.   Lewis, H. W. (1984). A structured group counseling program for reading disabled elementary school students. *School Counselor, 31,* 454-459.
       Compares a structured group counseling program with a nondirective program for 24 elementary school students in a remedial reading program. The structured group showed no significant gains in self-concept, anxiety scores, or reading rates, but demonstrated significantly higher reading comprehension.

108.   Lewis, W. (1980). A structured group counseling program for reading disabled elementary students. *Dissertation Abstracts International, 40*(08), 4493. (University Microfilms No. AAC80-04457)

109.   Little, L. F. (1981). The impact of Gestalt group psychotherapy on parents' perceptions of children identified as problematic. *Dissertation Abstracts International, 42*(02), 616A.

110.   March, J. S. (1995). Cognitive-behavioral psychotherapy for children and adolescents with OCD: A review and recommendations for treatment. *Journal of the American Academy of Child and Adolescent Psychiatry, 34,* 7-18.
       Critically reviews 32 articles on the use of cognitive-behavioral therapy—graded exposure and response prevention—in treating children and adolescents with obsessive-compulsive disorders (OCD). Concludes that the method is beneficial.

111.   Marmorale, A. M., & Brown, F. (1974). Mental health intervention in the primary grades. *Community Mental Health Journal, Monograph Series, 7,* 63.
       Describes a program that provided counseling, remedial reading, medical treatment, case work, consultation, and group work to a group of 145 first graders. After two years, no differences were found between program subjects' and controls' scores on a wide range of tests, including the Wechsler Intelligence Scale test.

112.   McCarthy, M. C. (1982). An investigation to determine if a model group counseling program can affect the A-Trait and A-State anxiety of children who are under stress. *Dissertation Abstracts International, 43*(03), 674. (University Microfilm No. AAC82-18294)

113.   McCollum, P. S., & Anderson, R. P. (1974). Group counseling and reading disabled children. *Journal of Counseling Psychology, 21,* 150-155.
       Compared 24 minimally brain damaged 10- to 14-year-olds who had participated in Adlerian group counseling sessions to 24 children who had not. Counseling group subjects displayed significant increases in oral and reading vocabulary skills, but not in sentence comprehension.

114.   McKinney, W. E. (1992). Training elementary students to cope with stressful change and their subsequent performance in junior high school. *Dissertation Abstracts International, 52*(11), 3829. (University Microfilm No. AAC92-12110)

115.   Meyer, D. J. (1982). Effects of rational-emotive group therapy upon anxiety and self-esteem of learning disabled children. *Dissertation Abstracts International, 42*(10), 4201. (University Microfilm No. AAC82-05578)

116.   Michielutte, W. L. (1977). The use of group tutorial and group counseling methods in the investigation of causal relationships between self-concept and reading achievement among underachieving sixth-grade boys. *Dissertation Abstracts International, 37*(08), 4155. (University Microfilms No. AAC77-03955).

117.   Millaway, J. H. (1975). A study of failure in first grade and second grade and intervention through group counseling. *Dissertation Abstracts International, 35*(09), 5823. (University Microfilm No. AAC75-07058)

118.   Mistur, R. J. (1978). Behavioral group counseling with elementary school children: A model. *Dissertation Abstracts International, 38*(12), 142. (University Microfilm No. AAC78-09294)

119.   Mitchum, N. T. (1979). The effects of group counseling on the self-esteem, achievement and sex role awareness of children. *Dissertation Abstracts International, 39*(07), 4062. (University Microfilm No. AAC79-00079).

120.   Mitchum, N. T. (1991). Group counseling for Navy children. *School Counselor, 38,* 372-377.
       Describes a group counseling program designed to help 22 fifth graders experiencing the naval deployment of their fathers.

121.   Moltane, D. H. (1988). Improving the behaviors, self-concept, and achievement of learning-disabled children through group counseling using relaxation therapy. *Dissertation Abstracts International, 48*(12), 3053. (University Microfilm No. AAC87-29885)

122.   Moses, M. D. (1979). The effects of an Adlerian group counseling approach utilizing rehearsal with puppetry in decreasing the social isolation of withdrawn children. *Dissertation Abstracts International, 40*(05), 2485.

123.   Moulton, L. P. (1991). The impact of group counseling and stress management on reported depression, anxiety, attitude toward divorce, school functioning, and behavior of children of divorce. *Dissertation Abstracts International, 52*(06), 2028. (University Microfilm No. AAC91-3003)

124.   Newcomer, B. L., & Morrison, T. L. (1974). Play therapy with institutionalized mentally retarded children. *American Journal of Mental Deficiency, 78,* 727-733.

125.   Nixon, C. D., & Singer, G. H. (1993). Group cognitive-behavioral treatment for excessive parental self-blame and guilt. *American Journal on Mental Retardation, 97*(6), 665-672.
        Randomly assigned 34 mothers of children with severe disabilities either to a treatment group, using behavioral and cognitive techniques to help mothers reduce their self-reported stress, or to a waiting list control condition. The mothers participated in counselor led classes, which covered topics relating to cognitive processes associated with guilt and self-blame. Results show significant reductions in measures of guilt, negative automatic thoughts, internal negative attributions, and depression. Briefly reviews theoretical and treatment literature concerning self-blame and guilt, and describes the derivative treatment.

126.   Nixon, R. (1983). The effects of group counseling on internal-external locus of control of children classified as learning disabled. *Dissertation Abstracts International, 43*(10), 3221. (University Microfilms No. AAC83-05371)
        Examined the effectiveness of intensive group counseling with 40 10- to 14-year-old low-income, inner-city elementary school males, classified as learning disabled. Found no significant differences between the treatment and control groups in locus of control and self-concept.

127.   O'Leary, M. A. (1985). A study of the effects of group counseling for parents who have exceptional children. *Masters Abstracts International, 23*(03), 324.

128.   Pasnau, R. O. (1976). Coordinated group psychotherapy of children and parents. *International Journal of Group Psychotherapy, 26,* 89-103.
        Compared the effectiveness of coordinated group psychotherapy of children and parents in the treatment of behaviorally disturbed boys from seven to nine years old. Both groups progressed; parents were better able to cope with problems and the children's behavior improved.

129.   Pedro-Carroll, J. L., Alpert-Gillis, L. J., & Cowen, E. L. (1992). An evaluation of the efficacy of a preventive intervention for fourth- to sixth-grade urban children of divorce. *Journal of Primary Prevention, 13,* 115-130.
        Evaluates the Children of Divorce Intervention Program (CODIP), a preventive intervention based on coping skills and social support, using fourth- to sixth-grade urban children of divorce. The subjects improved in levels of adjustment.

130.   Pendergast, M. M. (1992). The effects of brief interventions on children of divorce. *Dissertation Abstracts International, 52*(08), 4494. (University Microfilm No. AAC91-34990)

131.   Pevsner, R. K. (1981). Parent training and group therapy versus individual family therapy in the treatment of child behavior problems. *Dissertation Abstracts International, 41*(09), 3538B.

132.   Poitras-Martin, D., & Stone, G. L. (1977). Psychological education: A skill-oriented approach. *Journal of Counseling Psychology, 24,* 153-157.
        Compared the utility of two group approaches to problem solving with 30 sixth graders: skills-training, and exposure to films and discussions related to problem-solving skills. The training group generated more alternatives than the

film and discussion group, but both approaches resulted in improved problem-definition skills.

133.   Pringle, J. A. H. (1984). Divorce education and its effects on learning behavior and personal and social adjustment of children. *Dissertation Abstracts International, 45*(06), 1644. (University Microfilm No. AAC84-20359)

134.   Provenzano, A. J. (1985). Maladaptive school behavior during the child-adolescent transition: Parent-child perceptions and the impact of cognitive-behavioral counseling. *Dissertation Abstracts International, 45*(08), 2674. (University Microfilm No. AAC84-25168)

135.   Ramage, R. L. (1979). A study of the effects of activity group counseling on the self-concepts, teachers' ratings of student behavior, and achievement of fourth- and fifth-grade students with learning disabilities. *Dissertation Abstracts International, 40*(04), 1882. (University Microfilm No. AAC79-21769)

136.   Ratusnik, C. M., & Ratusnik, D. L. (1976). A therapeutic milieu for establishing and expanding communicative behaviors in psychotic children. *Journal of Speech and Hearing Disorders, 41,* 70-92.

137.   Raynor, C. M. (1992). Managing angry feelings: Teaching troubled children to cope. *Perspectives in Psychiatric Care, 28,* 11-14.
        Describes the incorporation of rational emotive therapy into an assertiveness training group aimed at teaching depressed, hyperactive children to cope with anger. Subjects were more able to express feelings verbally and to respond to and share with one another.

138.   Reid, H. A. (1989). Social learning therapy for families with aggressive boys: Individual family versus parent-group treatment. *Dissertation Abstracts International, 50*(06), 1566. (University Microfilm No. AAC89-21062)

139.   Rempel, K., Hazelwood, E., & McElheran, N. (1993). Brief therapy group for mothers of troubled children. *Journal of Systematic Therapies, 12*(1), 32-48.

140.   Rhodes, S. L. (1973). Short-term groups of latency-age children in a school setting. *International Journal of Group Psychotherapy, 23,* 204-216.
        Describes the effectiveness of conventional group therapy designed to solidify ego development, in the treatment of 22 children. Subjects were able to share their problems, explore feelings and make changes relative to their attitudes and behavior.

141.   Richmond, F. (1979). The effects of group counseling combined with audiotaped and videotaped feedback upon fourth- and sixth-grade children. *Dissertation Abstracts International, 39*(10), 5956. (University Microfilm No. AAC79-07155)

142.   Roberson, A. B. (1979). An elementary school cross-age group counseling program: Changes in self-concept, career goals, and career-related activities preference. *Dissertation Abstracts International, 40*(02), 681. (University Microfilm No. AAC79-17074)

143. Roe, V. (1993). An interactive therapy group. *Child Language Teaching and Therapy, 9,* 133-140.
Presents two case studies of selectively mute children and the development of an interactive therapy group using puppets, musical instruments and stories.

144. Rosal, M. L. (1993). Comparative group art therapy research to evaluate changes in locus of control in behavior disordered children. *Arts in Psychotherapy, 20,* 231-241.

145. Rose, C. C., & Rose, S. D. (1992). Family change groups for the early school age child. *Special Services in the Schools, 6,* 113-127.
Describes the successful use of reading, relaxation and imagery training, modeling, cognitive correction, token reinforcement, and interactive games and crafts in treating five- to seven-year-old children undergoing family changes.

146. Rosenberg, J., & Cherbuliez, T. (1979). Inpatient group therapy for older children and pre-adolescents. *International Journal of Group Psychotherapy, 29,* 393-405.
Describes a group therapy approach for treating severely disturbed 8- to 12-year-old inpatients which stressed restraint, direct involvement of the co-therapists, and group structure.

147. Rotar, F. E. (1980). A group counseling approach using the 'human development program' in grades kindergarten through six. *Dissertation Abstracts International, 40*(10), 5326. (University Microfilm No. AAC80-07312)

148. Rutledge, P. B. (1975). Effects of short-term multiple treatment group counseling on social interaction perceptions of isolate-rejectees in fifth and sixth grades. *Dissertation Abstracts International, 36*(03), 1315. (University Microfilm No. AAC75-18511)

149. Sabatini, S. G. (1976). An investigation of play group counseling. *Dissertation Abstracts International, 36*(12), 7875. (University Microfilm No. AAC76-13496)

150. Sameck, A. M. (1991). A structured small-group counseling intervention to assist children with adjustment to divorce. *Dissertation Abstracts International, 52*(03), 807. (University Microfilm No. AAC91-21655)

151. Sayger, T. V., Szykula, S. A., & Sudweeks, C. (1992). Treatment side effects: Maternal positive and negative attributes of child-focused family therapy. *Child and Family Behavior Therapy, 14*(1) 1-9.

152. Schectman, Z., Vurembrand, N., & Malajak, N. (1993). Development of self-disclosure in a counseling and therapy group for children. *Journal for Specialists in Group Work, 18,* 189-199.
Examined the development and self-disclosure of eight socially incompetent third grade girls who participated in a counseling and therapy group. Although self-disclosure increased over time, this was dependent upon specific activities, individual differences and length of treatment.

153. Schilling, R. F., Koh, N., Abramovitz, R., & Gilbert, L. (1992). Bereavement groups for inner-city children. Special Issue: Research and practice: Bridging the gap. *Research on Social Work Practice, 2,* 405-419.
      Describes a group intervention designed to help 38 inner-city 6- to 12-year-olds who had experienced the loss of a care giver. Differences between self-ratings and caregiver ratings of depression disappeared during treatment. Although the children remained depressed through the study, the program enabled them to develop a more mature concept of death.

154. Schofield, L. J., Hedlund, C., & Worland, J. (1974). Operant approaches to group therapy and effects on sociometric status. *Psychological Reports, 35,* 83-90.
      Examines the use of a behavior modification approach to group therapy with four hyperactive children, aged 8 to 10 years, living in a residential treatment center. Although subjects interacted more frequently with one another and showed increased attention to tasks, sociometric status remained unchanged.

155. Schofield, L. J., & Wong, S. (1975). Operant approaches to group therapy in a school for handicapped children. *Developmental Medicine and Child Neurology, 17,* 425-433.
      Describes the success of an operant approach to group therapy with mentally retarded and cerebral palsied children. Subjects showed improvement in social interaction, classroom behavior, and attention to tasks.

156. Schumacher, R. R. (1974). The influence of differential group composition on the effectiveness of group counseling with second-grade, third-grade, fourth-grade, and fifth-grade male children. *Dissertation Abstracts International, 35*(04), 1992. (University Microfilms No. AAC74-23261)

157. Scott, M. J., & Stradling, S. G. (1987). Evaluation of a group programme for parents of problem children. *Behavioural Psychotherapy, 15*(3), 224-239.
      Examined the results of a behaviourally based parental assistance program for low income and state-dependent single parents. Pre- and post-testing indicated that the program significantly reduced parental depression, inward and outward irritability, the perceived number and intensity of child behavior problems, and the level of perceived child conduct problems, impulsivity, and anxiety. The subjects' child management skills significantly improved. The reduction in child behavior problems was maintained at three and six month follow-up, and improvement in parental depression and irritability was maintained at three-month follow-up.

158. Shechtman, Z. (1991). Small group therapy and preadolescent same-sex friendship. *International Journal of Group Psychotherapy, 41,* 227-243.
      Examined the effectiveness of small group therapy in strengthening intimate same-sex friendships among 102 third- to sixth-grade students. Relative to controls, treatment subjects reported significant growth in intimate friendships.

159. Shechtman, Z. (1993). Group psychotherapy for the enhancement of intimate friendship and self-esteem among troubled elementary-school children. *Journal of Social and Personal Relationships, 10,* 483-494.

Evaluated the effect of group therapy on the close friendships and self-esteem of third- through sixth-grade Israeli students referred for social, learning, or emotional difficulties. Compared to controls, treatment subjects showed improved self-esteem and increased intimacy in close friendships.

160. Shechtman, Z. (1993). School adjustment and small group therapy: An Israeli study. *Journal of Counseling and Development, 72,* 77-81.
Examined the effects of small group therapy emphasizing interrelationships on 71 elementary school students with emotional, social, behavioral or learning difficulties. Subjects in the treatment group were viewed more positively by teachers, showed improved teacher and peer relationships and learning functions; they manifested reduced withdrawal, restlessness, depression, inattentiveness, aggression, disciplinary problems and absenteeism.

161. Shephard, C. S. (1975). The effect of group counseling on death anxiety in children with cancer. *Dissertation Abstracts International, 36*(05), 2723. (University Microfilm No. AAC75-25426)

162. Sheridan, J. T. (1982). Structured group counseling or explicit bibliotherapy as an in-school strategy for preventing problems in children from changing families. *Dissertation Abstracts International, 43*(03), 677. (University Microfilm No. AAC82-18935)

163. Shur, M. S. (1976). A group counseling program for low self-esteem preadolescent females in the fifth grade. *Dissertation Abstracts International, 36*(09), 5839. (University Microfilm No. AAC76-05475)

164. Silovsky, J. F., & Hembree-Kigin, T. L. (1994). Family and group treatment for sexually abused children: A review. *Journal of Child Sexual Abuse, 3,* 1-20.

165. Sinclair-Brown, W. (1981). A TA/redecision psychotherapy program for mothers who physically abuse and/or seriously neglect their children. *Dissertation Abstracts International, 42*(02), 788B.

166. Skuy, M., & Solomon, W. (1980). Effectiveness of students and parents in a psycho-educational intervention programme for children with learning problems. *British Journal of Guidance and Counselling, 8,* 76-86.
Divided thirty-eight 8 to 11 year old children into three conditions: youth counseling, youth counseling plus parent counseling, and control group. Effectiveness of the intervention program was supported, although not significantly.

167. Slosar, J. R. (1981). The psychological and behavioral effects of group counseling and megavitamin treatment in a school setting with handicapped children. *Dissertation Abstracts International, 42*(03), 1067.

168. Smith, C. S. (1979). Enhancing the self-concept of learning disabled children through group counseling. *Dissertation Abstracts International, 40*(02), 682. (University Microfilm No. AAC79-16238)

169. Snir, D., & Kuta, B. (1980). A group therapy experience using a social
      sensitivity game. *Israeli Journal of Psychology and Counseling in Education, 13,*
      102-106.
      Describes group therapy using a social sensitivity game, which included verbal
      self-expression, feedback, and the sharing of emotions. Encouraged self-control
      with tokens. Noted behavioral improvement in most of the seven 11-year-old
      subjects.

170. Sorsdahl, S. N., & Sanche, R. P. (1985). The effects of classroom meetings on
      self-concept and behavior. *Elementary School Guidance and Counseling, 20,* 49-
      56.
      Examined the effectiveness of group counseling in improving self-concept and
      classroom behavior of ninety-one 4th-grade students. Group counseling
      improved the subjects' behavior in meetings and in classrooms. During
      classroom meetings, self-concept improved but at post-test, it did not differ from
      controls.

171. Spitzer, A., Webster-Stratton, C., & Hollinsworth, T. (1991). Coping with
      conduct-problem children: Parents gaining knowledge and control. *Journal of
      Clinical Child Psychology, 20*(4), 413-427.

172. Srivastava, K. I. (1985). Socio-psychological factors of stammering and the
      problem of rehabilitation of statements. *Indian Psychological Review, 29,* 24-34.
      Examined the effect of group therapy on the stammering of 80 subjects, 10 years
      or older. Subjects showed improved adjustment in family, schools, offices and
      other public places. Found stammering to be related to physical and
      sociopsychological factors.

173. Staggs, A. M. (1980). Group counseling of learning disabled children in the
      intermediate grades enrolled in the public school special education program:
      Training in cognitive behavior modification. *Dissertation Abstracts International,
      40*(12), 6157. (University Microfilm No. AAC80-12141)

174. Stamps, L. W. (1973). The effects of intervention techniques on children's fear
      of failure behavior. *Journal of Genetic Psychology, 123,* 85-97.

175. Strunk, C. S., & Witkin, L. J. (1974). The transformation of a latency-age
      girls' group from unstructured play to problem-focused discussion. *International
      Journal of Group Psychotherapy, 24,* 460-470.
      Describes the effectiveness of a structured group comprised of an equal number
      of girls who were: impulsive and acting-out; inhibited and conforming.
      Following treatment, subjects improved behaviors and adopted more age
      appropriate patterns.

176. Sugar, M. (1993). Research in child and adolescent group psychotherapy.
      Journal of Child and Adolescent Group Therapy, 3, 207-226.

177. Sumlin, D. L. (1979). An affective-cognitive group counseling procedure for use
      with parents of handicapped children: A comparative study of its effectiveness
      for changing attitudes and training parents in a method of child guidance.
      Dissertation Abstracts International, 39(07), 4186A.

178.   Sutton, C. (1992). Training parents to manage difficult children: A comparison of methods. *Behavioural Psychotherapy, 20*(2), 115-139.
       Parents of preschool children participated in one of four parent training conditions: group, home visit, telephone, or waiting list control. Assessments conducted pre- and post-intervention and at 12 to 18 month follow-up indicated clinical improvement for all three active intervention conditions, compared to the control condition. However, there were no significant differences among the three active intervention conditions at post-intervention and follow-up.

179.   Swink, D. F., & Buchanan, D. R. (1984). The effects of sociodramatic goal-oriented role play and non-goal-oriented role play on locus of control. *Journal of Clinical Psychology, 40,* 1178-1183.
       Compared goal-oriented role play (GO) to non-goal-oriented role play therapy (NonGo) with 53 Black fifth graders. Compared to the NonGo subjects, GO subjects significantly increased their internal locus of control.

180.   Tannenbaum, M. J. (1992). Social-cognitive group therapy for children. *Dissertation Abstracts International, 53*(04), 2076. (University Microfilm No. AAC92-24620)

181.   Tarnow, P. M. (1988). Group therapy in orthopedagogical context. *Dissertation Abstracts International, 26*(01), 25.

182.   Taylor, W. F., & Hoedt, K. C. (1974). Classroom-related behavior problems: Counsel parents, teachers, or children? *Journal of Counseling Psychology, 21,* 3-8.
       Compared the effectiveness of group counseling with parents and teachers and group counseling with students alone in reducing classroom behavior problems of 372 children. Analysis showed that the indirect approach with the adults was more effective than the direct approach with the children.

183.   Terkelson, C. (1976). Making contact: A parent-child communication skill program. *Elementary School Guidance and Counseling, 11*(2), 89-99.
       Six elementary school students and 6 parents attended 12 counseling sessions aimed at developing skills in listening, conflict resolution, and value identification. Parents and children were counseled separately during the first six sessions and together in the remaining six sessions. Comparison of pre- and post-treatment responses showed some positive gains in parent-child communication. The children reported a greater change in their parents' behavior toward them than the parents reported about themselves.

184.   Thompson, W. R., & Randolph, D. L. (1973). A comparison of the relative effectiveness of two different group approaches to counseling with sixth-grade pupils. *Southern Journal of Educational Research, 7,* 66-79.
       Compared the effects of a structured versus unstructured approach to group therapy. The two groups of sixth graders showed no difference in self-concept, interpersonal relationships and school adjustment scores.

185.   Tidwell, R., & Bachus, V. A. (1977). Group counseling for aggressive school children. *Elementary School Guidance and Counseling, 12,* 2-7.

186.   Tiedemann, G. L., & Johnston, C. (1992). Evaluation of a parent training
       program to promote sharing between young siblings. *Behavior Therapy, 23,* 299-
       318.
       Evaluates the effectiveness of individual and group formats of a parenting
       program in promoting sharing between young siblings.   Parents were given
       information and taught behavioral techniques.   The observations and reports of
       sharing behavior evinced the program's positive effects, sustained over a six
       week follow-up period.

187.   Tobin, G. A. (1987). The design, implementation, and evaluation of an
       encouragement therapy group counseling process for elementary school children.
       Dissertation Abstracts International, 47(10), 3668. (University Microfilm No.
       AAC87-01988)

188.   Todd, J. F. (1989). The effects of problem-solving group counseling on
       academic social skills training for learning disabled children. *Dissertation
       Abstracts International, 51*(01), 120. (University Microfilms No. AAC90-
       9005682)
       Divided 34 learning disabled children into two groups, a treatment group and a
       control group, which focused on problem-solving and feelings, respectively.
       Each group received eight sessions of group counseling. Both groups displayed
       significant improvement in the areas of self-concept, teacher ratings and
       inappropriate classroom behaviors.

189.   Twardosz, S., Nordquist, V. M., Simon, R., & Botkin, D. (1983). The effect
       of group affection activities on the interaction of socially isolate children.
       Analysis and intervention in Developmental Disabilities, 3, 311-338.
       Describes two studies that used group affection activities to improve three isolate
       preschool children's peer interaction. In both studies, peer interaction increased
       after treatment.

190.   Ulman, L. T. (1974). A study of maternal group counseling in the elementary
       schools. *Dissertation Abstracts International, 35*(03), 264. (University Microfilm
       No. AAC74-20470)

191.   Utay, J. M. (1992). Effectiveness of a cognitive-behavioral group play therapy
       intervention on selected aspects of social skills of third- through sixth-grade
       students with learning disabilities. *Dissertation Abstracts International, 52*(08),
       2826. (University Microfilm No. AAC92-02167)

192.   Wagner, C. A. (1975). Selected characteristics of children differentially referred
       for group counseling. *Dissertation Abstracts International, 35*(08), 5042.
       (University Microfilm No. AAC75-03675)

193.   Wagner, R. P. (1989). An evaluation of school social work services from a kid's
       eye view. *Masters Abstracts International, 27*(03), 348. (University Microfilm
       No. AAC13-34972)

194.   Weingarten, M. A. (1985). A pilot study of the multidisciplinary management
       of childhood asthma in a family practice. *Journal of Asthma, 22,* 261-265.

Discusses the ventilatory capacity improvement in asthmatic children from 8 to 11 years old after participating in group and individual therapy. Addresses the potential of nonpharmaceutical therapy for childhood asthma.

195.   Weist, M. D., Vannatta, K., Waylan, K. K., & Jackson, C. Y. (1993). Social skills training for abused girls: Interpersonal skills training for sexually abused girls. *Behavior Change, 10,* 244-252.
Examined a group training program focused on improving interpersonal skills of four sexually abused girls aged 8 to 11. Subjects showed improvement in all trained behaviors, in perceived academic competence, peer functioning, appearance and in global self-concept.

196.   Westmoreland, S. C. (1975). Outdoor activity group experience and group counseling with institutionalized children and adolescents. *Dissertation Abstracts International, 35*(09), 5837. (University Microfilm No. AAC75-07072)

197.   Wiggins, J. D., & Wiggins, M. M. (1992). Elementary students' self-esteem and behavioral ratings related to counselor time-task emphases. *School Counselor, 39*(5), 377-381.
Examined the efficacy of classroom guidance (CG) versus individual counseling (IC) techniques in increasing elementary school students' self-esteem and positive behavior. Self-ratings changed in both groups, but IC students showed greater improvement.

198.   Wilkinson, G. S. (1977). Small group counseling with elementary school children of divorce. *Dissertation Abstracts International, 37*(10), 6287. (University Microfilm No. AAC77-08241)

199.   Wodarski, J. S., & Pedi, S. J. (1978). The empirical evaluation of the effects of different group treatment strategies against a controlled treatment strategy on behavior exhibited by antisocial children, behaviors of the therapist, and two self-rating scales that measure antisocial behavior. *Journal of Clinical Psychology, 34,* 471-481.

200.   Zacharias, M. A. (1993). The effectiveness of group psychotherapies with children from divorced families: An interaction of client and therapy variables. *Dissertation Abstracts International, 54*(02), 1118. (University Microfilm No. AAC93-10466)

201.   Ziegler, E. W., Scott, B. N., & Taylor, R. L. (1991). Effects of guidance intervention on perceived school behavior and personal self-concept: A preliminary study. *Psychological Reports, 68,* 50.
Describes the success of a structured guidance intervention group in improving fifth-grade girls' self-concept and school behavior.

202.   Zimmerman, G. A. (1987). Investigation of behavior therapy groups in a children and youth partial hospitalization program. *Dissertation Abstracts International, 48*(04), 885. (University Microfilm No. AAC87-11435)

203.   Zimmerman, W. M. (1980). Effects of short-term group counseling on gifted
       elementary students. *Dissertation Abstracts International, 40*(12), 6214.
       (University Microfilm No. AAC80-13891)

2

Adolescents

204. Abbott, W. J. (1985). The effect of reality therapy-based group counseling on the self-esteem of learning disabled sixth, seventh, and eighth graders. *Dissertation Abstracts International, 45*(07), 1989A.
Following treatment, the experimental group showed a significant and positive change on the Self-Esteem Inventory (SEI) Total score, the SEI General scale score, the SEI School scale score, and the Self form of the Jesness Behavior Checklist, as compared to the control group. A post-test analysis found no significant difference in the number of referrals in the experimental group compared to the control group.

205. Adams, B. N., Brownstein, C. A., Rennalls, I. M., & Schmitt, M. H. (1976). The pregnant adolescent: A group approach. *Adolescence, 11,* 467-485.

206. Albert, J. J. (1976). A comparison of changes in attendance, GPA, discipline referrals, and self-concept between tenth-grade students who were in short-term group counseling and tenth-grade students whose parents were in short-term group counseling. *Dissertation Abstracts International, 37*(02), 871. (University Microfilm No. AAC76-18319)

207. Allwood, L. V. (1981). The effects of transactional analysis groups on locus of control, self-concept, academic achievement, and attendance in an urban high school. *Dissertation Abstracts International, 41*(12), 4975. (University Microfilm No. AAC81-09057)

208. Anderson, L., Fodor, I., & Alpert, M. (1976). A comparison of methods for training self-control. *Behavior Therapy 7,* 649-658.

209. Andrews, D. A., & Young, J. G. (1974). Short-term structured group counseling and prison adjustment. *Canadian Journal of Criminology and Corrections, 16,* 5-13.
Compared 32 16- to 21-year-old male delinquents who participated in either group counseling designed to address the aspects of institutional life, or a routine orientation program. Counseling sessions had a significant effect on only the 16- to 17-year-old males.

210.   Apter, A., Sharir, I., Tyano, S., & Wijsenbeek, H. (1978). Movement therapy with psychotic adolescents. *British Journal of Medical Psychology, 51,* 155-159. Compared individual and group movement therapy with 13- to 18-year-old psychotic adolescents. Movement therapy was effective.

211.   Ashley, P. A. (1975). The effect of group counseling on the self-concept of high school females. *Dissertation Abstracts International, 36*(02), 698A.

212.   Babouri, E. M. (1985). Use of the group modality in the prevention of sexually transmitted diseases among adolescent girls. *International Journal of Adolescent Medicine and Health, 3-4,* 325-336.
       Examined the effectiveness of a group education approach to the prevention of sexually transmitted diseases (STDs) in a group of 34 Black and Hispanic adolescent girls from low socioeconomic, inner-city junior and senior high schools. Control subjects had an increase in STDs, while treatment subjects had no STDs during or at a 12 month follow-up.

213.   Baker, B. A. (1984). The effects of group counseling on junior high remedial reading students' self-concept. *Dissertation Abstracts International, 45*(02), 411A.
       Divided 90 junior high remedial reading students into three groups: a control group, a group who attended daily remedial reading class only (RR), and a group who attended daily remedial reading class plus daily group counseling (RR+C). Within a six-week period, RR+C did not significantly affect the students' self-concept. There was a significant difference in the reported happiness and satisfaction factor of self-concept for the RR students.

214.   Baker, C. R. (1987). A comparison of individual and group therapy as treatment of sexually abused adolescent females (Family dynamics, incest, victims. *Dissertation Abstracts International, 47*(10), 105. (University Microfilm No. AAC86-29832)
       Group therapy was at least as effective as individual therapy in treating depression, anxiety, and low self-concept in sexually abused adolescent females.

215.   Baldassano, J. (1991). The effects of interpersonal cognitive problem-solving group training on the classroom behavior of adolescent psychiatric patients. *Dissertation Abstracts International, 51*(10), 5020. (University Microfilm No. AAC91-07072)
       Adolescent psychiatric patients with a history of antisocial and disruptive classroom behavior participated in either training in Interpersonal Problem Solving Thinking training (IPST) or standard group therapy (SGT). Patients who received IPST training improved in areas of aggression, delinquent and externalizing behavior, while those receiving SGT did not.

216.   Bardill, D. R. (1977). A behavior-contracting program of group treatment for early adolescents in a residential treatment setting. *International Journal of Group Psychotherapy, 27,* 389-400.
       Describes the use of a behavior-contracting approach with adolescent boys to reduce impulsive acting-out behavior during group treatment. The program was successful in allowing group therapy to continue without many disruptions; the

boys also learned self-control, effective expression of emotions and ideas, and alternatives to aggressive behavior.

217. Bellus, S. B. (1984). The WISC-R in predicting success in group psychotherapy with juvenile delinquents. *Dissertation Abstracts International, 44*(07), 2234. (University Microfilm No. AAC83-25330)
The Wechsler Intelligence Scale for Children-Revised (WISC-R) did not predict success rate of the 95 adjudicated juveniles who participated in group psychotherapy.

218. Benavides, R. (1988). The effects of individual feedback tutoring on adolescents' verbalization performance in group therapy. *Dissertation Abstracts International, 48*(09), 2279. (University Microfilm No. AAC87-27339)

219. Benson, R. L. (1984). The comparison of the effect of two sex education models for families upon sex knowledge, general communication, and sexual communication. *Dissertation Abstracts International, 45*(03), 748A.

220. Berkovitz, I. H., & Sugar, M. (1976). An experience in teaching adolescent group psychotherapy: Observers become participants. *International Journal of Group Psychotherapy, 26,* 441-453.
Describes a project designed to increase trust between the teenage-participants in group therapy and the professionals conducting therapy. The project seemed to increase therapeutic effect and to encourage learning in the professionals.

221. Bernfeld, G., Clark, L., & Parker, G. (1984). The process of adolescent group psychotherapy. *International Journal of Group Psychotherapy, 34,* 111-126.
Examined the group development process of 22 13- to 17-year-old psychiatric inpatients participating in group therapy. Group role scores increased over time, individual role scores increased then decreased, task role scores decreased then stabilized, and clinical appropriateness scores increased over time.

222. Biasco, F., & Redfering, D. (1976). Effects of counselor supervision on group counseling Client's perceived outcomes. *Counselor Education and Supervision 15,* 216-220.
Examined the effect of supervision on counselor's effectiveness with Neighborhood Youth Corps participants. Those participating in groups in which the counselor was supervised had more positive feelings toward their experiences than those participating in groups in which the counselor was unsupervised.

223. Bibby, C. J. (1988). The effect of self-acceptance training on academic achievement and self-esteem in minority high school youth. *Dissertation Abstracts International, 49*(06), 1371. (University Microfilm No. AAC88-16396)
Examined whether self-acceptance training conducted in group counseling would significantly enhance self-esteem and academic achievement in 78 high school students. While treatment improved self-esteem scores, it did not improve academic achievement.

224. Birmingham, D. R. (1975). The effects of counselor-led group counseling and leaderless group counseling on anxiety, self-concept, and study habits among

high school seniors. *Dissertation Abstracts International, 35*(07), 4151. (University Microfilm No. AAC75-00870)

225.   Blackman, M., Pitcher, S., & Rauch, F. (1986). A preliminary outcome study of a community group treatment programme for the emotionally disturbed adolescents. *Canadian Journal of Psychiatry, 31,* 112-118.
Examined the progress of 31 emotionally disturbed adolescents, from ages 11 to 17, who participated in either day or evening programs. All participants reported significant positive changes in all areas, but these improvements were not substantiated by family members.

226.   Blanchard, C. W. (1994). Effects of ropes course therapy on interpersonal behavior and self-esteem of adolescent psychiatric inpatients. *Dissertation Abstracts International, 55*(02), 584B.

227.   Brandt, D. E. (1973). A descriptive analysis of selected aspects of group therapy with severely delinquent boys. *Journal of the American Academy of Child Psychiatry, 12,* 473-481.
Describes group therapy sessions at a day treatment facility for delinquent males, from 14 'to 17 years old. Staff contributed 50% of all responses, with participants discussing interpersonal relationships more positively than other topics.

228.   Brannon, J. M., & Troyer, R. (1991). Peer group counseling: A normalized residential alternative to the specialized treatment of adolescent sex offenders. *International Journal of Offender Therapy and Comparative Criminology, 35,* 225-234.

229.   Brennan, M. M. (1979). Self-concept change among pregnant adolescent girls as a result of small group counseling. *Dissertation Abstracts International, 39*(11), 5538B.

230.   Brenner, M. I. (1988). The impact of short-term group counseling on the social self-esteem of a seventh-grade Cambodian male. *Masters Abstracts International, 26*(01), 59.

231.   Brewster, R. J. (1978). Group counseling as an alternative to school suspension for high school smoking violators: Help or hindrance? *Dissertation Abstracts International, 39*(01), 370. (University Microfilm No. AAC78-00181)

232.   Brooks, B. D. (1975). Contingency management as a means of reducing school truancy. *Education, 95,* 206-211.
Describes the successful use of a modified token economy, a contract, and group guidance meetings in reducing truant behavior in 20 high school students.

233.   Brown, W., & Kingsley, R. F. (1975). The effect of individual contracting and guided group interaction upon behavior-disordered youth's self-concept. *Journal of School Health, 45*(7), 399-401.

234.   Bruyere, D. H. (1975). The effects of client-centered and behavioral group counseling on classroom behavior and self-concept of junior high school students

who exhibited disruptive classroom behavior. *Dissertation Abstracts International, 36*(03), 1299. (University Microfilm No. AAC75-18723)

235. Buldas, J. J. (1985). Using group psychotherapy for enhancing late adolescent self-concept: Comparing the effects of hypnosis and rational-emotive therapy. *Dissertation Abstracts International, 46*(01), 296B.

236. Burdsal, C., Force, R., C., & Klingsporn, M. J. (1989). Treatment effectiveness in young male offenders. *Residential Treatment for Children and Youth, 7*, 75-88.

237. Burton, G. M. (1988). A modified assertiveness training program using group counseling with Korean-American adolescents. *Dissertation Abstracts International, 48*(08), 2450. (University Microfilm No. AAC87-25691)

238. Carl, J. L. (1984). The effect of aerobic exercise and group counseling on the reduction of anxiety in special education students. *Dissertation Abstracts International, 44*(07), 2090A.
Found no significant difference on measured anxiety scales between the counseling treatment (CT) group and control group, or between the aerobic exercise (AE) treatment group and the control group. Indicates that nine weeks of AE or GC did not effect a difference between treatment and control groups in anxiety scores of special education students.

239. Carpenter, P., & Sandberg, S. (1985). Further psychodrama with delinquent adolescents. *Adolescents, 20*, 599-604.
Describes the consolidation of behavioral-cognitive techniques with psychodrama group therapy. Delinquent adolescents demonstrated improvement in ego strength and introversive tendencies.

240. Carroll, D. E. (1985). A study of the effects of nonsexist group counseling on androgyny in ninth-grade females. *Dissertation Abstracts International, 45*(12), 3547. (University Microfilm No. AAC85-02976)

241. Carswell, R. W. (1976). A study of the effects of an experimental learning model in group counseling with juvenile delinquents. *Dissertation Abstracts International, 36*(11), 7201. (University Microfilm No. AAC76-10492)

242. Casella, D. A., & Schrader, D. R. (1975). "Tripping" with borderline dropouts. *School Counselor, 23*, 48-50.
Describes a counseling program in which borderline dropout students went into the community with a teacher/counselor and met with successful workers. Students exhibited improvements in self-concept only, relative to controls.

243. Cassorla, A. A. (1986). A preliminary investigation of the experience of shame in psychiatrically hospitalized, conduct disordered adolescents. *Dissertation Abstracts International, 47*(04), 1715B.
Administered semi-structured interviews in conjunction with several structured scenarios to nine male and seven female conduct disordered adolescents during a period of psychiatric hospitalization. The most significant finding was that shame is a common affect with powerful motivating functions in this population.

Also addressed are the following issues: the explication of sources of self-reported shame, defenses employed in relation to shame, and the relationship between shame and sexuality, as well as between shame and depression. Explores gender-linked differences and discusses implications for treatment.

244.   Chase, J. L. (1991). Inpatient adolescent and latency-age children's perspectives on the curative factors in group psychotherapy. Special Issue: Child and Adolescent group psychotherapy. *Group, 15,* 95-108.
Examined which factors were deemed most curative by group therapy members, who were 33 adolescent and 11 child psychiatric inpatients. Level of functioning and age had a minimal effect on perceptions, and members valued hope, cohesiveness, and universality.

245.   Chase, J. L., & Kelly, M. M. (1993). Adolescents' perceptions of the efficacy of short-term, inpatient group therapy. *Journal of Child and Adolescent Group Therapy, 3,* 155-161.

246.   Chiu, P. (1980). Group counselling with emotionally disturbed school children in Taiwan. *School Psychology International, 1,* 27-30.
Reports on the success of a group counseling program in reducing adjustment problems for 29 emotionally disturbed junior high school Taiwanese males. The program did not succeed in improving social anxiety or personal and social adjustment.

247.   Clark, R. B. (1982). The effects of selected counseling approaches on low-achieving grade-ten students. *Dissertation Abstracts International, 42*(08), 3507. (University Microfilm No. AAC81-26347)
Compared the utility of individual and group counseling with low-achieving 10th-grade students. Individual counseling improved attitudes toward school and attendance. Individual and group counseling similarly affected self-concept, scholastic achievement and classroom behavior.

248.   Clarke, G., Hops, H., Lewinsohn, P. M., & Andrews, J. (1992). Cognitive-behavioral group treatment of adolescent depression: Prediction of outcome. *Behavior Therapy, 23,* 341-354.

249.   Coleman, S. B. (1978). Sib group therapy: A prevention program for siblings from drug-addicted families. *International Journal of the Addictions, 13,* 115-127.
While weekly group therapy sessions with 15 to 20 younger, latency age siblings of addicted adolescents helped decrease extreme group acting-out behavior, they did not seem to change underlying psychodynamics. There was some evidence of experimentation with alcohol; the siblings wanted to continue their group therapy.

250.   Comiskey, P. E. (1993). Using Reality Therapy group training with at-risk high school freshmen. *Journal of Reality Therapy, 12,* 59-64.
Describes the success of a combined group counseling program with school accommodation in changing behaviors and attitudes related to dropout in a group of at-risk ninth-grade students.

251.   Copeland, E. J. (1974). Peer-counselor effect on the self-concept and academic adjustment of educational opportunity students who participated in group counseling. *Dissertation Abstracts International, 35*(04), 1974. (University Microfilm No. AAC74-23431)

252.   Corder, B. F. (1981). An experimental study of the effect of structured videotape feedback on adolescent group psychotherapy process. *Journal of Youth and Adolescence, 10,* 255-262.

253.   Corder, B. F., Cornwall, T., & Whiteside, R. (1984). Techniques for increasing effectiveness of co-therapy functioning in adolescent psychotherapy groups. *International Journal of Group Psychotherapy, 34*(4), 643-654.
       Subjects found use of a questionnaire beneficial in reducing initial anxiety levels, predicting potential problem areas, and facilitating planning.

254.   Costantino, G., Malgady, R. G., & Rogler, L. H. (1988). Folk hero modeling therapy for Puerto Rican adolescents. Special Issue: Mental health research and service issues for minority youth. *Journal of Adolescence, 11,* 155-165.

255.   Creange, N. C. (1983). The effects of individual and peer group counseling on a sample of disruptive high school students. *Dissertation Abstracts International, 44*(05), 1336. (University Microfilm No. AAC83-21615)

256.   Cuff, B. J. (1985). The implementation and evaluation of a drug/alcohol intervention program on the secondary school level. *Dissertation Abstracts International, 46*(06), 1517. (University Microfilm No. AAC85-17972)
       Describes implementation of a drug/alcohol intervention program designed for students already involved in substance abuse. The program consists of informational lectures, films, informal Socratic sessions, self-esteem groups, individual and group counseling, and programmed recreation. Initial feedback indicates that the program increases drug/alcohol knowledge and is well received.

257.   Cullen, T. J. (1986). Group therapy with the mentally retarded: Effects of control and intimacy. *Dissertation Abstracts International, 47*(05), 2155. (University Microfilm No. AAC86-11828)

258.   Deesch, J. B. (1976). The use of the Ohlsen Model of group counseling with secondary school students identified as being disruptive to the educational process. *Dissertation Abstracts International, 36*(07), 4253. (University Microfilm No. AAC75-29876)

259.   Deluca, F. (1976). The effects of group counseling as influenced by group size on junior high school students in academic difficulty. *Dissertation Abstracts International, 36*(08), 5037. (University Microfilm No. AAC76-02979)

260.   Dequine, E. R., & Pearson, D. S. (1983). Videotaped improvisational drama with emotionally disturbed adolescents: A pilot study. *Arts in Psychotherapy, 10,* 15-21.

Examined the effectiveness of using improvised dramas in treating 14 emotionally disturbed 12- to 17-year-olds. Relative to the control group, treatment subjects increased prosocial behaviors and attitudes.

261.   Desalvo, J. M. (1983). The effect of group counseling on achievement and self-concept among alternative high school students. *Dissertation Abstracts International, 43*(08), 2617. (University Microfilm No. AAC83-00765)

262.   De Shon, F. A. (1984). Influence of democratic self-management group therapy on greater congruence of real and ideal self of delinquent teenage girls in a German institution. *Dissertation Abstracts International, 44*(11), 3522. (University Microfilm No. AAC84-04716)

263.   Desmarais, H, L. (1981). The effects of 'innerchange' counseling with a group of habitual truants at the high school level. *Dissertation Abstracts International, 42*(11), 4721. (University Microfilm No. AAC82-07755)

264.   Desrats, R. G. (1975). The effects of developmental and modeling group counseling on adolescents in child-care institutions. *Dissertation Abstracts International, 36*(05), 2625. (University Microfilm No. AAC75-23985)

265.   Devinante, S. (1980). Group counseling with teachers: Effect of "C group" on the student's self-concept. *Canadian Counselor, 14*(3), 141-145.
        Examined whether the Adlerian "C group" technique would improve teachers' attitudes in interpersonal relations with their students, and cause a positive change in the students' self-concept. Statistical analysis indicated that C group subjects achieved a positive change in how they perceived their teachers and in self-concept, as compared to controls. Teacher attitudes and self-concept also improved.

266.   Dishion, T. J., Patterson, G. R., & Kavanagh, K. A. (1992). An experimental test of the coercion model: Linking theory, measurement, and intervention. In J. McCord & R. E. Tremblay (Eds.), *Preventing antisocial behavior: Interventions from birth through adolescence* (pp. 253-282). New York: Guilford Press.
        Shows the linkage of the measurement model to coercion theory development in a sample of 119 at-risk families who participated in the field experiment.

267.   Dobbins, D. P. F. (1991). Effects of a group counseling program on grade point average and noncognitive factors of self-concept among underachieving secondary school students. *Dissertation Abstracts International, 52*(02), 428. (University Microfilm No. AAC91-09054)
        Examined the effects of a structured group counseling program on 101 underachieving secondary school students. Students improved on measures of grade point average; perceived levels of aspiration; academic interest and satisfaction; leadership and initiative; anxiety; and, identification with school environment.

268.   Dooley, B. K. (1976). Family communication during the process of multifamily group counseling and its effect on the school performance of the adolescent

family members. *Dissertation Abstracts International, 37*(03), 1400. (University Microfilm No. AAC76-20416)

269. Downes, M. A. (1987). The development of an adolescent females' psychotherapy group: A feminist psychological orientation. *Dissertation Abstracts International, 48*(05), 1149. (University Microfilm No. AAC87-16080)
Examined an adolescent female psychotherapy group using the stage model of group development. Discusses implications for future research and training.

270. Eaker, H. A., Allen, S. S., Gray, J., & Heckel, R. V. (1982). A factor-analytic study of a group therapy screening scale for children and adolescents. *Journal of Clinical Psychology, 38,* 742-743.
Describes the usefulness of factor analysis in evaluating a group prediction scale administered to 200 delinquent youths.

271. Etters, L. E. (1975). Adolescent retardates in a therapy group. *American Journal of Nursing, 75,* 1174-1175.

272. Feindler, E. L., Ecton, R. B., Kinsley, D., & Dubey, D. R. (1986). Group anger control training for institutionalized psychiatric male adolescents. *Behavior Therapy, 17,* 109-123.
Ten inpatient psychiatric male adolescents participated in a cognitive-behavioral technique aimed at self-control of anger and aggressive behavior. The program effectively taught self-control and increased appropriate verbalizations.

273. Feldman, R. A. (1992). The St. Louis Experiment: Effective treatment of antisocial youths in prosocial peer groups. In J. McCord & R. E. Tremblay (Eds.), *Preventing antisocial behavior: Interventions from birth through adolescence* (pp. 233-252). New York: Guilford Press.
As a result of the prosocial peer groups, significantly less post-test antisocial behavior was reported on the 14O referred youths for whom parents provided pre- and post-test data.

274. Felton, G. S., & Davidson, H. R. (1973). Group counseling can work in the classroom. *Academic Therapy, 8,* 461-468.
Describes the success of small group psychotherapy in teaching internalization and responsible behavior to 61 low-achieving high school students.

275. Fiedler, P. E. (1979). Effects of assertive training on hospitalized adolescents and young adults. *Adolescence, 14*(55), 523-528.

276. Fine, S., Forth, A., Gilbert, M., & Haley, G. (1991). Group therapy for adolescent depressive disorder: A comparison of social skills and therapeutic support. *Journal of American Academy of Child and Adolescent Psychiatry, 30*(1), 79-85.
Compared two forms of short-term group therapy, social skills training (SST) and therapeutic support (TS), with 66 adolescents. Treatment outcome was based on self-report and semi-structured clinical interviews for depression, measures of self-concept, and cognitive distortions. Subjects in TS groups showed significantly greater reductions in clinical depression and significant

increases in self-concept. However, these group differences were no longer evident at a nine month follow-up.

277. Fine, S., Knight-Webb, G., & Breau, K. (1976). Volunteer adolescents in adolescent group therapy: Effects on patients and volunteers. *British Journal of Psychiatry, 129,* 407-413.

278. Fine, S., Knight-Webb, G., & Vernon, J. (1977). Selected volunteer adolescents in adolescent group therapy. *Adolescence, 12,* 189-197.
    Examined the utility of volunteers in the group treatment of adolescence, finding that 21 adolescent group members modeled their behavior and attitudes after three volunteers.

279. Fischer, J., & Coyle, B. (1977). A specialised treatment service for young problem drinkers (16-30 years): Treatment results obtained during the first six months of the treatment programme. *British Journal of Addiction, 72*(4), 317-319.
    Established a special bi-weekly group therapy program for young problem drinkers. Results obtained during the first six months of the program were encouraging, suggesting that separate treatment for young alcohol abusers merits further exploration.

280. Flynn, D. (1992). Adolescent group work in a hospital in-patient setting with spina bifida patients and others. *Journal of Child Psychotherapy, 18,* 87-107.

281. Fraggetti, G. (1990). An investigation into the effects of assertion training on parents' behavior and the assessment of assertive and aggressive responses in parent-adolescent relationships. *Dissertation Abstracts International, 51*(05), 2618B.

282. French, M. S. (1986). A study of the interaction of cerebral palsy and group process. *Dissertation Abstracts International, 47*(02), 499.
    Examined the adaptive coping behavior and communication of 28 junior and senior high school cerebral palsied students participating in group therapy.

283. Freudenberger, L. B. (1990). The successful incompetent in group therapy: The drug-abusing adolescent and group therapy. *Dissertation Abstracts International, 51*(06), 3129. (University Microfilm No. AAC90-29117)

284. Friedman, A. S., & Utada, A. T. (1992). Effects of two group interaction models on substance-using adjudicated adolescent males. Special Issue: Programs for change: Office for Substance Abuse Prevention demonstration models. *Journal of Community Psychology, 20,* 106-117.
    Describes an early intervention program used with 62 adolescent substance abusers. An anti-violence and values clarification model was more successful than a life skills training model in improving behavior and attitudes.

285. Fulliton, W. L. (1991). The effects of treatment rationale information on acceptability of treatment and response in treatment by psychiatrically hospitalized adolescents. *Dissertation Abstracts International, 51*(12), 6102. (University Microfilm No. AAC91-12895)

286. Gallegos, R. L. (1983). The effect of a reward-based group counseling system on self-concept, achievement and attendance patterns of minority high school students. *Dissertation Abstracts International, 44*(01), 57. (University Microfilm No. AAC83-11391)

287. Gathers, M. A. (1977). The comparative effectiveness of two methods of group counseling of potential dropouts in an urban high school. *Dissertation Abstracts International, 37*(07), 4130. (University Microfilm No. AAC77-00448)

288. Gatz, M., Tyler, F. B., & Pargament, K. I. (1978). Goal attainment, locus of control, and coping style in adolescent group counseling. *Journal of Counseling Psychology, 25,* 310-319.

289. George, D. A. (1993). Impact of structured group therapy on problematic sexualized and non-sexualized behaviors in victims of child sexual abuse. *Dissertation Abstracts International, 54*(06), 3339. (University Microfilm No. AAC93-24337)
      Examined the use of a Parallel Group Treatment Program with 25 Latino and 36 Caucasian victims of childhood sexual abuse, ranging from 4 to 16 years old. Discusses cultural impact on participation in group therapy.

290. Glatt, F. K. (1978). The effect of group counseling on the self-concepts of hearing impaired adolescents. *Masters Abstracts International, 17*(01), 34.

291. Golant, M. C. (1980). The effects of group counseling on locus of control with pregnant teenagers. *Dissertation Abstracts International, 40*(10), 5321A.

292. Gold, M., Mattlin, J., & Osgood, D. W. (1989). Background characteristics and responses to treatment of two types of institutionalized delinquent boys. *Criminal Justice and Behavior, 16,* 5-33.
      Examined the differences of two types of delinquent boys in terms of etiology of their behavior and response to group treatment. The two types of boys revealed significant differences in life experiences, delinquent behavior and response to treatment.

293. Goodman, J. C. (1976). Group counseling with seventh graders. *Personnel and Guidance Journal, 54,* 519-520.
      Reports positive behavioral changes in the classroom behavior of nine seventh graders after participating in group counseling.

294. Gottheil, E., Rieger, J. A., Farwell, B., & Lieberman, D. L. (1977). An outpatient drug program for adolescent students: Preliminary evaluation. *American Journal of Drug and Alcohol Abuse, 4,* 31-41.

295. Gottsegen, M. G., & Grasso, M. (1973). Group treatment of the mother-daughter relationship. *International Journal of Group Psychotherapy, 23,* 69-81. Describes a group designed to explore and change difficulties within the mother-daughter relationship. The group was found to be useful.

296. Gould, E. O. (1979). A comparison of the relative effectiveness of Adlerian Group Counseling and Adlerian Parent Education on Middle School youth with

classroom adjustment problems. *Dissertation Abstracts International, 40*(05), 2480. (University Microfilm No. AAC79-25404)

297. Grainer, M. S. (1987). An investigation of the efficacy of group counseling with emotionally disturbed middle school students. *Dissertation Abstracts International, 47*(10), 3703. (University Microfilm No. AAC87-00425)

298. Gruner, L. (1984). Membership composition of open and closed therapeutic groups: A research note. *Small Group Behavior, 15,* 222-232.
Reports on the lack of development in open-ended groups relative to close-ended groups, using the Hill Interaction Matrix to analyze the four different groups of delinquent boys.

299. Gutter, M. L. (1987). The effect of aerobic physical fitness training combined with counseling on the self-concept of junior high school students. *Dissertation Abstracts International, 47*(11), 3981A.

300. Guyer, C. G. (1978). The effects of nonverbal warm-up exercises upon group counseling effectiveness with adolescent groups. *Dissertation Abstracts International, 39*(05), 2754. (University Microfilm No. AAC78-19917)

301. Hagan, A. K. (1982). The quantitative and qualitative evaluations of a group intervention for junior high school students with divorced or separated parents. *Dissertation Abstracts International, 43*(04), 1254. (University Microfilm No. AAC82-20931)

302. Hagborg, W. J. (1993). Middle-school student satisfaction with group counseling: An initial study. *Journal for Specialists in Group Work, 18,* 80-85.
Examined client satisfaction of 48 fifth to eighth-grade students participating in counseling for social and emotional problems. Client satisfaction was related to attendance but not to background characteristics, outcome variables, or ratings of global improvement.

303. Hahn, W. O. (1985). A theme-centered approach to changing self-concept in a group of adolescent boys. *Dissertation Abstracts International, 45*(11), 3281A.
Divided 30 adolescent boys into three groups: a group using Cohn's modified Theme-Centered Interaction method, traditional group counseling, and a no-treatment control. Found no significant differences in self-concept scores among the three groups in pre- and post-testing. Adolescents in the theme-centered group showed significant positive differences in their feelings about the sessions, desire to attend the sessions, and perception of the group leader's helpfulness and understanding of the group.

304. Hains, A. A., Herrman, L. P., Baker, K. L., & Graber, S. (1986). The development of a psycho-educational group program for adolescent sex offenders. *Journal of Offender Counseling, Services, and Rehabilitation, 11,* 63-67.
Examined the effects of psycho-educational group therapy on seventeen 16 to 18 year old male sex offenders. While sexual knowledge increased and problem solving ability and attitudes improved, the subjects' moral judgment remained unaffected.

305. Haldeman, D. E., & Baker, S. B. (1992). Helping female adolescents prepare to cope with irrational thinking via preventive cognitive self-instruction training. *Journal of Primary Prevention, 13*(2), 161-169.

306. Hanson, J. T., & Sander, D. L. (1973). Differential effects of individual and group counseling on realism of vocational choice. *Journal of Counseling Psychology, 20,* 541-544.
Describes the successful use of group counseling in providing more realistic career goals to llth- and 12th-grade boys who were extreme overshooters or extreme undershooters.

307. Heckel, R. V., Hursh, L., & Hiers, J. M. (1977). Analysis of process data from token groups in a summer camp. *Journal of Clinical Psychology, 33,* 241-244.
Forty-two 8- to 15-year-olds attending summer camp for disturbed children were treated with group therapy combined with a token economy, using peer judgements as the basis for token awards. After treatment, irrelevant responses and leader-directed responses declined, while group responses and decision-making increased.

308. Henshaw, H. V. (1986). A qualitative study of the self-concept system of adolescents admitted to psychiatric hospitals. *Dissertation Abstracts International, 46*(11), 4037B.
Used structured interviews and participant observation to examine six adolescent subjects' self-concept system. Results suggested that all subjects felt inadequate about their ability to do and to achieve, felt alienated and cut off from others, and tended to feel badly about themselves. Concluded that inpatient psychiatric units could be used to help facilitate proper need satisfaction; this could be achieved though individual and group psychotherapy, activity groups, and school vocational programs.

309. Herman, L. L. (1986). The relationship between self-esteem and perceived cohesiveness in peer group counseling groups. *Dissertation Abstracts International, 47*(06), 2025A.
Two trained peer group leaders led treatment groups, composed of 10 freshmen; groups met twice a week for 16 weeks. The control group remained in study hall while the treatment groups met. Results showed no differences between the treatment and no-treatment groups. Found reciprocal predictive relationships between self-esteem and cohesiveness, with such relationships being significantly more predictive for males than females.

310. Heyman, J. (1986). An investigation of the effect of group counseling on self-reported change of self-concept scores of bright high school underachievers from low-income families who attended an upward bound program. *Dissertation Abstracts International, 46*(08), 2259. (University Microfilm No. AAC85-21965)

311. Hicks, J. S., & Wieder, D. (1973). The effects of inter-generation group counseling on clients and parents in a vocational rehabilitation agency. *Rehabilitation Literature, 34,* 358-363.
Compares two types of group therapy for parents and young adult clients in a vocational rehabilitation program. Fifty clients and 66 parents attended either inter-generational groups or separate group therapy sessions for parents and

clients. Parents favored the inter-generational condition, while clients preferred the separate condition. Presents suggestions for short-term programs.

312. Hock, R. A., Rodgers, C. H., Reddi, C., & Kennard, D. W. (1978). Medico-psychological interventions in male asthmatic children: An evaluation of physiological change. *Psychosomatic Medicine, 40,* 210-215.

313. Hodges, W. E. (1975). The effects of an intensive group counseling process on failing Chicano Males. *Dissertation Abstracts International, 36*(05), 2630. (University Microfilm No. AAC75-23542).

314. Hodges-Bongirno, M. F. (1982). Group counseling: Its effect on ninth-grade high school Hispanic females. *Dissertation Abstracts International, 42*(10), 4364. (University Microfilm No. AAC82-06171)

315. Hoffmann, F. J. (1975). Use of the Adlerian model in secondary school counseling and consulting. *Individual Psychology, 12,* 27-32.
Describes the effectiveness of four types of treatment for students who exhibited attention-seeking behavior. These treatments are, in order of effectiveness: counseling of both teacher and student, counseling of teacher only, counseling of student only, and no counseling.

316. Holleran, J. P. (1981). Effect of group counseling on locus of control and academic achievement: Reality therapy with underachieving junior high school students. *Dissertation Abstracts International, 41*(12), 4980. (University Microfilm No. AAC81-12250)

317. Holt, E. W. (1979). The effects of behavioral group counseling using self-verbalization on the self-responsibility and academic achievements of culturally different adolescents. *Dissertation Abstracts International, 39*(11), 6546A.

318. Houser, C. A. (1989). Effects of group counseling on the self-esteem, creative thinking, and problem-solving skills of gifted tenth- and eleventh-grade students. *Dissertation Abstracts International, 49*(11), 3269A.
Forty-eight gifted 10th- and 11th-grade students participated in one of three groups for 12 weeks: group counseling either with a leader-structured approach (LSA) or a group-structured approach (GSA), or a control group. The two counseling groups met for 45 minutes weekly. Found no statistical difference among the three groups on measures of self-esteem, self-acceptance, social adjustment, figural creative thinking, and problem-solving. This unexpected finding suggests that using group counseling with gifted students needs additional exploration.

319. Huey, W. C. (1985). Informational-processing groups: A peer led orientation approach. *School Counselor, 33,* 3-8.
Describes a program designed to facilitate adjustment for eighth graders preparing to enter high-school. Peers led the groups, which were based on information-processing, and consisted of 357 Black suburban students of lower socioeconomic status. Participants reported fewer failures and absences and better conduct than controls.

320. Hunter, A. (1975). An assessment of a group counseling program in the secondary schools. *Dissertation Abstracts International, 36*(06), 3510. (University Microfilm No. AAC75-26047)

321. Isaacs, L. D. (1977). Art-therapy group for latency age children. *Social Work, 22,* 57-59.
Describes the success of a group therapy program consisting of sharing art materials, producing artwork, and discussing artwork, in improving withdrawn and aggressive behavior in four girls, aged 9 to 11 years.

322. Jakubik, C. (1982). The relative effectiveness of three types of group counseling leadership on selected personality and behavioral variables. *Dissertation Abstracts International, 43*(05), 1427A. (University Microfilm No. AAC82-22547)

323. Jensen, J. L. (1978). Eliminating self-defeating behavior group counseling: Its effects on self-concept and locus of control of economically disadvantaged high school students. *Dissertation Abstracts International, 39*(06), 3375A.

324. Jessell, J. C., & Bush, J. F. (1973). Effects of principal actor time structuring on goal attainment in group counseling. *Counselor Education and Supervision, 13*(2), 105-110.
Examined whether the structuring of principal actor time in a series of group counseling experiences (PATS) influenced clients' individual goal attainment, and whether PATS affected the groups' therapeutic climate. PATS did not result in differential goal attainment between subjects in structured or unstructured groups. Noted no significant difference in the measured therapeutic relationship achieved between counselors and subjects in the different groups.

325. Joanning, H., Quinn, W., Thomas, F., & Mullen, R. (1992). Treating adolescent drug abuse: A comparison of family systems therapy, group therapy, and family drug education. *Journal of Marital and Family Therapy, 18,* 345-356.
Compared the effectiveness of family systems therapy (FST), adolescent group therapy (AGT) and family drug education (FDE) in adolescent drug abuse treatment. FST was more effective in stopping adolescent drug abuse.

326. Johnson, C. L., & Johnson, J. A. (1991). Using short-term group counseling with visually impaired adolescents. *Journal of Visual Impairment and Blindness, 85,* 166-170.
Reports on a group counseling program aimed at enhancing self-concept in 14 congenitally visually impaired adolescents. Subjects showed improvement in self-concept, attitudes toward blindness, and internality of locus of control.

327. Johnson, C. L., Jr. (1990). Using group procedures to improve self-concept, attitudes toward blindness and internality among congenitally blind adolescents. *Dissertation Abstracts International, 50*(09), 4223B.

328. Johnston, J. C., Healey, K. N., & Tracey-Magid, D. (1985). Drama and interpersonal problem solving: A dynamic interplay for adolescent groups. *Child Care Quarterly, 14,* 238-247.

Fifteen Black foster-care youths with interpersonal conflicts participated in a group counseling approach, which combined drama therapy and interpersonal problem-solving dialoguing. Post-test results showed significant improvement in interpersonal cognitive problem solving.

329.   Kaggwa, G. H. (1980). The effects of client centered group counseling and relaxation on the self-concept and negative behavior of junior high school students who are disciplinary problems. *Dissertation Abstracts International, 40*(07), 3782A.

330.   Kane, R. A. (1991). Effects of student support group counseling in a student assistance program (SAP) on grades, attendance, discipline, and suicidal orientation. *Dissertation Abstracts International, 52*(04), 1154. (University Microfilms No. AAC91-28261)
       Examined the effects of counseling support groups on 44 middle school students. Counseling participants had significantly fewer discipline referrals than the 40 nonparticipants; participants' absenteeism, failing grades, and suicidal orientation also decreased, but not significantly.

331.   Kantor, I. M. (1990). An assessment of some personal and interpersonal characteristics of sexually abused adolescent girls. *Dissertation Abstracts International, 51*(02), 989. (University Microfilm No. AAC90-17600)

332.   Klarreich, S. H. (1981). A study comparing two treatment approaches with adolescent probationers. *Corrective and Social Psychiatry and Journal of Behavior Technology, Methods, and Therapy, 27,* 1-13.

333.   Kochendofer, S. A. (1975). Group preparation: Interview versus questionnaire. *School Counselor, 23,* 38-42.
       Compared the usefulness of individual interviewing versus a group administered counseling questionnaire in preparing junior and senior high school students for group counseling. The only between-group difference was related to the questionnaire participants' acknowledgement of their greater involvement in, and more responsibility for, their problems.

334.   Kostoulas, K. K., Berkovitz, I. H., & Arima, H. (1991). School counseling groups and children of divorce: Loosening attachment to mother in adolescent girls. *Journal of Child and Adolescent Group Therapy, 1,* 177-192.
       Examines the evaluation of a middle school counseling group for nine 12- to 14-year-old girls from divorced families. Most of the subjects believed the group improved their self-esteem and mood, but few felt more in control of their lives.

335.   Kunze, K. S. (1992). The effects of group counseling on low-achieving and/or underachieving ninth graders participating in an alternative education program. *Dissertation Abstracts International, 53*(06), 1800. (University Microfilm No. AAC92-31483)
       Examines the usefulness of group counseling in improving the achievement, self-concept and locus of control of 66 low- and under-achieving ninth-grade students. Parental involvement predicted significant improvement, but participating in group counseling did not.

336. Laird, G. S. (1981). The effects of progressive relaxation on anxiety among high school students. *Dissertation Abstracts International, 42*(04), 1552A.
Divided students into four groups: those trained in progressive relaxation with biofeedback, those trained in progressive relaxation only, those in a values clarification counseling group, and those in the no-treatment control group. Those trained in progressive relaxation, with or without biofeedback, showed greater changes in the direction of reduced anxiety than the clarification counseling or control group. Discusses the results' practical meanings and theoretical implications for further research.

337. Larsen, J. A. (1991). The effect of group counseling on the self-esteem of students with learning disabilities. *Masters Abstracts International, 29*(03), 362.

338. Larsen, P. T. (1976). A study of the effects of group counseling on absentee-prone high school sophomores. *Dissertation Abstracts International, 37*(06), 3311. (University Microfilm No. AAC76-27907)

339. Leeman, L. W., Gibbs, J. C., Fuller, D. (1993). Evaluation of a multicomponent group treatment program for juvenile delinquents. *Aggressive Behavior, 19,* 281-292.
Describes the improvement in institutional conduct and recidivism rates of 19 male juvenile offenders, from 15 to 18 years old, after participating in multicomponent group treatment.

340. Lena, E. A. (1988). A cognitive psychological group therapy approach to counseling of male adolescents in a residential treatment facility. *Dissertation Abstracts International, 49*(04), 767. (University Microfilm No. AAC88-09586)

341. Lenz, E. A. (1988). A cognitive psychological group therapy approach to counseling of male adolescents in a residential treatment facility. *Dissertation Abstracts International, 49*(04), 767. (University Microfilm No. AAC88-09586)

342. Loera, P. A. (1987). Group counseling with deaf adolescents in residential schools: A survey of residential school counselors. *Dissertation Abstracts International, 48*(06), 1420A.
Examines information on the frequency with which group counseling is used with deaf adolescents in residential schools, the major characteristics of counseling groups with this population, and the group training background of residential school counselors.

343. Lucero, K. F. (1980). The effects of group counseling on self-concept and academic performance of a select group of seventh-grade students in a remedial reading program. *Dissertation Abstracts International, 41*(04), 1406. (University Microfilm No. AAC80-22817)

344. Lyon, J. M. (1991). Conflict resolution in an inner-city middle school: An alternative approach. *School Counselor, 39*(2), 127-130.
Eight 8th graders, identified as having dispute-resolution problems, participated in a pilot group counseling program, which used skits, role-reversals, and simulations for four weeks, followed by four weeks of once weekly individual

sessions. Within four weeks of termination of the program, all subjects were involved in major incidents resulting in suspensions or police citations.

345.   Lyons, L. G. (1983). The effects of a human-relations and rational-emotive peer group counseling program upon high school students. *Dissertation Abstracts International, 44*(04), 1244. (University Microfilm No. AAC83-19171)
       Compared peer group counseling with adolescent males using either a human relations or a rational emotive framework. Found no difference between the two groups.

346.   MacKay, B., Gold, M., & Gold, E. (1987). A pilot study in drama therapy with adolescent girls who have been sexually abused. Special Issue: Childhood Sexual Abuse. *Arts in Psychotherapy, 14,* 77-84.
       Describes drama therapy used with five 12- to 18-year-old girls who had been sexually abused. Following therapy, subjects reported less depression, hostility and psychotic symptoms.

347.   Maher, C. A. (1982). Behavioral effects of using conduct problem adolescents as cross-age tutors. *Psychology in the Schools, 19,* 360-364.
       Compared the improvement of 18 9th- to 12th-grade emotionally disturbed youths, randomly assigned to one of three groups: In the first group, subjects furnished cross-age tutoring to educable mentally retarded students, in the second, they received peer tutoring, and in the third, they received group counseling. The cross-aged tutors improved significantly more on social science and language arts grades, and significantly reduced their absenteeism and disciplinary referrals.

348.   Maher, C. A., & Barback, C. R. (1982). Preventing high school maladjustment: Effectiveness of professional and cross-age behavioral group counseling. *Behavior Therapy, 13,* 259-270.
       Describes a group counseling program aimed at the prevention and remediation of maladjusted ninth graders. Subjects improved their attendance and GPA, and disciplinary and special education referrals decreased.

349.   Maier, K. J. V. (1985). Children of Divorce: Adolescent female self-concept, attitudes, counseling needs, and father-daughter relationships. *Dissertation Abstracts International, 45*(07), 1993. (University Microfilm No. AAC84-22283)

350.   Majumder, R. K., Greever, K. B., Holt, P. R., & Friedland, B. U. (1973). Counseling techniques tested: Field study shows effective internal/external counseling. *Journal of Rehabilitation, 39,* 19-22.

351.   March, J. S. (1995). Cognitive-behavioral psychotherapy for children and adolescents with OCD: A review and recommendations for treatment. *Journal of the American Academy of Child and Adolescent Psychiatry, 34,* 7-18.
       Critically reviews 32 articles on the use of cognitive-behavioral therapy—graded exposure and response prevention—in treating children and adolescents with obsessive-compulsive disorders (OCD). Concludes that the method is beneficial.

352.   Marlowe, R. H. (1978). Severe classroom behavior problems: Teachers and counselors. *Journal of Applied Behavior Analysis, 11,* 53-66.

Examined the effectiveness of behavioral, client-centered, and no counseling groups in reducing disruptive and inappropriate classroom behavior in twelve 7th-grade Black male students. Found that teachers more effectively reduced inappropriate behavior than any counseling group.

353.   Maroon, E. L. (1977). The effects of the tenth-grade administration of the PSAT/NMSQT and group counseling experience on the eleventh-grade performance on the PSAT/NMSQT. *Dissertation Abstracts International, 38*(05), 2559. (University Microfilm No. AAC77-25178)

354.   Marshall-Liebing, M. (1986). Adolescent group counseling and outdoor survival trips: Two school programs designed to modify character traits common to high school dropouts. *Dissertation Abstracts International, 46*(07), 1878.
       Compares two programs designed to encourage potential dropout students to stay in high school, survival trips and group counseling. Survival trip participants' self-concept, family self-concept, moral/ethical self-concept increased, and paranoid ideation decreased. Counseling group participants' psychotic symptoms and physical self-concept decreased.

355.   Martens, B. A. (1993). The implementation of a dropout prevention program for at-risk secondary students. *Dissertation Abstracts International, 53*(08), 2759. (University Microfilm No. AAC92-37374)

356.   Marvit, R. C., Lind, J., & McLaughlin, D. G. (1974). Use of videotape to induce attitude change in delinquent adolescents. *American Journal of Psychiatry, 131,* 996-999.
       Examined the use of peer groups and videotape techniques in the treatment of antisocial attitudes in 44 Hawaiian adolescents. The technique increased reality testing and reduced denial.

357.   Maskin, M. B. (1976). The differential impact of work-oriented vs. communication-oriented juvenile correction programs upon recidivism rates in delinquent males. *Journal of Clinical Psychology, 32,* 432-433.
       Compares recidivism rates among 60 males, aged 15 to 17 years, assigned to work-oriented or communication-oriented juvenile delinquency programs. In both residential and aftercare programs, the work-oriented group had the highest recidivism rates.

358.   Massie, B. M. (1981). Signs in psychological assessment data predicting success or failure in adolescent group therapy. *Dissertation Abstracts International, 42*(03), 1182. (University Microfilm No. AAC81-19159)

359.   May, M. K. (1993). The effects of group counseling on the self-esteem of sexually abused adolescent females (girls). *Dissertation Abstracts International, 54*(06), 2057. (University Microfilm No. AAC93-31637)

360.   McCaffrey, T., & Lyon, E. (1993). Teaching children to be good friends: Developmental group work with vulnerable children. *Educational and Child Psychology, 10*(3), 75-77.
       Used conflict management techniques to address peer relationship difficulties and behavioral management problems with two groups of vulnerable secondary

school students. The students and schools determined that the subjects had made gains in the areas of communication skills and in understanding the meaning of co-operative working, and deemed both projects to be successful.

361. McCann, B. (1990). Develop individual potential: Individual student growth through group counseling. In D. J. S. Blum (Ed.), *Group counseling for secondary schools* (pp. 115-122). Springfield, IL: Charles C. Thomas.
Presents instruments used to evaluate the growth groups that the author has conducted each semester for approximately 16 years.

362. McDonald, D. G. (1993). A study of Krumboltz's decision-making process in the use of group and individual counseling of epileptic high-school-aged students. *Dissertation Abstracts International, 53*(11), 3804. (University Microfilm No. AAC93-09071)

363. Mendelowitz, D. E. (1991). The effect of a group counseling and problem-solving model for college-bound high school seniors on perceived adjustment to college. *Dissertation Abstracts International, 52*(06), 2028A.
Forty college-bound students volunteered to participate in an eight week intervention before beginning college. Half the subjects participated in the small group counseling and problem solving treatment, and the remainder in the no treatment control condition. Results indicated that a first semester college student's academic and social adjustment to college can be improved by participating in a high school based group counseling and problem solving program.

364. Merrill, O. W. (1974). Group psychotherapy with American Indian adolescents: A study of reported changes. *Dissertation Abstracts International, 35*(03), 1392. (University Microfilm No. AAC74-20537)

365. Miles, J. M. H. (1975). A comparative analysis of the effectiveness of verbal reinforcement group counseling and parent effectiveness training on certain behavioral aspects of potential dropouts. *Dissertation Abstracts International, 35*(12), 7655. (University Microfilm No. AAC75-12493)

366. Miller, A. H. (1973). The spontaneous use of poetry in an adolescent girls' group. *International Journal of Group Psychotherapy, 23*, 223-227.
Examined the use of poetry in group therapy with eight adolescent girls. Surprise, pleasure, learning and insight were reported outcomes of this approach.

367. Miran, M., Lehrer, P. M., Koehler, R., & Miran, E. (1974). What happens when deviant behavior begins to change? The relevance of social systems approach for behavioral programs with adolescents. *Journal of Community Psychology, 2*, 370-375.
Discusses the need for primary prevention and systems-oriented consultation with a group of 14 eighth- to ninth-grade boys with conduct problems. External reinforcers, presented during group and behavior therapy, appeared to reduce suspensions.

368.   Mirrow, G. S. (1978). A study of the effect of group counseling on the self-concept and level of self-actualization of high school students. *Dissertation Abstracts International, 38*(10), 5928A.

369.   Mistilis, B. A. (1978). An investigation of goal attainment scaling as an adjunct in group counseling with high school students. *Dissertation Abstracts International, 39*(06), 3477A.

370.   Mondell, S. H. (1980). A measure of child psychosocial competence and its usefulness in child psychotherapy evaluation. *Dissertation Abstracts International, 41*(06), 2338. (University Microfilm No. AAC80-27123)

371.   Moody, T. J. (1981). The effects of group assertion training on aggressive behaviors of seventh- and eighth-grade males. *Dissertation Abstracts International, 42*(05), 1964. (University Microfilm No. AAC81-23845)

372.   Moore, K. J., & Shannon, K. K. (1993). The development of superstitious beliefs in the effectiveness of treatment of anger: Evidence for the importance of experimental program evaluation in applied settings. *Behavioral Residential Treatment, 8*(2), 147-161.

373.   Morgan, S. B., Fulliton, W., & Nabors, L. (1993). Adolescents' perceptions of acceptability of inpatient treatments: Does exposure to the treatment make a difference? *Residential Treatment for Children and Youth, 10,* 85-99.

374.   Moser, A. J. (1975). Structured group interaction: A psychotherapeutic technique for modifying locus of control. *Journal of Contemporary Psychotherapy, 7,* 23-28.
       Describes the success of small group therapy in shaping internalization behaviors in 24 adolescent felons.

375.   Nearpass, G. L. (1990). Counseling and guidance effectiveness in North American high schools: A meta-analysis of the research findings. *Dissertation Abstracts International, 50*(07), 1948. (University Microfilm No. AAC89-23518)

376.   Nesbit, M. J. (1977). Effects of social skill training and group counseling on adolescent self and peer perceptions. *Dissertation Abstracts International, 37*(12), 7645. (University Microfilm No. AAC77-11562)

377.   Nixon, R. (1983). The effects of group counseling on internal-external locus of control of children classified as learning disabled. *Dissertation Abstracts International, 43*(10), 3221. (University Microfilms No. AAC83-05371)
       Examined the effectiveness of intensive group counseling with 40 10- to 14-year-old low-income, inner-city elementary school males, classified as learning disabled. Found no significant differences between the treatment and control groups in locus of control and self-concept.

378.   O'Connor, L. C. (1983). The relationship between psychodrama and the intrapersonal and interpersonal development of the adolescent. *Dissertation Abstracts International, 44*(02), 595. (University Microfilm No. AAC83-15101)

379.   O'Donnell, W. E. (1978). The relative effectiveness of Transactional Analysis
       Group Counseling vs. Gestalt Group Counseling in effecting change in male
       junior high school truants. *Dissertation Abstracts International, 38*(11), 6542.
       (University Microfilm No. AAC78-05735)

380.   O'Sullivan, T. (1980). The effect of short-term behavioral group counseling on
       academic achievement and behavior with adolescent boys in a residential
       treatment program. *Dissertation Abstracts International, 41*(01), 109. (University
       Microfilm No. AAC80-14090)

381.   Ochoa, M. L. (1981). Group counseling Chicana troubled youth: An exploratory
       group counseling project. *Dissertation Abstracts International, 42*(03), 1013.
       (University Microfilm No. AAC81-18033)

382.   Pate, C. (1986). Social skills and problem solving training: A study with
       adolescent offenders (Moral development). *Dissertation Abstracts International,
       46*(09), 2818. (University Microfilm No. AAC85-26362)

383.   Patton, D. B. (1975). The effects of a group counseling program on the self-
       concept and locus of control orientation of pre-college disadvantaged students.
       Dissertation Abstracts International, 35(11), 7067A.

384.   Peitler, E. J. (1980). A comparison of the effectiveness of group counseling and
       Alateen on the psychological adjustment of two groups of adolescent sons of
       alcoholic fathers. *Dissertation Abstracts International, 41*(04), 1520. (University
       Microfilm No. AAC80-21807)
       Compared the effectiveness of group counseling versus Alateen, with males from
       14 to 16 years old, whose fathers were alcoholics. Group counseling was more
       effective than Alateen.

385.   Phelix, B. R. (1988). A comparison of two counseling approaches which are
       compatible versus incompatible with the sociological learning style preferences
       of Black and Hispanic males adolescents on moral judgement issues. *Dissertation
       Abstracts International, 48*(07), 1662. (University Microfilm No. AAC87-22158)

386.   Porter, B. A. (1982). Differential effects of a cognitive counseling approach
       with preadolescent children. *Dissertation Abstracts International, 42*(12), 5027.
       (University Microfilm No. AAC82-11079)

387.   Posmer, K. M. (1975). The effect of two modalities of group counseling for
       secondary school seniors upon their locus-of-control expectancies. *Dissertation
       Abstracts International, 36*(10), 6483A.

388.   Rachman, A. W. (1974). The role of "fathering" in group psychotherapy with
       adolescent delinquent males. *Corrective and Social Psychiatry and Journal of
       Behavior Technology Methods and Therapy, 20,* 11-22.
       Describes group therapy with 25 delinquent males who had negative and
       conflictual relationships with their fathers. Therapy included "fathering" by the
       therapists. While in therapy, 84% of the subjects did not become involved in
       legal difficulties.

389. Rankin, P. P. (1975). Looking at change in the area of body image and self-concept in adolescent females after exposure to two types of small group counseling experiences. *Dissertation Abstracts International, 35*(09), 5828A.

390. Redfering, D. L. (1973). Durability of effects of group counseling with institutionalized delinquent females. *Journal of Abnormal Psychology, 82,* 85-86. The effects of group counseling were still present in 36 female delinquents at one year follow-up: Subjects continued to give more positive connotative meanings to the concepts of father, mother and self, and significantly more group counseling subjects had been released without being recommitted to the institution.

391. Redfering, D. L. (1975). Differential effects of group counseling with Black and White female delinquents: One year later. *Journal of Negro Education, 44,* 530-537.

392. Regas, S. J. (1984). A comparison of functional family therapy and peer group therapy in the treatment of hyperactive adolescents. *Dissertation Abstracts International, 44*(08), 2566. (University Microfilm No. AAC83-24051) Compared family therapy and peer group therapy, using 18 families. Both therapies were equally effective in improving the hyperactive adolescents' behavior and in reducing emotional distance between family members.

393. Reiss, D., & Costell, R. (1977). The multiple family group as a small society: Family regulation of interaction with nonmembers. *American Journal of Psychiatry, 134,* 21-24. Describes the inter-generational dynamics of 18 families participating in group counseling. Changes in either the parents' or the adolescents' group participation levels were rapidly matched by the other generation.

394. Reyes, L. S. (1991). A treatment program for juvenile homicidal offenders: Impact on hostility-aggression, empathy and locus of control (homicidal offenders, psychodrama). *Dissertation Abstracts International, 52*(01), 529. (University Microfilm No. AAC91-16960)

395. Rice, P. A. (1988). The effects of a structured group counseling program on the self-esteem of a sample of Black juvenile delinquent males. *Dissertation Abstracts International, 49*(05), 1065A.

396. Richmond, L. H., & Gaines, T. (1979). Factors influencing attendance in group psychotherapy with adolescents. *Adolescence, 14,* 715-720.

397. Rivera, E. J. (1981). The efficacy of a group counseling approach direct decision therapy with bilingual, bicultural Chicano students. *Dissertation Abstracts International, 41*(11), 4276. (University Microfilm No. AAC81-09646)

398. Roberts, J. P. (1979). An investigation of select personality dimensions of peer group counseling leaders in a junior high school setting. *Dissertation Abstracts International, 40*(03), 1367. (University Microfilm No. AAC79-20960)

399.   Rogeness, G. A., & Stewart, J. T. (1978). The positive group: A therapeutic technique in the hospital treatment of adolescents. *Hospital and Community Psychiatry, 29,* 520-522.
       Describes a group therapy program in which only positive comments were allowed. Through role-modeling, participants learned to accept and make positive comments.

400.   Rosene, D. K. (1987). The impact of short-term participation in a non-traditional activity group therapy program on selected developmental variables in boys, ages 7-11. *Dissertation Abstracts International, 47*(12), 4336. (University Microfilm No. AAC87-05501)

401.   Rosenstock, H. A. (1979). Parental involvement as a requisite for successful adolescent therapy. *Journal of Clinical Psychiatry, 40,* 132-134.
       Examines the effect of parental involvement in a treatment program for 63 adolescent patients. There was a 64% success rate for patients whose parents participated and a nearly 100% failure rate for those whose parents did not.

402.   Rosenstock, H. A., Galle, M., & Levy, H. J. (1978). Early A. M. group therapy. *Journal of the National Association of Private Psychiatric Hospitals, 9,* 37-38.
       Describes a group therapy program with inpatient adolescents designed to increase group cohesiveness and reduce resistance and denial.

403.   Rosenstock, H. A., & Hansen, D. B. (1974). Toward better school adaptability: An early adolescent group therapy experiment. *American Journal of Psychiatry, 131,* 1397-1399.
       Describes the improvement of eight 7th graders with behavior problems after receiving in-school group therapy. The therapy appeared effective in increasing student adaptability to the academic and interpersonal school environment.

404.   Rosentover, I. F. (1974). Group counseling of the underachieving high school student as related to self-image and academic success. *Dissertation Abstracts International, 35*(06), 3433. (University Microfilm No. AAC74-27342)

405.   Ross, R. R., & Palmer, W. R. (1976). Modification of emotional expressiveness in adolescent offenders. *Crime and Justice, 4,* 125-133.
       Operant verbal conditioning increased female adolescent offenders' emotional expressiveness; contingent reinforcement was more effective than noncontingent reinforcement. Training in emotional expressiveness generalized to group therapy situations.

406.   Roundtree, G. A., Parker, J. B., & Jones, A. (1979). Behavioral management in the re-socialization of a group of adjudicated delinquents. *Corrective and Social Psychiatry and Journal of Behavior Technology, Methods and Therapy, 25,* 15-17.

407.   Rubin, J. A., & Rosenblum, N. (1977). Group art and group dynamics: An experimental study. *Art Psychotherapy, 4,* 185-193.

408. Russell, B. M. (1980). Didactic group counseling as it affects the trainable
       mentally retarded's self-concept, communication skills, peer acceptance and
       perceived social standing. *Dissertation Abstracts International, 41*(06), 2523A.
       Trainable mentally retarded students at a county special education center
       participated in either a treatment condition, where two therapists conducted 30
       weekly, 30-minute didactic group counseling sessions in a standardized context;
       or a control condition, where subjects spent equal time in non-counseling
       activities.   Results indicated that didactic group counseling significantly
       increased the subjects' self-concept and peer relations. The results rejected the
       hypothesis concerning communication skills and perceived social standing.

409. Samsel, R. L. (1976). Effect of group counseling on career maturity of students
       grades seven through twelve. *Dissertation Abstracts International, 37*(06), 3428.
       (University Microfilm No. AAC76-27344)

410. Samulewicz, E. (1975). The effects of critical thinking and group counseling
       upon behavior problem students. *Dissertation Abstracts International, 36*(05),
       2645.

411. Savin, H. A. (1976). Multimedia group treatment with socially inept
       adolescents. *Clinical Psychologist, 29,* 14-17.
       Determined improvements in interpersonal social behavior in 38 13- to 19-year-
       old males who participated in group treatment. Measured improvement by eye
       contact, physical posture, verbal following and expression of feelings.

412. Schmulowitz, J. S. (1976). Effectiveness of group counseling as a function of
       state/trait anxiety in reducing problematic speech in children. *Dissertation
       Abstracts International, 37*(04), 1928. (University Microfilm No. AAC76-23287)

413. Schnike, S. P., Schilling, R. F., & Gilchrist, L. D. (1986). Prevention of drug
       and alcohol abuse in American Indian youths. *Social Work Research and
       Abstracts, 22,* 18-19.

414. Schroeder, E. D. (1983). Adolescent women at risk: Group therapy for
       increasing self-esteem. *Dissertation Abstracts International, 44*(04), 1208A.
       Evaluated a counseling intervention for female adolescent prostitutes and women
       with histories of arrest, running away, or living on the streets. Treatment goals
       included increases in self-esteem, in interpersonal problem-solving skills, and in
       women's health knowledge. Results indicate that the counseling intervention met
       these treatment goals.

415. Schweisheimer, W., & Walberg, H. J. (1976). A peer counseling experiment:
       High school students as small-group leaders. *Journal of Counseling Psychology,
       23,* 398-401.
       Reports on the use of 16 peer counselors in group therapy with 122 potential
       high school dropouts. Treatment subjects improved significantly in attendance
       and decisiveness relative to controls.

416. Scott, K. L. (1985). The effects of selected group counseling topics on the self-
       concepts of gifted high school students in a rural area. *Dissertation Abstracts
       International, 45*(10), 3073A.

417.   Shanklin, P. A. (1984). The effects of a theme-centered group counseling experience on the self-concept and self-actualization of confined adolescent females. *Dissertation Abstracts International, 44*(11), 3290A.

418.   Sharma, K. L. (1975). Rational group counselling with anxious underachievers. *Canadian Counsellor, 9,* 132-137.
Compared 84 high school underachievers in one of four conditions: rational group counselling, teaching of rational ideas, teaching of study skills, or no treatment. Subjects receiving rational group counseling showed significantly greater reduction in irrational beliefs and greater improvement in grades than those in other conditions.

419.   Silveria, D. D. (1994). Cognitive-behavioral group therapy for sexually abused adolescent males. *Dissertation Abstracts International, 55*(03), 1194.
Examined the use of group therapy with 20 sexually abused adolescent males. Sexual knowledge and self-esteem improved after therapy, and there was some evidence that depression decreased.

420.   Simmons, C. H., & Parsons, R. J. (1983). Developing internality and perceived competence: The empowerment of adolescent girls. *Adolescence, 18,* 917-922.
Describes a small group workshop designed to complement the traditional Big Sisters of Colorado program in empowering adolescent girls. The workshop was successful with working class girls but not with lower class sixth-grade girls.

421.   Sims, G. K., & Sims, J. M. (1973). Does face-to-face contact reduce counselee responsiveness with emotionally insecure youth? *Psychotherapy: Theory, Research and Practice, 10*(4), 348-351.
Hypothesized that, as a consequence of inappropriate punishment, low levels of positive reinforcement, and reciprocal social interaction among the child's family members, emotionally insecure children may be inhibited by the cues they receive from the physical presence of an adult counselor. Comparison of 12 bi-weekly sessions with direct groups versus indirect groups, in which the counselor communicated by phone, supports the hypothesis.

422.   Smeak, I. E. (1985). Comparison of the effectiveness of role-playing and group therapy in teaching social skills to severely emotionally handicapped students. *Dissertation Abstracts International, 46*(06), 1598. (University Microfilm No. AAC85-18052)

423.   Smillie, A. L. (1991). The effects of group interventions on attitudes and stress in parents of learning-disabled and educable mentally impaired adolescents. *Dissertation Abstracts International, 52*(03), 808A.
Evaluated the effects of a support group, counseling group, and educational group on the attitudes and stress levels of parents of learning-disabled and educable mentally impaired adolescents. Results indicated significant change in parents' attitudes but no significant decrease in parents' stress levels. There were no significant findings regarding birth order, type of disability, and income level of family. Discusses the need for future research.

424.   Smith, C. L. (1991). The effects of one youth shelter on adolescent runaways. *Masters Abstracts International, 29*(04), 592. (University Microfilm No. AAC13-44498).

425.   Smith, V. L. (1980). Effects of group therapy on adolescents experiencing parental absence due to divorce or marital separation. *Dissertation Abstracts International, 41*(03), 947. (University Microfilm No. AAC80-19150)
       Examined the effectiveness of a group therapy model with 24 adolescents aged 12 to 17, whose parents were absent due to divorce or marital separation. Measured subjects' levels of self-esteem, anxiety and attitudes toward their parents. Findings were inconclusive.

426.   Smith, W. (1981). The effect of Project Turnabout on the self-concept and attitude toward school of low achieving students. *Dissertation Abstracts International, 42*(01), 149A.
       This study included low achieving subjects who remained in the Project Turnabout treatment program for at least two months. Treatment included individual and group counseling; conferences with teachers, school administrators and parents; home visits; telephone calls to parents; and contacts with community agencies and other resources. Results indicated that treatment was effective in bringing about a change in self-concept but not in changing subjects' attitude toward school.

427.   Smuts, H. E. (1982). Group therapy with deaf adolescents. *Masters Abstracts International, 20*(02), 215.

428.   Smyth, J. P., & Walberg, H. J. (1974). Group counseling effects on several adjustment problems. *Small Group Behavior, 5*(3), 331-340.
       Examined the effects of group and individual counseling services on 236 urban high school students who met in 25 groups, two times weekly for one year. Adjustment gains made in group counseling are discussed.

429.   Solomon, S. E. (1986). The influence of a moral intervention program for emotionally disturbed adolescents in a nonresidential alternative school. *Dissertation Abstracts International, 47*(04), 1259A.
       The results did not support the hypothesized relationship between higher stages of principled moral thinking and participation in the Just Community program, a moral intervention program for emotionally disturbed adolescents. However, significant positive changes in sociomoral reasoning and self-concept suggest that a Just Community program, with moral development training and group counseling, can be applied effectively to emotionally disturbed adolescents in nonresidential settings.

430.   Soong, W. L. (1986). Differential effects of two interventions for promoting ego development in late adolescence. *Dissertation Abstracts International, 47*(01), 88A. (University Microfilm No. AAC86-00318)

431.   Spencer, E. G. (1986). An outcome study of social-behavioral skill development in male adolescent delinquency. *Dissertation Abstracts International, 47*(05), 1891. (University Microfilm No. AAC86-18153)

432. Spencer, T. W. (1987). The effect of an Adlerian-based group counseling/education program on the self-concept, locus-of-control, and family environment of alternative high school students. *Dissertation Abstracts International, 47*(08), 2894A.

433. Srivastava, K. I. (1985). Socio-psychological factors of stammering and the problem of rehabilitation of statements. *Indian Psychological Review, 29,* 24-34. Examined the effect of group therapy on the stammering of 80 subjects, 10 years or older. Subjects showed improved adjustment in family, schools, offices and other public places. Found stammering to be related to physical and sociopsychological factors.

434. Stallard, P., & Law, F. D. (1993). Screening and psychological debriefing of adolescent survivors of life-threatening events. *British Journal of Psychiatry, 163,* 660-665.

435. Stehouwer, R. S., Bultsma, C. A., & Blackford, I. T. (1985). Developmental differences in depression: Cognitive-perceptual distortion in adolescent versus adult female depressives. *Adolescence, 20,* 291-299. Examined the success of group psychotherapy in reducing the cognitive-perceptual distortion of 50 depressed 13- to 54-year-old female psychiatric inpatients; compared cognitive-perceptual distortion in the adolescent and adult subjects.

436. Stephenson, R. M., & Scarpitti, F. R. (1974). *Group interaction as therapy: The use of the small group in corrections.* Westport, CT: Greenwood Press. Evaluates the experimental group program for 16- or 17-year-olds by comparing 943 subjects assigned to probation, with 100 youths assigned to each of the three experimental programs by means of MMPIs, background data, in-program progress, and recidivism rates.

437. Stewart, J. B., Hardin, S. B., Weinrich, S., & McGeorge, S. (1992). Group protocol to mitigate disaster stress and enhance social support in adolescents exposed to Hurricane Hugo. *Issues in Mental Health Nursing, 13*(2), 105-119. Evaluated the effectiveness of a nursing group intervention protocol designed to enhance cognitive understanding of disaster stress and to promote social support among adolescents who experienced the effects of Hurricane Hugo. Findings suggest that subjects valued both the small- and large-group components of the program.

438. Stoner, S., & Fiorillo, M. (1976). A program for self-concept improvement and weight reduction for overweight adolescent females. *Psychology, 13,* 30-35.

439. Strough, B. S. (1993). Assessment of a group counseling intervention with at-risk students: Effects on self-concept and attitude toward school. *Masters Abstracts International, 31*(04), 1448. (University Microfilm No. AAC13-52132)

440. Strub, R. F. (1974). The perceptions of selected group regarding the effect of cross-cultural group counseling on reducing tension in a racially mixed school. *Dissertation Abstracts International, 35*(06), 3437. (University Microfilm No. AAC74-27265)

441.   Sugar, M. (1993). Research in child and adolescent group psychotherapy. *Journal of Child and Adolescent Group Therapy, 3,* 207-226.

442.   Sullivan, A. K. (1986). The effect of group counseling on academic achievement and achievement motivation of alternative high school students. *Dissertation Abstracts International, 47*(05), 191. (University Microfilm No. AAC86-16838)

443.   Sullivan, M. J. (1986). Interaction in multiple family group therapy: A process study of aftercare treatment for runaways. *Dissertation Abstracts International, 47*(05), 139. (University Microfilm No. AAC86-08865)

444.   Summers, T. W. (1978). The examination of outcome evaluation procedures for a multiple family and adolescent group counseling program. *Dissertation Abstracts International, 38*(12), 6180. (University Microfilm No. AAC78-08186)

445.   Tarakoff, J. A. (1992). The effects of structured cognitive and affective group bereavement counseling on the emotional reactions, coping behaviors and understanding of death concepts of middle school students. *Dissertation Abstracts International, 52*(12), 4227A.
       Four groups of 7 to 10 students met weekly for eight structured sessions with certified school counselors. Pre- to post-testing results indicate a significant change in the understanding of human death concepts for all groups. While not statistically significant, a decrease in depression and anxiety followed the group bereavement counseling.

446.   Taves, R. A., Hutchinson, N. L., & Freeman, J. G. (1992). The effect of cognitive instruction in the development of employment interview skills in adolescents with learning disabilities. *Canadian Journal of Counselling, 26,* 87-95.
       Describes the successful use of cognitive instruction in small group counselling with a group of 10 learning disabled high school students seeking job interviewing skills. Subjects learned appropriate interview behaviors, enhanced their knowledge of the interview process, and increased their metacognitive awareness.

447.   Thomas, F. N. (1988). Therapy with substance abusing adolescents and their families: A comparison of three treatment conditions. *Dissertation Abstracts International, 49*(10), 4578. (University Microfilm No. AAC88-19426)
       Compared three treatment modalities, family therapy, adolescent group therapy, and educational groups, for their effectiveness in treating adolescents with substance abuse problems. Found no significance differences among treatment groups.

448.   Thompson, D. G. (1979). Effectiveness of values clarification and broad-spectrum behavioral group counseling with ninth-grade boys in a residential school. *Dissertation Abstracts International, 39*(08), 185A.

449.   Thompson, D. G., & Hudson, G. R. (1982). Values clarification and behavioral group counseling with ninth-grade boys in a residential school. *Journal of Counseling Psychology, 29,* 394-399.

Compared the effectiveness of values clarification and behavioral counseling in reducing the maladaptive and interfering behaviors of ninety-six 9th-grade males. Found both therapies equally effective in reducing negative behaviors.

450. Tice, T. N. (1988). Factors that influence positive growth of adolescents in group counseling within the school setting. *Dissertation Abstracts International, 49*(05), 1101A.
Presents open-ended, semi-structured interviews with nine adolescents, analyzing each case thematically and further analyzing whole sets of cases. Also reviews literature, which provides four thematic categories important to effective counselor leadership of adolescent groups: group atmosphere, interpersonal interplay, self-understanding and transformation, and lore of the group. Discusses future research areas and applications within school settings.

451. Toffoli, G., & Allan, J. (1992). Group guidance for English as a Second Language students. *School Counselor, 40,* 136-145.
Examined a guidance curriculum addressing the emotional issues of newly immigrated high school students. The program, which included relaxation, guided imagery, drawing, writing, and preparatory discussions, successfully addressed issues of cultural confusion, desires to keep heritage and memories alive, and the need to have positive and negative feelings validated.

452. Towberman, D. B. (1982). Counselor-client similarity and the client's perception of the treatment environment. *Dissertation Abstracts International, 43*(05), 1431. (University Microfilm No. AAC82-23942)

453. Towberman, D. B. (1993). Group vs. individual counseling: Treatment mode and the client's perception of the treatment environment. *Journal of Group Psychotherapy, Psychodrama & Sociometry, 45,* 163-174.
Compared the impact of group (GC) versus individual counseling (IC) on 96 female delinquent offenders. Subjects in GC had significantly higher and more positive perception ratings of interpersonal relationships and of the treatment program than did those in IC.

454. Truax, C. B., & Wittmer, J. (1973). The degree of the therapists's focus on defense mechanisms and the effect on therapeutic outcome with institutionalized juvenile delinquents. *Journal of Community Psychology, 1,* 201-203.

455. Tyler, F. B. (1979). Psychosocial competence differences among adolescents on entering group counseling. *Psychological Reports, 44,* 811-822.

456. Tyler, F. B., & Gatz, M. (1977). Development of individual psychosocial competence in a high school setting. *Journal of Consulting and Clinical Psychology, 45*(3), 441-449.

457. Tyler, F. B., & Pargament, K. I. (1981). Racial and personal factors and the complexities of competence-oriented changes in a high school group counseling program. *American Journal of Community Psychology, 9,* 697-714.
Reports on the effect of group counseling with 218 high school students. Stresses the importance of developing individualized change strategies that reflect the social/community context.

458. Uhren, K. K. (1981). The effects of three types of group counseling on the self-actualization, self-concept, and level of dogmatism of adolescents. *Dissertation Abstracts International, 42*(05), 2042A.
Each of the three groups met for a total of 12 hours of group counseling: the traditional group met once weekly for one hour, the marathon group met for a single 12-hour session, and the final group met for one hour each week for six weeks plus one continuous six-hour session. The three group counseling methods did not produce significant changes in self-actualization, self-concept, and level of dogmatism. No one method was superior to any other in producing change.

459. Urioste, M. M. (1978). Multicultural Experiential Group Counseling versus Multicultural Didactic Instruction on the attitudes of high school females. *Dissertation Abstracts International, 39*(08), 4743. (University Microfilm No. AAC79-03094)

460. Vang, A. T. (1993). A descriptive study of academically proficient Hmong high school girl dropouts. *Dissertation Abstracts International, 53*(10), 3463. (University Microfilm No. AAC93-03173)

461. Verleur, D., Huges, R. E., & de Rios, M. D. (1986). Enhancement of self-esteem among female adolescent incest victims: A controlled comparison. *Adolescence, 21,* 843-854.

462. Vernot, G. G. (1975). A study of the effectiveness of group counseling using a human relations treatment program with disruptive tenth-grade boys. *Dissertation Abstracts International, 36*(06), 3420. (University Microfilm No. AAC75-26825)

463. Vreeland, A. D. (1982). Evaluation of face-to-face: A juvenile aversion program. *Dissertation Abstracts International, 42*(10), 4597.

464. Wadowski, V. C. (1992). The effects of didactic and experiential group counseling on the self-concept, locus-of-control, and problematic beliefs of seventh and eighth graders from families of divorce. *Dissertation Abstracts International, 53*(12), 4216A.

465. Wagner, R. P. (1989). An evaluation of school social work services from a kid's eye view. *Masters Abstracts International, 27*(03), 348. (University Microfilm No. AAC13-34972)

466. Wallace, S. B. (1980). Efficacy of the use of group psychotherapy with adolescents who have a seizure disorder. *Dissertation Abstracts International, 40*(08), 3976. (University Microfilm No. AAC80-04844)

467. Washington, E. L. (1974). Effects of group counseling and role-playing upon selected behaviors of institutionalized male delinquents. *Dissertation Abstracts International, 35*(05), 2703. (University Microfilm No. AAC74-25536)

468.   Wearne, T. D., & Powell, J. C. (1977). The differential long-term effects of
        client-centered, developmental counselling with individuals and group. *Canadian
        Counsellor, 11,* 83-92.

469.   Weber, L. A. (1980). The effect of videotape and playback on an inpatient
        adolescent group. *International Journal of Group Psychotherapy, 30,* 213-227.
        Examined the effect of videotape and playback conducted in group therapy with
        adolescents diagnosed with borderline personality disorder. Hostility and flight
        responses decreased and warmth responses increased; the group also became
        more cohesive.

470.   Weinberger, D. M. (1975). Frequency of group counseling as a variable
        affecting student self-esteem and classroom behavior with male students at the
        seventh-grade level. *Dissertation Abstracts International, 36*(03), 1517B.

471.   Weinstock, A. (1979). Group treatment of characterologically damaged,
        developmentally disabled adolescents in a residential treatment center.
        International Journal of Group Psychotherapy, 29, 369-381.

472.   Weiss, B. (1989). Predictors of clinical change in children and adolescents
        receiving psychotherapy in outpatient clinics. *Dissertation Abstracts
        International, 49*(12), 5536. (University Microfilm No. AAC89-05693)

473.   Westmoreland, S. C. (1975). Outdoor activity group experience and group
        counseling with institutionalized children and adolescents. *Dissertation Abstracts
        International, 35*(09), 5837. (University Microfilm No. AAC75-07072)

474.   Wilder, B. (1979). The effects of group counseling on the self-concept and
        adjustment of Black juvenile delinquents. *Dissertation Abstracts International,
        39*(12), 7171. (University Microfilm No. AAC79-14003)

475.   Wodarski, J. S., & Pedi, S. J. (1978). The empirical evaluation of the effects
        of different group treatment strategies against a controlled treatment strategy on
        behavior exhibited by antisocial children, behaviors of the therapist, and two
        self-rating scales that measure antisocial behavior. *Journal of Clinical
        Psychology, 34,* 471-481.

476.   Woody, R. H., & Wood, J. D. (1975). Behavioral group counseling for
        adolescent females with behavioral problems. *Psychological Reports, 36,* 421-
        422.
        Describes the success of a program aimed at integrating and implementing
        humanistic and behavioral group methods with 29 adolescent females with
        behavioral problems.

477.   Zakus, G. (1979). A group behavior modification approach to adolescent
        obesity. *Adolescence, 14,* 481-490.

478.   Zimmerman, G. A. (1987). Investigation of behavior therapy groups in a
        children and youth partial hospitalization program. *Dissertation Abstracts
        International, 48*(04), 885. (University Microfilm No. AAC87-11435)

479. Zimpfer, D., & Waltman, D. (1982). Correlates of effectiveness in group counseling. *Small Group Behavior, 13,* 275-290.
Describes a client-centered group counseling program for 70 adolescents with behavior or learning problems. Group composition and counselor variables were related to how the subjects interacted, how much value they placed on the group, and changes in their self-image.

480. Zongaro, A. J. (1987). A multivariate analysis of recidivism: Discriminating recidivists from non-recidivists among non-incarcerated male delinquents in a group counseling program. *Dissertation Abstracts International, 47*(09), 3379. (University Microfilm No. AAC86-27540)

481. Zweback, S. (1976). Use of concrete reinforcement to control content of verbal initiations in group therapy with adolescents. *Psychological Reports, 38,* 1051-1057.

3

College Students

482. Altmaier, E. M., & Woodward, M. (1981). Group vicarious desensitization of test anxiety. *Journal of Counseling Psychology, 28*(5), 467-469.

483. Anderson, D. (1977). The effects of group counseling on the incidence of fear of success motives, role orientation and personal orientation of college women. *Dissertation Abstracts International, 38*(04), 1881A.

484. Anderson, J. D. (1978). Growth groups and alienation: A comparative study of Rogerian encounter, self-directed encounter, and Gestalt. *Group and Organization Studies, 3*(1), 85-107.
      Compared short-term variants of Rogerian encounter, Gestalt sensory awareness, and self-directed encounter treatments in terms of intermember empathy and cohesiveness, and outcome measurement levels of alienation and autonomy. All growth-group experience significantly decreased feelings of alienation and increased sense of autonomy. Discusses implications for practice and additional findings.

485. Andrews, D. A. (1973). The attitudinal effects of group discussions between young criminal offenders and community volunteers. *Journal of Community Psychology, 1,* 417-422.
      Compared attitudes toward the law and law violations in a control group of young incarcerated offenders and community volunteers, and a group that participated in short-term structured group counseling. At post-test, control offenders showed increased identification with other criminals and increased tolerance for law violations, while experimental offenders showed significant decrease in identification and no change in tolerance. Treatment effects were minimal among the community volunteers.

486. Anton, W. D. (1976). An evaluation of outcome variables into the systematic desensitization of test anxiety. *Behavior Research and Therapy, 14,* 217-224.
      Compared the effects of group counseling (GC) and group systematic desensitization (GSD) on the academic performance and anxiety of 54 undergraduates. The GSD group showed significant decreases in test anxiety

relative to the GC group, but neither group showed any change in trait anxiety or academic achievement.

487. Arabatgis, J. S. (1974). Group counseling with college students through the implementation of a decision-making model. *Dissertation Abstracts International, 35*(02), 813A.

488. Avis, J. (1991). The effects of integrity therapy group counseling on peer relationships of college students. *Dissertation Abstracts International, 51*(08), 2678A.

489. Baither, R. C., & Godsey, R. (1979). Rational emotive education and relaxation training in large group treatment of test anxiety. *Psychological Reports, 45*(1), 326.
      One hundred fifty underachieving freshmen enrolled in a study skills course received one of three test anxiety treatments: rational emotive education (RE), relaxation training (RT), or control. Administered the Alexander-Husak Anxiety Differential pre- and post-treatment with this result: The RE and control groups' scores suggest that an RE approach may be more useful than RT.

490. Bander, K. W., Steinke, G. V., Allen, G. J., & Mosher, D. L. (1975). Evaluation of three dating-specific treatment approaches for heterosexual dating anxiety. *Journal of Consulting and Clinical Psychology, 43,* 259-265.
      Compared the utility of a re-educative therapy with a human relations training program in reducing heterosexual dating anxiety in 84 male undergraduates. According to self-report and behaviorally rated outcome criteria, re-educative therapy was more effective.

491. Barrera, A. R. (1981). The effectiveness of group psychotherapy and study skills training on academic achievement of Mexican American freshmen. *Dissertation Abstracts International, 42*(04), 1539.
      Assesses the effectiveness of the combination of group psychotherapy, study skills training and tutoring on the academic achievement of Mexican American college freshmen. The treatment did not significantly affect the participants' grade point average or attrition but did appear to facilitate their adjustment to the university environment.

492. Berah, E. F. (1981). Influence of scheduling variations on the effectiveness of a group assertion-training program for women. *Journal of Counseling Psychology, 28,* 265-268.
      Compared four types of group assertion: massed practice, distributed practice, combined practice, and no treatment. No differences were found between the groups, except that assertiveness training produced greater increases in assertiveness.

493. Berlin, J. S., & Dies, R. R. (1974). Differential group structure: The effects on socially isolated college students. *Small Group Behavior, 5*(4), 462-472.
      Compared the relative efficacy of encounter marathon (EM) versus theme-oriented marathon (TOM) techniques, using a structured workshop control group format with 25 socially isolated undergraduates. Assessed change resulting from the group experience immediately following, and four weeks after the group

experience. The TOM approach resulted in significant follow-up changes in participant self-concept and more frequent reporting of long-term effect.

494. Blumer, C. H., & McNamara, J. R. (1985). Preparatory procedures for videotaped feedback to improve social skills. *Psychological Reports, 57,* 549-550.
Compared videotaped feedback coupled with three types of group treatment: didactic lectures, behavioral problem solving, and exercises to raise group cohesion. Over time, the combination of videotaped feedback and group treatment improved social skills in the undergraduate subjects.

495. Bohart, J. B., & Bergland, B. W. (1979). The impact of death and dying counseling groups on death anxiety in college students. *Death Education, 2*(4), 381-391.

496. Bonfandini, J. E. (1976). Assessing and changing the student-teacher and his learning environment with student ratings and peer group counseling sessions. *Dissertation Abstracts International, 37*(04), 2119. (University Microfilm No. AAC76-23210)

497. Borkovec, T. D., Kaloupek, D. G., & Slama, K. M. (1975). The facilitative effect of muscle tension-release in the relaxation treatment of sleep disturbance. *Behavior Therapy, 6*(3), 301-309.
Students with sleep difficulty were assigned to one of four treatment conditions: progressive relaxation with muscle tension release (PR), relaxation without tension release, placebo, and no treatment. Prior to the final session, PR produced significantly greater improvement in reported latency to sleep onset than the other three conditions, and after the final session, PR was the only group to display greater improvement than the no treatment condition. On a five month follow-up, the PR group had made further gains.

498. Brandt, H. P. (1975). Effects of developmental group counseling and creativity training on creativity, adjustment, and achievement. *Dissertation Abstracts International, 35*(08), 5009A.

499. Caffey, C. A. (1983). A study of the effects of group counseling on self-esteem, attitude, and reading efficiency of athletes at the University of Mississippi. *Dissertation Abstracts International, 44*(06), 1728A.

500. Caldwell, T. A. (1981). The effectiveness of peer group counseling using integrity therapy in producing personality improvement in incoming college freshmen. *Dissertation Abstracts International, 42*(04), 1581B.

501. Calef, R. A. (1974). Facilitation of group desensitization of test anxiety. *Psychological Reports, 35*(3), 1285-1286.
Used a modified desensitization procedure, which called for pairing a stimulus tone with relaxation training, then presenting the stimulus while subjects completed the test-anxiety hierarchy. Subjects were then divided into four groups: one group received the modified group-desensitization procedure (MGDP); a second group received conventional group desensitization (CGD),

and two control conditions (CCs) were included. MGDP was more effective than CGD and the CCs.

502. Cooker, P. G., & Caffey, C. A. (1984). Addressing the cognitive and affective needs of college athletes: Effects of group counseling on self-esteem, reading skills, and coaches' perception on attitudes. *Journal of Sport Psychology, 6*(4), 377-384.
Examined three counseling approaches with 43 college football players: a reading instruction program; reading plus counseling, focusing on personal growth and self-awareness; and, a no treatment control group. The treatment group showed significantly higher post-test scores on reading rate and efficiency but not on comprehension. Students in the counseling condition reported benefits in problem solving, interpersonal relationship building, and the expression of feelings.

503. Corvin, S. A. (1986). Analyses of differences in support seeking between two groups of women returning to college. *Dissertation Abstracts International, 46*(11), 3290A. (University Microfilm No. AAC86-01141)
Identified differences between women returning to college who were interested in participating in supportive group counseling and those who were not. The largest numbers of those interested were found in the Junior and Senior classes. Those not interested were significantly less concerned about course work and grades, arranging child-care, relations with significant others, remaining young-looking, attractive, and depression; they perceived greater emotional support from people and were more successful in dealing with their return to college.

504. Crafts, G. (1975). The effect of group counseling on self-concept and reading improvement on selected community college students. *Dissertation Abstracts International, 35*(07), 4181A.

505. Danford, R. D., Jr. (1981). A comparison of experiential and didactic group counseling techniques/activities for improving the vocational and personal development of Black evening students. *Dissertation Abstracts International, 41*(09), 3881A. (University Microfilm No. AAC81-05568)

506. Davis, M. M. (1978). The effects of group counseling on the self-concept and achievement of Black college freshmen. *Dissertation Abstracts International, 39*(03), 1335A.

507. Davis, R. C., & Horne, A. M. (1986). The effect of small-group counseling and career course on career decidedness and maturity. *Vocational Guidance Quarterly, 34*, 255-262.
Compared the effectiveness of a career course and small group counseling on 102 undergraduates' career decidedness and maturity. Both treatment groups significantly changed but there was no difference between the two groups.

508. Dies, R. R., & Cohen, L. (1976). Content considerations in group therapist self-disclosure. *International Journal of Group Psychotherapy, 26*(1), 71-88.
Studied therapy (T) versus encounter (E) group members' attitudes toward varying degrees of therapist self-disclosure. Subjects, 108 undergraduate psychology majors, evaluated whether a leader's statements made during group

discussion were helpful or harmful to the group. E groups showed a more positive attitude toward leader openness than did T groups. Time affected subjects' disclosure ratings. Discusses the pros and cons of therapist self-disclosure.

509. Dobson, J. E., & Campbell, N. J. (1986). Laboratory outcomes of personal growth groups. *Journal for Specialists in Group Work, 11,* 9-15.
Required Master's level counselor candidates to participate in one of six personal growth groups, which provided a forum for examining themselves and how they relate to others. Post-treatment and follow-up results showed significant improvement.

510. Dowling, S. M. E. (1984). A group counseling approach to reducing death anxiety in nursing students. *Dissertation Abstracts International, 44*(07), 2228.
Assigned 43 nurses to one of three treatments: wait-list control (WL); a group using structured counseling and activities (SC&A) designed to have subjects explore their feelings about death; and, a group which used films relating to death followed by group discussion (F&GD). Results failed to support these contentions: (a) that the SC&A group was superior to either the WL group or the F&GD group, or (b) that there would be a higher correlation between death anxiety and trait anxiety than between death anxiety and state anxiety.

511. Ely, A. L., Guerney, B. G., & Stover, L. (1973). Efficacy of the training phase of conjugal therapy. *Psychotherapy: Theory, Research and Practice, 10,* 201-207.
Assigned married graduate and undergraduate students, with varying degrees of marital problems, to either conjugal therapy training in meaningful communication, designed to improve mutual understanding, or a no therapy control. Pre- and post-therapy questionnaires demonstrated significant between-group differences in amount of improvement.

512. Felton, G. S., & Biggs, B. E. (1973). Psychotherapy and responsibility: Teaching internalization behavior to Black low achievers through group therapy. *Small Group Behavior, 4,* 147-155.
Describes the use of group therapy and a weekend encounter experience with 15 low achieving Black students. Subjects' internal scores increased at post-test on the Rotter Internal-External scale.

513. Foulds, M. L., Guinan, J. F., & Hannigan, P. (1974). Marathon group: Changes in scores on the California Psychological Inventory. *Journal of College Student Personnel, 15*(6), 474-479.
Administered the CPI to 18 undergraduates immediately before and after participation in a 24-hour marathon group; 18 control subjects completed the CPI but did not participate in the marathon group. Found significant positive changes on 11 of 18 scales of the CPI for the experimental subjects, suggesting that an experiential-Gestalt group enhances feelings of intra- and inter-personal adequacy; fosters a stronger sense of values and a greater acceptance of different values; and, increases motivation in both academic and social activities.

514. Foulds, M. L., Guinan, J. F., & Warehime, R. G. (1974). Marathon group: Changes in a measure of dogmatism. *Small Group Behavior, 5*(4), 387-392.

515.   Foulds, M. L., Guinan, J. F., & Warehime, R. G. (1974). Marathon group: Changes in perceived locus of control. *Journal of College Student Personnel, 15*(1), 8-11.
        Administered Rotter's Internal-External Control Scale (I-E) to 15 undergraduates before and after participation in a 24-hour marathon group exercise; 50 undergraduates matched on I-E pretest scores served as controls. Found significant increases in internality in the marathon subjects. Presents suggestions for future research.

516.   Foulds, M. L., & Hannigan, P. S. (1976). Effects of psychomotor group therapy on locus of control and social desirability. *Journal of Humanistic Psychology, 16*(2), 81-88.
        Subjects in the experimental group met for eight weekly sessions of four hours each. Tested all subjects pre- and post-treatment, and at a six-month follow-up. Pre- to post-treatment comparisons disclosed significant positive changes on both tests in the experimental group, and follow-up data revealed that this change remained constant. The control group showed no significant changes. Psychomotor therapy seemed to foster increased internality and decreased social desirability responding in growth-seeking college students.

517.   Foulds, M. L., & Hannigan, P. S. (1976). A Gestalt marathon workshop: Effects on extraversion and neuroticism. *Journal of College Student Personnel, 17*(1), 50-54.
        Examined the effects of a Gestalt marathon workshop on 18 college students' Eysenck Personality Inventory (EPI) scores. It was hypothesized that subjects would show significant increases in extraversion and decreases in neuroticism, while the 18 control subjects would not. Found significant change in neuroticism and extraversion-introversion.

518.   Francis, K. C., McDaniel, M., & Doyle, R. E. (1987). Training in role communication skills: Effect on interpersonal and academic skills of high-risk freshmen. *Journal of College Student Personnel, 28*(2), 151-156.
        Measured 39 disadvantaged college freshmen's interpersonal communication skills; study habits and attitudes; and academic achievement. Using these subjects, compared a didactic academic counseling group (DAC) with group counseling (GC), which emphasized interpersonal communication skills. The GC subjects showed improvement on the dependent measure and in GPA scores compared to the DAC group.

519.   Fukuyama, M. A., & Coleman, N. C. (1992). A model for bicultural assertion training with Asian-Pacific American college students: A pilot study. Special issue: Group counseling with multicultural populations. *Journal for Specialists in Group Work, 17*(4), 210-217.
        Offers a theoretical basis for culture-specific group work, including the concepts of acculturation and ethnic identity development of Asian-Pacific Americans. Discusses group procedures, group themes, cultural specific topics, benefits from participation and selection criteria for group participants in an Asian-Pacific American bicultural assertion training program.

520.   Gamble, D. H. (1982). The effects of group counseling vs. self-directed reading on androgyny, self-actualization and academic achievement of college females

of varying academic ability. *Dissertation Abstracts International, 42*(08), 3399. (University Microfilm No. AAC82-02081)

521.   Golden, B. R., Corazzini, J. G., & Grady, P. (1993). Current practice of group therapy at university counseling centers: A national survey. *Professional Psychology: Research and Practice, 24*(2), 228-230.
Surveyed 232 directors, with a response rate of 64%, to determine current practices of group psychotherapy at university counseling centers. Results indicate that the typical group consists of five to eight members, is co-led, meets weekly in the late afternoon, and lasts for 1.5 hours. Discusses shortage of treatment, implications for practice, and future research.

522.   Gonzalez, G. (1991). Structured group counseling for university students of alcoholic parentage. *Dissertation Abstracts International, 52*(05), 1642. (University Microfilm No. AAC91-21635)

523.   Gordon, W. K. (1983). Combination of cognitive group therapy and subliminal stimulation in treatment of test-anxious college males. *Dissertation Abstracts International, 43*(11), 3731. (University Microfilm No. AAC83-07927)
Compared the effectiveness of cognitive group therapy (CGT) and subliminal stimulation (SS) in reducing test anxiety in 34 male students. Students in the SS condition demonstrated no significant effect, but those who received both treatments demonstrated significant decreases in test anxiety.

524.   Grottkau, B. J. (1986). The effects of a group counseling intervention on self-concept, self-esteem, anxiety and grade point average of female, nontraditional students. *Dissertation Abstracts International, 47*(02), 386A.

525.   Grouling, T. E. (1977). An investigation comparing the effectiveness of biofeedback and group counseling in reducing test anxiety. *Dissertation Abstracts International, 37*(09), 5604. (University Microfilm No. AAC77-05535)

526.   Hadiyono, J. E. P. (1986). The effect of the native language and English during interactional group psychotherapy with Indonesian and Malaysian students, and the effectiveness of this method for foreign students from non-Western countries. *Dissertation Abstracts International, 46*(10), 3594B.

527.   Hilyer, J. C., & Mitchell, W. (1979). Effect of systematic physical fitness training combined with counseling on the self-concept of college students. *Journal of Counseling Psychology, 26*(5), 427-436.
Investigated the effect of systematic physical fitness training combined with counseling on measured self-concept. For ten weeks, subjects participated in one of three conditions: fitness program only (FP), fitness program plus counseling (FP+C), or a control condition. The FP group made significant gains in self-concept; those in the FP+C who had had low self-concept on the pretest measure made significant positive changes in self-concept.

528.   Howard, J. R. (1974). The effect of group counseling techniques on feelings of alienation of Black college freshmen. *Dissertation Abstracts International, 35*(05), 2533A.

529.   Jacobs, E., & Croake, J. W. (1976). Rational emotive theory applied to groups. *Journal of College Student Personnel, 17,* 127-129.
       Examined whether a short-term learning program, based on Ellis and Harper's (1961) principles of rational emotive therapy, would positively affect rational thinking, anxiety, and self-reported problems in college students. Results indicate that rational emotive therapy techniques helped produce desirable changes in these areas.

530.   Jacobs, M., Jacobs, A., Feldmann, G., & Cavior, N. (1973). Feedback: II. The "credibility gap": Delivery of positive and negative and emotional and behavioral feedback in groups. *Journal of Consulting and Clinical Psychology, 41*(2), 215-223.
       Forty-eight undergraduates participated in six programmed sensitivity training groups receiving either behavioral, emotional, or combined feedback; feedback was either positive or negative in nature. Consistently rated all positive feedback as more credible than negative feedback. Positive feedback groups reported greater cohesion. Discusses other findings concerning the credibility, desirability, and impact of feedback, and sensitivity groups' evaluations.

531.   Johnson, S., & Johnson, N. (1979). Effects of various group approaches on self-actualization of graduate counseling students. *Journal of Counseling Psychology, 26*(5), 444-447.
       Compared group approaches to determine whether growth groups affect the participants' self-actualization. Assigned subjects by gender to one of four conditions: a marathon group, a shorter session group, a combination of marathon and shorter-session group, or a control group. While treatment groups indicated significant positive movement, no single approach was found to be more effective than the others.

532.   Jones, D. S., & Medvene, A. M. (1975). Self-actualization effects of a marathon growth group. *Journal of Counseling Psychology, 22*(1), 39-43.
       Examined the effects of a marathon group experience on 34 female and 23 male undergraduates' levels of self-actualization at two days, and at six weeks after the experience. Assessed the relationship between ego strength and extent of change in self-actualization during a marathon growth group. Gains in self-actualization due to marathon group participation were found to depend upon an individual's level of ego strength upon group entry.

533.   Jones, F. D. (1975). The effect of personal growth group counseling on the self-concepts and academic achievement of college freshman. *Dissertation Abstracts International, 36*(05), 2631A.

534.   Karpeles, K. (1978). Differential effectiveness of structured and non-structured group counseling as a function of facilitation for sexual attitude change and sexual behavior change among sexually normal university students. *Dissertation Abstracts International, 39*(02), 678.

535.   Kennedy, B. R. J. (1990). The effects of a structured group counseling program on grade point averages and noncognitive factors among nontraditional freshmen college students. *Dissertation Abstracts International, 50*(08), 2389. (University Microfilm No. AAC89-18802)

536. Kilmann, P. R. (1976). Effects of a marathon group on self-actualization and attitudes toward women. *Journal of Clinical Psychology, 32,* 154-157.
      Female undergraduates participated in a 16-hour marathon session, designed to increase levels of self-actualization and to improve attitudes towards women. Discusses improvements in the participants in the areas of independence and self-supportedness.

537. Kilmann, P. R., Albert, B. M., & Sotile, W. M. (1975). Relationship between locus of control, structure of therapy, and outcome. *Journal of Consulting and Clinical Psychology, 43,* 588.
      Evaluated the relationship between locus of control and structure of group therapy with undergraduates, who participated either in a 16-hour marathon or in group therapy sessions. Results tentatively support pairing external subjects with a structured therapist model, and internal subjects with an unstructured therapist model, for maximum therapy benefits.

538. Kimball, R., & Gelso, C. J. (1974). Self-actualization in a marathon growth group: Do the strong get stronger? *Journal of Counseling Psychology, 21*(1), 38-42.
      Examined self-actualization of 20 male and 8 female college students at one and four weeks after their weekend marathon group experience. Analysis of pre- and post-scores indicate that, in general, group experience increased self-actualization, which persisted through the four week follow-up. Discusses the possibility of a sleeper effect, and offers hypotheses on conditions necessary for marathon groups to be effective.

539. Kimbrough, F. H. (1981). Effects of a group career/life planning counseling model on the sex role and career self-concept of female undergraduates. *Dissertation Abstracts International, 42*(03), 1009A. (University Microfilm No. AAC81-18274)

540. Kirshner, L. A. (1974). A follow-up of a freshman group counseling program. *Journal of the American College Health Association, 22*(4), 279-280.

541. Klinefelter, H. F., III. (1983). Cognitive and experiential group counseling for university students of alcoholic parentage. *Dissertation Abstracts International, 43*(10), 3218A. (University Microfilm No. AAC83-02254)
      Evaluated two kinds of structured group counseling, designed for university students with an alcoholic parent. Randomly assigned subjects to cognitive counseling, experiential counseling, or a delayed treatment control group. The counseling groups showed significant increases in knowledge about alcoholism; the cognitive group showed significantly more knowledge gains in the area of responsible drinking than the other groups, and more significant improvement in coping attitudes than in the control group; and, the experiential group showed improved coping behaviors.

542. Lesh, K. C. (1981). The effects of support services on the self-concept, locus of control and goal attainment of physically disabled college students. *Dissertation Abstracts International, 42*(03), 1011A. (University Microfilm No. AAC81-17739)

Evaluated two kinds of support services for physically disabled college students by assigning volunteer subjects to one of three conditions: Adaptive Physical Education classes, counseling group, or no-support control. The two support conditions did not effect significant changes in self-concept or locus of control, and there were no significant differences among the groups.

543. Lindquist, C. U., & Lowe, S. R. (1978). A community-oriented evaluation of two prevention programs for college freshman. *Journal of Counseling Psychology, 25*(1), 53-60.

544. Linehan, E., & O'Toole, J. (1982). Effect of subliminal stimulation of symbiotic fantasies on college student self-disclosure in group counseling. *Journal of Counseling Psychology, 29*(2), 151-157.
Three main groups of 12 female college student subjects, consisting of six experimentals and six controls in each group, participated in three group counseling sessions. Pre-session subliminal messages, "Mommy and I are one" and "People are walking" were given to the experimental and control subjects, respectively. Group 1 was exposed to eight counselor self-disclosures (CSDs), Group 2 received 4 CSDs, and Group 3 received no CSDs. Results indicated that the "Mommy" message produced more subject self-disclosure.

545. Maffeo, P. A. (1984). The influence of a supportive, problem-solving, group intervention on the health status of students with great recent life change. *Journal of Psychosomatic Research, 28,* 275-278.
Assigned college students with high life-change and illness scores to one of two conditions: supportive, problem-solving, group therapy treatment or a control group. The control group fared significantly worse in illness frequency and days disabled than did the treatment group.

546. Marx, M. B., Somes, G. W., Garrity, T. F., Reeb, A. C., & Maffeo, P. A. (1984). The influence of a supportive, problem-solving, group intervention on the health status of students with great recent life change. *Journal of Psychosomatic Research, 28,* 275-278.
Describes an intervention group (IG) designed to help college seniors cope with life changes and interpersonal problems. IG participants did significantly better in areas of number of illnesses and length of impairment than control subjects.

547. May, R. J., & Tierney, D. E. (1976). Personality changes as a function of group transactional analysis. *Journal of College Student Personnel, 17*(6), 485-488.
Sixteen college dormitory residents participated in transactional analysis (TA) groups. Pre- and post-test scores on the Omnibus Personality Inventory showed that, compared with the control group, the experimental group had significantly decreased Complexity scores and increased Aestheticism scores. Discusses the use of TA groups in university programs.

548. McMillan, R. L. (1978). The effect of group counseling on the self-concept of Black college students. *Dissertation Abstracts International, 39*(04), 2067A.

549. Mendonca, L. (1982). Group counseling: Its effects on the perception of self and others and on the adjustment of students from India. *Dissertation Abstracts International, 42*(09), 3873A.

550. Meyers-Arvin, M. A. (1991). Structured group counseling for university students of alcoholic parentage. *Dissertation Abstracts International, 52*(05), 1642A. (University Microfilm No. AAC91-21635)
       Evaluated structured group counseling for changes in knowledge, ego development, attitude and behavior. Randomly assigned college students with alcoholic parentage either to structured group therapy or to an informational control group. Both groups showed significant increases in knowledge, there were significant between group differences in ego development, but there were no differences in attitude and behavior.

551. Moore, J. C. (1978). Relationship of group counseling and personality factors to attrition of freshman nursing students. *Dissertation Abstracts International, 38*(11), 6540. (University Microfilm No. AAC78-06091)

552. Parsons, J. A. (1980). Effects of therapist modeling of feedback delivery on member feedback and self-concept in group therapy with EMR students. *Dissertation Abstracts International, 41*(03), 1122B.

553. Pittman, W. M. (1977). The relative effectiveness of three group counseling approaches in reducing loneliness among college students. *Dissertation Abstracts International, 37*(08), 4870A.

554. Poole, P. H. (1977). Constructive personality change in relation to a new class of contextual variables in the general linear equation called paratherapeutic praxis for university students involved in group counseling. *Dissertation Abstracts International, 37*(09), 5613A.

555. Porter, B. L. (1977). The effects of a behavioral group counseling method on the study habits, attitudes and academic achievement of some differently qualified students. *Dissertation Abstracts International, 38*(01), 184. (University Microfilm No. AAC77-15196)

556. Qualia, L. R. (1988). Effects of group counseling and group discussion on selected personality variables on first-year theology students. *Dissertation Abstracts International, 48*(08), 1989.

557. Rabin, M. A. (1974). The differential effects of short-term preventive experiential group counseling with residential and commuter college students. *Dissertation Abstracts International, 35*(03), 1510A.

558. Ramirez-Cancel, C. M. (1975). Effects of verbal reinforcement and modeling in group counseling on the career-information-seeking behavior of college freshmen. *Dissertation Abstracts International, 36*(05), 2719. (University Microfilm No. AAC75-25133)

559. Redick, R. J. (1974). Behavioral group counseling and death anxiety in student nurses. *Dissertation Abstracts International, 35*(04), 1989A.

560. Richards, P. S., Owen, L., & Stein, S. (1993). A religiously oriented group counseling intervention for self-defeating perfectionism: A pilot study. *Counseling and Value, 37*(2), 96-104.
      Describes a religiously oriented group counseling approach developed to treat self-defeating perfectionism. Treatment with 15 religiously devout university students included relaxation exercises, religious bibliotherapy exercises, religious imagery, and discussions about religious concepts of perfection. During the course of treatment, subjects became less perfectionistic and depressed, and experienced more positive self-esteem and feelings of existential well-being.

561. Robertson, L. M. (1975). The effects of individual and group counseling on the self-concept of physically handicapped college students. *Dissertation Abstracts International, 35*(09), 5873A.

562. Rockwell, W. J., Moorman, J. C., Hawkins, D., & Musante, G. (1976). Individual versus group: Brief treatment outcome in a university mental health service. *Journal of the American College Health Association, 24*(4), 186-190.

563. Ross, R. G. (1982). Staying in school: Peer support group intervention with high risk community college students. *Dissertation Abstracts International, 42*(08), 3444. (University Microfilm No. AAC82-01389)

564. Roush, K. L. (1987). Structured group counseling for college students of alcoholic parentage. *Dissertation Abstracts International, 48*(06), 1423A. (University Microfilm No. AAC87-20057)
      Compared structured group counseling with an educational lecture control group in the treatment of college students of alcoholic parents. Measured knowledge, coping attitude, and behavior change as it related to parental alcoholism. Both groups showed significant knowledge increase, maintained through follow-up. The treatment group showed improved coping attitude, with qualification. There was no significant improvement in behavior.

565. Rubin, H. S., & Cohen, H. A. (1974). Group counseling and remediation: A two-faceted intervention approach to the problem of attrition in nursing education. *Journal of Educational Research, 67*(5), 195-198.
      Investigated whether using brief group therapy to address underachievement and remediation to address deficiencies in basic skills would reduce the attrition rate of student nurses. Interviewed subjects whose entrance scores indicated risk of academic failure: high scorers received therapy, low scorers with no motivational problems received remediation, and low scorers with motivational problems received both. Use of these techniques resulted in a significant decrease in attrition rate.

566. Saunders, M. P. (1976). The effects of group counseling on open admission students. *Dissertation Abstracts International, 37*(02), 895A.

567. Schoonmaker, B. J. (1980). The relative effectiveness of a short-term structured psychological education model on the inner-directedness, time competence and personal goal attainment of college sophomores. *Dissertation Abstracts International, 41*(10), 224. (University Microfilm No. AAC81-07668)

568. Schutter, W. J. (1982). Practicum seminar instruction: A comparison of the relative efficacy of psychodrama and discussion formats. *Dissertation Abstracts International, 43*(04), 1050A.

569. Schwartz, L., Kieff, J. S., & Winers, J. A. (1976). Group experience for nonpatient undergraduates with difficulties in making decisions. *Journal of the American College Health Association, 24*(4), 195-197.
      Describes a group therapeutic counseling program developed for students experiencing career decision-making difficulties. The group leaders used a nondirective, facilitative approach. Initially, group members had guarded reactions; in later sessions, group members began revealing themselves; and by the end of the project, considerable group cohesion had developed. All subjects completed the project, and two reported definite increases in self-esteem.

570. Scissons, E. H., & Njaa, L. J. (1973). Systematic desensitization of test anxiety: A comparison of group and individual treatment. *Journal of Consulting and Clinical Psychology, 41*(3), 470.
      Assigned 30 college students with high test anxiety to group or individual desensitization therapy, or to a no-treatment control group. Results clearly demonstrate the efficacy of both individual and group desensitization in treating high test anxiety.

571. Sellers, J. E. (1983). The effects of stress inoculation training and conversation skills training on shy college students. *Dissertation Abstracts International, 43*(09), 2895A.

572. Smith, R. E., & Nye, S. L. (1973). A comparison of implosive therapy and systematic desensitization in the treatment of test anxiety. *Journal of Consulting and Clinical Psychology, 41*(1), 37-42.
      Compared the efficacy of two techniques for reducing test anxiety with 34 undergraduates. Both desensitization and implosive therapy resulted in significant decreases in anxiety scores. Discusses results in relation to a number of conceptual and methodological issues.

573. Sowa, C. J. (1992). Understanding clients' perceptions of stress. Special Issue: Wellness throughout the life span. *Journal of Counseling and Development, 71*(2), 179-183.
      Presents a framework for understanding clients' perceptions of stress. Systematic rationalization (SR), based on the concept of learned helplessness, focuses on the perceptions and attributions of clients who have difficulty coping with stressful events in their lives. Divided 48 clients at a university counseling center into an SR group and a general stress management group. At post-test, SR subjects reported significantly less perceived stress than did controls.

574. Starke, M. C. (1987). Enhancing social skills and self-perceptions of physically disabled young adults: Assertiveness training versus discussion groups. *Behavior Modification, 11*, 3-16.
      Assigned physically disabled undergraduates to one of three conditions: assertiveness training (AT), discussion-support (DS) or a waiting list control group. Those in AT showed greater improvement in social responses and assertiveness. Additional results are addressed.

575.   Steward, R. J. (1993). Black women and White women in groups: Suggestions for minority-sensitive group services on university campuses. *Journal of Counseling and Development, 72,* 39-41.

576.   Swarr, R. R., & Ewing, T. N. (1977). Outcome effects of eclectic interpersonal-learning-based group psychotherapy with college student neurotics. *Journal of Consulting and Clinical Psychology, 45*(6), 1029-1035.

577.   Sweet, M. J. (1994). Gay, lesbian, and bisexual young adults: Satisfaction with counseling experiences. *Dissertation Abstracts International, 54*(08), 4410. (University Microfilm No. AAC93-22558)
       Surveyed gay male, lesbian and bisexual college students to determine their satisfaction with counseling experiences. Findings include: high satisfaction with, and a preference for peer support group counseling; a preference for openly gay male, lesbian and bisexual counselors/leaders; greater satisfaction with current than with previous counseling. The most frequently cited reasons for counseling were loneliness and sexual orientation issues.

578.   Sweet, T. W. (1989). A study of an intensive student developmental counseling program with the student athlete. *Dissertation Abstracts International, 49*(12), 3631. (University Microfilm No. AAC89-05975)

579.   Swisher, J. D., Warner, R. W., Spence, C. C., & Upcraft, M. L. (1973). Four approaches to drug abuse prevention among college students. *Journal of College Student Personnel, 14,* 231-235.
       Compared four group approaches to drug abuse prevention for changes in drug knowledge, attitude toward drug use, and drug usage. Undergraduates participated in one of four groups: discussion, relationship counseling, or one of two types of reinforcement groups—one with and another without reformed drug users. Knowledge was nondifferentially increased in all groups; all groups adopted a more liberal attitude toward drug use; and there were no significant changes in drug use.

580.   Talbott-Green, M. A. (1989). A comparative study of feminist group psychotherapy and poetry therapy as an adjunctive treatment to increase self-actualization on the personal orientation inventory. *Dissertation Abstracts International, 49*(08), 3425. (University Microfilm No. AAC88-20360)

581.   Tardd, A. C. (1989). The effects of rational self-counseling as an independent study course. *Dissertation Abstracts International, 49*(07), 1708. (University Microfilm No. AAC88-11990)

582.   Thomas, B. L. (1985). Topical group counseling as an intervention with women. *Dissertation Abstracts International, 46*(05), 1422. (University Microfilm No. AAC85-14160)
       Evaluates whether Topical Group Counseling (TPG) effects an attitudinal change in females with sex-role conflicts. Compared subjects in TPG to a no-treatment control group, with no significant results.

583.   Thompson, A., & Miller, A. (1973). A criterion system for measuring outcomes of counseling. *Journal of College Student Personnel, 14*(6), 483-489.

584.   Thompson, P. N. (1991). The effectiveness of social problem-solving therapy
        in reducing anxiety. *Dissertation Abstracts International, 52*(01), 576B.
        Compared Problem-Solving Therapy (PST) for its effectiveness in reducing
        anxiety with a wait-list control condition (WLCC) and a nondirective group
        therapy regimen, Problem-Focused Therapy (PFT). By post-test, subjects in the
        PST group had significantly reduced their anxiety compared to those in the
        WLCC, as measured by the Beck Anxiety Inventory (BAI). PST did not
        significantly differ from PFT on the BAI. PST subjects rated PST therapy and
        therapists more positively than their PFT counterparts. Results support the
        hypothesis that PST more effectively reduces anxiety in college students than the
        WLCC.

585.   Thorn, M. E., & Boudewyns, P. A. (1976). A behaviorally oriented weight loss
        program for counseling centers. *Journal of Counseling Psychology, 23*(1), 81-82.
        Compared the effectiveness of several weight loss programs offered through a
        university counseling center, using 80 undergraduates. Although subjects met
        for only two treatment sessions, at follow-up, those in the behavior therapy
        group had lost significantly more weight than subjects in the rational therapy,
        self-directed, and no-treatment control groups.

586.   Torrance, M. I. (1993). The design of a competence-based group psychotherapy
        training program for psychology graduate students. *Dissertation Abstracts
        International, 53*(07), 3758B.

587.   Tredwell, V. (1977). Group and individual counseling: Effects on college
        grades. *Journal of Non-White Concerns in Personnel and Guidance, 5,* 73-82.
        Compared the effectiveness of group (GC) versus individual counseling (IC) on
        the academic performance of 20 Black freshmen. Academically, GC subjects
        achieved more than those receiving IC. At one year follow-up, half of the IC
        subjects had left school, compared to one drop-out from the GC condition.

588.   Wade, J. D. (1982). Effect of improved self-concept on retention of Black
        students at the University of Oregon. *Dissertation Abstracts International,
        43*(06), 1904A.

589.   Weddington, W. G. (1981). Comparison of group systematic desensitization on
        pretest and test anxiety among community college students. *Dissertation
        Abstracts International, 42*(03), 1069A.

590.   Wessel, T. R. (1981). The relationship of self-concept and sex to anxiety,
        depression, and hostility among select Black college freshmen. *Dissertation
        Abstracts International, 42*(04), 1564A.

591.   West, M. A., & Kirkland, M. (1986). Effectiveness of growth groups in
        education. *Journal for Specialists in Group Work, 11*(1), 16-24.

592.   Whyte, C. B. (1978). Effective counseling methods for high-risk college
        freshmen. *Measurement and Evaluation in Guidance, 10,* 198-200.
        Examined the effectiveness of various counseling methods with high-risk college
        freshmen, using 63 subjects. The most effective treatment included study skills

instruction, group counseling, and individual internal/external locus of control counseling.

593.   Wingett, W. R. (1976). A comparison of two models of group counseling in teaching communication skills to nursing students. *Dissertation Abstracts International, 36*(07), 4278A.

594.   Wright, W., Morris, K. T., & Fettig, B. (1974). Comparative effects of social skill development. *Small Group Behavior, 5,* 211-221.
        Compared a structured (SG), an unstructured (UG), and a no-treatment control group (CG) for effects on the freshmen college subjects' self-concept, as measured by the Tennessee Self-Concept Scale and self-report. The UG showed significant increases in Self-Satisfaction, Personal Self, Social Self, Positive Self; CG scores increased in Positive Self; the SG remained the same.

595.   Zibili, A. S. (1989). Effects of group counseling on self-concept and academic achievement of Black college freshmen at Texas Southern University. *Dissertation Abstracts International, 49*(09), 2545A.

4

Adults

596. Abend, S. A. (1981). Sexism and psychotherapists: The relationship between sex of therapists, their level of training, and their sex-role stereotyping. *Dissertation Abstracts International, 42*(01), 134.

597. Abney, V. D., Yang, J. A., & Paulson, M. J. (1992). Transference and countertransference issues unique to long-term group psychotherapy of adult women molested as children: Trials and rewards. *Journal of Interpersonal Violence, 7,* 559-569.
Examines transference and countertransference in the long-term, psychodynamic, group treatment of women who had been molested as children. Includes an account of the therapists' countertransference reactions to the clients, approaches to transference and countertransference, and success of intervention.

598. Abraham, S. T. (1981). The effects of systematic desensitization group therapy on learned helplessness tendencies. *Dissertation Abstracts International, 42*(06), 2564A.

599. Abramowitz, C. V., Abramowitz, S. I., Roback, H. B., & Jackson, C. (1974). Differential effectiveness of directive and nondirective group therapies as a function of client internal-external control. *Journal of Consulting and Clinical Psychology, 42*(6), 849-853.

600. Abramowitz, S. I. (1976). Sex bias in psychotherapy: A failure to confirm. *American Journal of Psychiatry, 133,* 706-709.
Examined how gender affects countertransference and bias in psychotherapy. Relative to gender, found minimal differences in therapists' responses.

601. Abramowitz, S. I., & Abramowitz, C. V. (1974). Psychological-mindedness and benefit from insight-oriented group therapy. *Archives of General Psychiatry, 30*(5), 610-615.

602. Abramowitz, S. I., & Jackson, C. (1974). Comparative effectiveness of there-and-then versus here-and-now therapist interpretations in group psychotherapy. *Journal of Counseling Psychology, 21*(4), 288-293.

603.   Abston, N. (1985). The influence of patients' ethnicity and gender on ratings of suitability for various psychiatric treatments. *Dissertation Abstracts International, 46*(06), 2053.(University Microfilm No. AAC85-18309)

604.   Acton, R. G., & During, S. M. (1992). Preliminary results of aggression management training for aggressive parents. *Journal of Interpersonal Violence, 7*(3), 410-417.
       Twenty-nine parents completed a 13 week treatment program for aggression management training, which focused on anger management, communication skills, problem-solving skills, and enhancement of empathy. After treatment, parents reported less anger and improvements in relationships with children. Post-treatment scores on evaluation questionnaires moved from the clinical to the normal range.

605.   Adams, R., & Vetter, H. J. (1981). Social structure and psychodrama outcome: A ten year follow-up. *Journal of Offender Counseling, Services, and Rehabilitation, 6,* 111-119.
       At a 10 year follow-up, assessed criminality rate of males who had participated in psychodrama therapy while at a juvenile correction facility, and found that psychodrama was associated with increased criminality.

606.   Agan, H. W., Jr. (1982). A comparison of group chemotherapy and individual chemotherapy in treatment of outpatient schizophrenic patients. *Dissertation Abstracts International, 43*(02), 364. (University Microfilm No. AAC82-10423)

607.   Ahmad, Z. A. (1983). The effects of group counseling, situational message, microteaching, and relaxation training on the reduction of teaching anxiety. *Dissertation Abstracts International, 44*(06), 1690A.

608.   Ahumada, J. L., Abiuso, D., Baiguera, N., & Gallo, A. (1974). On limited-time group psychotherapy: I. Setting, admission, and therapeutic ideology. *Psychiatry, 37,* 254-260.
       Describes a group psychotherapy program consisting of very structured and well-defined parameters.

609.   Akin, C., & Kunzman, G. G. (1974). A group desensitization approach to public speaking anxiety. *Canadian Counsellor, 8*(2), 106-111.
       Outlines a program designed to reduce symptoms of public speaking anxiety in university students, using a mixed behavioral format and emphasizing practice situations. Results are similar to traditionally operant or desensitization formats, with less attrition in attendance.

610.   Alarcon, F.M. (1974). The effects of human potential group counseling on the self-concept and anxiety level of drug addicts in a therapeutic rehabilitation program. *Dissertation Abstracts International, 35*(02), 813. (University Microfilm No. AAC74-17324)

611.   Albrecht, E., & Brabender, V. (1983). Alcoholics in inpatient, short-term interactional group psychotherapy: An outcome study. *Group, 7*(3), 50-54.
       Examined 100 psychiatric inpatients, some of whom had secondary alcoholism and some of whom did not. Data from a battery of tests indicate that secondary

alcoholics did not differ from the other subjects in regard to treatment outcome, although they displayed more distinct active/aggressive personality features. Group outcomes did not differ according to the presence or absence of alcoholic members.

612.   Alden, A. R., Weddington, W. W., Jacobson, C., & Gianturco, D. T. (1979). Group aftercare for chronic schizophrenia. *Journal of Clinical Psychiatry, 40,* 249-252.

613.   Alexander, P. C., Neimeyer, R. A., Follette, V. M. (1991). Group therapy for women sexually abused as children: A controlled study and investigation of individual differences. *Journal of Interpersonal Violence, 6,* 218-231.

614.   Alfred, A. R. (1991). Members' perceptions of co-leaders' influence and effectiveness in group psychotherapy. *Dissertation Abstracts International, 51*(07), 3551. (University Microfilm No. AAC90-32238)

615.   Alfred, A. R. (1992). Members' perceptions of co-leaders' influence and effectiveness in group psychotherapy. *Journal for Specialists in Group Work, 17*(1), 42-53.
        Investigated whether group members in group therapy perceive male and female co-leaders differently in terms of influence and effectiveness. As the group progressed, members saw both co-leaders as more influential and effective. There were no definite findings regarding differences between male and female co-leaders.

616.   Alger, S. K. (1975). The effect of readiness on group counseling outcomes. *Dissertation Abstracts International, 35*(09), 5803. (University Microfilm No. AAC75-03685)

617.   Allen, J. C., & Barton, G. M. (1976). Patient comments about hospitalization: Implications for change. *Comprehensive Psychiatry, 17,* 631-640.

618.   Almeida, K. A. (1990). A group therapy project within the pastor-parish setting. *Dissertation Abstracts International, 51*(02), 528. (University Microfilm No. AAC90-15219)
        Describes the success of a long-term group counseling program within a Protestant parish and discusses implications for the pastor-parishioner relationship.

619.   Alyn, J. H., & Becker, L. A. (1984). Feminist therapy with chronically and profoundly disturbed women. *Journal of Counseling Psychology, 31,* 202-208. Psychiatrically chronically disturbed women who participated in a women's awareness group made significant gains in self-esteem and sexual knowledge as compared to the control group, which had no gain. Neither group's scores changed on the Attitudes Toward Women Scale.

620.   Amodeo, M., & Kurtz, N. (1990). Cognitive processes and abstinence in a treated alcoholic population. *International Journal of the Addictions, 25*(9), 983-1009.

Explored the cognitive processes affecting recovery in 46 White male alcoholics, who were abstinent either for 13 to 36 months, or for 37 to 108 months. Interviewed subjects about the precipitants to abstinence, the decision to remain abstinent, maintenance of abstinence, temptations to drink, and casual thoughts on drinking. Subjects reported that their decision to stop drinking was accompanied by an awareness that their lives were in crisis; most indicated two or more motivators, constituting a mental set, that helped them maintain sobriety; and, subjects cited various treatment modalities as useful in maintaining abstinence.

621. Anchor, K. N., Vojtisek, J. E., & Patterson, R. L. (1973). Trait anxiety, initial structuring and self-disclosure in groups of schizophrenic patients. *Psychotherapy: Theory, Research and Practice, 10,* 155-158.
Examined the relationship between trait anxiety, as measured by the State-Trait Anxiety Inventory, and self-disclosure in group psychotherapy, in 24 hospitalized schizophrenic males. High A-trait schizophrenics were inclined toward self-disclosure in group psychotherapy.

622. Anderson, A. T. (1978). Alcoholics in the mental hospital: Socialization and length of stay in treatment. *Journal of Studies on Alcohol, 39*(5), 914-917.
Examined whether the socialization of alcoholics among mental patients would arouse negative stereotyped concepts of mental disorder, resulting in premature termination of treatment. The nine-week treatment consisted of a core of confrontational group therapy supplemented with individual and family counseling, recreational activities, educational programs, and a job placement service. Comparison of the length of stay between members of the groups showed similar mean durations. Findings do not support the hypothesis.

623. Anderson, G. T. (1984). The effect of a form of group treatment with violent, chronic schizophrenic patients. *Dissertation Abstracts International, 44*(11), 3514. (University Microfilm No. AAC84-04033)
Evaluated the effect of group treatment on violent, chronic, schizophrenic patients. Tabulated violent incidents, where the patient was dangerous to self or others, for one year for 106 subjects, randomly assigned to group treatment (GT) or to no treatment. The GT condition had a significantly reduced number of violent episodes and demonstrated improvement in all aspects of day to day living.

624. Andrews, J. (1976). An investigation into the attitudes and sexual behavioral patterns of Black mentally retarded adults. *Journal of Black Psychology, 3,* 20-33.
Compared the sexual attitudes and behavior of educable mentally retarded adults and trainable mentally retarded adults participating in individual and group counseling. Noted a number of differences between the two groups, but both appeared selfishly motivated.

625. Annis, H. M., & Chan, D. (1983). The differential treatment model: Empirical evidence from a personality typology of adult offenders. *Criminal Justice Behavior, 10*(2), 159-173.

626. Antonuccio, D. O. (1984). An exploratory study: The psycho-educational group treatment of drug-refractory unipolar depression. *Journal of Behavior Therapy and Experimental Psychiatry, 15,* 309-313.
      Examined the utility of psycho-educational groups in teaching skills such as relaxation, constructive thinking, social skills, and generation of a self-change plan to patients diagnosed with unipolar depression.

627. Antonuccio, D. O., Davis, C., Lewinsohn, P. M., & Breckenridge, J. S. (1987). Therapist variables related to cohesiveness in a group treatment for depression. *Small Group Behavior, 18,* 557-564.

628. Antonuccio, D. O., Lewinsohn, P.M., & Steinmetz, J. L. (1982). Identification of therapist differences in a group treatment for depression. *Journal of Consulting and Clinical Psychology, 50*(3), 433-435.

629. Apolinsky, S. R. (1991). Symbolic confrontation as a counseling technique to enhance self-concept and decrease depression for adult survivors of childhood sexual abuse. *Dissertation Abstracts International, 51*(10), 3361. (University Microfilm No. AAC91-05943)
      Used the symbolic confrontation (SC) technique in group counseling and measured its effect on the self-concept and depression of adult-participants, who had experienced childhood sexual abuse. SC increased self-concept but its effect on depression was unclear.

630. Apolinsky, S. R., & Wilcoxon, S. A. (1991). Symbolic confrontation with women survivors of childhood sexual victimization. *Journal for Specialists in Group Work, 16,* 85-90.
      Women who experienced childhood sexual abuse participated either in group counseling using symbolic confrontation (SC) or in a control group. SC was significant in raising self-concept and decreasing depression.

631. Appelbaum, P. S., & Greer, A. (1993). Confidentiality in group therapy. *Hospital and Community Psychiatry, 44*(4), 311-312.

632. Arbes, B. H., & Hubbell, R. N. (1973). Packaged impact: A structured communication skills workshop. *Journal of Counseling Psychology, 20*(4), 332-337.
      Two experimental groups received a seven-week structured workshop treatment program, while the control group received no treatment; participants were self-referred clients, who expressed problems in feeling uncomfortable in their relationships. Pre- and post-test results indicated a significant difference between scores on the criterion measures. The workshop group reduced anxiety in interpersonal situations, and reported an increase in establishing interpersonal relationships.

633. Archer, J., & Reisor, J. S. (1982). A group approach to stress and anxiety management. *Journal for Specialists in Group Work, 7*(4), 238-244.

634. Armstrong, J. H., Jr. (1978). The effect of group counseling on the self-concept, academic performance, and reading level of a selected group of high school students. *Dissertation Abstracts International, 39*(03), 1332A.

635.   Armstrong, R. G. (1974). A comparison between group therapists and members of the desired degree of self-disclosure by therapists. *Newsletter for Research in Mental Health and Behavioral Sciences, 16*, 20-21.
       Examined therapists' self-disclosing behavior in view of group members' desires. Although some therapists agreed with the idea of self-disclosure, few practiced it effectively.

636.   Aronoff, R. (1976). Parent group or student group counseling: A question of efficiency. *Dissertation Abstracts International, 36*(07), 4249. (University Microfilm No. AAC76-00179)

637.   Aronstam, M. (1990). A phenomenological study of power and authority in group psychotherapy. *Dissertation Abstracts International, 51*(06), 3118.

638.   Aumack, L. (1981). Drinking decisions: Evaluation of a short-term behavioral self-assessment program for problem drinkers. *Dissertation Abstracts International, 42*(05), 2040B.

639.   Azim, H. F., & Joyce, A. S. (1986). The impact of data-based program modifications on the satisfaction of outpatients in group psychotherapy. *Canadian Journal of Psychiatry, 31*, 119-122.
       Modifications made within a group therapy program resulted in increased patient satisfaction.

640.   Azrin, N. H. (1976). Improvements in the community-reinforcement approach to alcoholism. *Behaviour Research and Therapy, 14*(5), 339-348.
       Evaluated a modified community reinforcement program for testing alcoholics, which incorporated a buddy system, a daily report procedure, group counseling, and a special social motivation program to ensure the self-administration of disulfiram. The 19 subjects in this program drank less, worked more, spent more time at home and less time institutionalized than did their matched controls who received standard hospital treatment. These results were stable over a two-year period and the program appeared even more effective and less time-consuming than the previous program.

641.   Babb, W. A. (1976). The effects of group counseling in a naval correctional facility. *Dissertation Abstracts International, 37*(02), 797. (University Microfilm No. AAC76-18088)

642.   Bachar, E., Kindler, S., Schefler, G., & Lerer, B. (1991). Reminiscing as a technique in the group psychotherapy of depression: A comparative study. *British Journal of Clinical Psychology, 30*, 375-377.
       Describes the usefulness of reminiscing techniques compared to traditional reflective nondirective group therapy approaches with a population of severely depressed hospital patients.

643.   Baider, L., Amikam, J. C., & De Nour, A. K. (1984). Time-limited thematic group with post-mastectomy patients. *Journal of Psychosomatic Research, 28*(4), 323-330.

644. Bailis, S. S., Lambert, S. R., & Bernstein, S. B. (1978). The legacy of the group: A study of group therapy with a transient membership. *Social Work in Health Care, 3,* 405-418.
Examined whether stable group membership was required for the group to develop and grow. Found that group norms passed from one generation of group members to the next and that the group evolved, despite highly transient membership.

645. Baker, B. L., & Brightman, R. P. (1984). Training parents of retarded children: Program-specific outcomes. *Journal of Behavior Therapy and Experimental Psychiatry, 15*(3), 255-260.
Randomly assigned 14 families with a retarded child to a parents as teachers (PT) group or to a parents as advocates (PA) group. Administered pre- and post- training measures of behavior modification skills and knowledge, and of advocacy knowledge. PA subjects showed gains in knowledge about targeting and teaching self-help skills and managing behavior problems, while PA subjects showed gains in understanding parental rights and in finding legally relevant information. Neither condition resulted in a significant gain in teaching skills.

646. Balch, P., & Ross, A. W. (1974). A behaviorally oriented didactic-group treatment of obesity: An exploratory study. *Journal of Behavior Therapy and Experimental Psychiatry, 5,* 239-243.

647. Balgooyen, T. J. (1974). A comparison of the effect of Synanon game verbal attack therapy and standard group therapy practice on hospitalized chronic alcoholics. *Journal of Community Psychology, 2*(1), 54-58.

648. Balmer, D. H. (1987). Counselling in a hospital setting: An introduction to the CARE project. *Journal of British Guidance and Counselling, 15*(2), 150-157.

649. Balmer, D. H. (1988). The CARE project: The development stages of group counselling for patients with rheumatoid arthritis. *British Journal of Guidance and Counselling, 16*(1), 63-72.
Investigated whether group counseling could illuminate the psychological concomitants of rheumatoid arthritis and prove to be a therapeutic intervention. Group counseling followed four developmental stages: ice-breaking and climate creation, information exchange, self-disclosure, and enhanced self-concept and self-esteem.

650. Balmer, D. H. (1989). The CARE project: The evaluation of group counselling as a therapeutic intervention for patients with rheumatoid arthritis. *British Journal of Guidance and Counselling, 17*(3), 304-316.

651. Bancroft, J. (1989). *Human sexuality and its problems* (2nd ed.). London: Churchill Livingstone.
Comments on several uncontrolled studies and on the efficacy of group treatment, noting difficulties confronting researchers in evaluating sex therapy conducted with marital couples in groups.

652.   Banik, S. N., & Mendelson, M. A. (1978). Group psychotherapy with a paraplegic group, with an emphasis on specific problems of sexuality. *International Journal of Group Psychotherapy, 28*(1), 123-128.
        Subjects came from underprivileged backgrounds, had been involved in conflicts with ward staff members and other patients, were confined to wheelchairs, and had varying functional ability in their upper bodies. The group was organized to increase adaptation to hospitalization and to increase functioning in the outside world after release. Sexual capacity was a major focus of concern; group leaders provided information and facilitated group member discussion of their feelings. Lack of sexual satisfaction appeared to be a significantly greater problem for males than for females; however, females may have felt socially constrained from discussing their sexual concerns.

653.   Banken, D. M. (1994). Group versus individual cognitive-behavioral treatment for depression. *Dissertation Abstracts International, 54*(12), 6452. (University Microfilm No. AAC94-14766)
        Compared the use of Coping Therapy in individual and group settings, finding significant improvement in both conditions.

654.   Barbach, L. G. (1974). Group treatment of pre-orgasmic women. *Journal of Sex and Marital Therapy, 1,* 139-145.

655.   Barbaro, J. A. (1982). The effectiveness of a short-term, didactic, group psychotherapy in eliminating self-defeating behavior, increasing internal locus of control and increasing self-esteem. *Dissertation Abstracts International, 42*(12), 4924B.

656.   Barlow, D. H., O'Brien, G. T., & Last, C. G. (1984). Couples treatment of agoraphobia. *Behavior Therapy, 15*(1), 41-58.
        Divided agoraphobic women into two treatment groups: those who received cognitive restructuring and self-initiated exposure exercises with their husbands, and those who received the same treatment without their husbands. Results indicated that those treated with their husbands had a substantial advantage, particularly when attrition was considered.

657.   Barlow, L. O. (1983). A comparison of the effectiveness of group therapy on divorce adjustment and depression for separated and divorced persons. *Dissertation Abstracts International, 43*(07), 2462A.

658.   Barnett, S. H. (1981). The effect of preparatory training in communication skills on group therapy with lower socioeconomic class alcoholics. *Dissertation Abstracts International, 41*(07), 2744B.

659.   Barr, J. E. (1979). A study of relationships between premature termination in group counseling and select client variables. *Dissertation Abstracts International, 39*(09), 5319. (University Microfilm No. AAC79-05983)

660.   Barrera, M. (1979). An evaluation of a brief group therapy for depression. *Journal of Consulting and Clinical Psychology, 47,* 413-415.

Evaluated brief group therapy aimed at depressed outpatients. While the effectiveness of immediate treatment was not supported, subjects receiving delayed treatment increased pleasurable activities and decreased depression.

661. Barth, R. P., Blythe, B. J., Schinke, S. P., & Schilling, R. F. (1983). Self-control training with maltreating parents. *Child Welfare, 62*(4), 313-324.

662. Basler, H. D. (1985). Psychological group treatment of obese essential hypertensives by lay therapists in rural general practice settings. *Journal of Psychosomatic Research, 29*(4), 383-391.

663. Basler, H. D. (1993). Group treatment for pain and discomfort. Special issue: Psychosocial aspects of rheumatic diseases. *Patient Education and Counseling, 20*(2-3) 167-175.
Chronic pain patients suffering from back pain, tension headaches, rheumatoid arthritis, and ankylosing spondylitis participated in a group cognitive-behavioral treatment program which included relaxation, cognitive restructuring and the promotion of well-being. Pain reduction was greatest in low back pain and least in ankylosing spondylitis. Patients with inflammatory rheumatic diseases showed some improvement in self-reported physical complaints and in their feelings of well-being.

664. Basler, H. D., Brinkmeier, U., Binserr, K., Haehn, K., & Molders-Kober, R. (1982). Psychological group treatment of essential hypertension in general practice. *British Journal of Clinical Psychology, 21*(4), 295-302.
Compared obese patients with essential hypertension in one of five conditions: modification of nutritional patterns; modification of nutritional patterns plus self-monitoring of blood pressure and social competence training; modification of nutritional patterns plus relaxation training; learning about the causes and consequences of high blood pressure; or, no treatment control. Found no differential effect among the four treatments; all treatments significantly reduced the participants' blood pressure values, and distinctly reduced their body weight.

665. Basler, H. D., Brinkmeier, U., Buser, K., & Gluth, G. (1992). Nicotine gum assisted group therapy in smokers with an increased risk of coronary disease: Evaluation in a primary care setting format. *Health Education Research, 7*(1), 87-95.

666. Battegay, R., & von Marschall, R. (1978). Results of long-term group psychotherapy with schizophrenics. *Comprehensive Psychiatry, 19,* 349-353.
Outcome of long-term group psychotherapy in 21 schizophrenics was: decreased hospitalizations; enhanced social contact (14 subjects) and capacity to enjoy life (14 subjects); and, increased work capacity (12 subjects).

667. Battle, A. O. (1984). Group therapy for the survivors of suicide. *Crisis, 5,* 45-58.
Examined the utility of group therapy with individuals whose loved ones had committed suicide by comparing subjects to those who had never attended group therapy.

668. Baumgartner, D. D. (1986). Sociodrama and the Vietnam combat veteran: A
      therapeutic release for a wartime experience. *Journal of Group Psychotherapy,
      Psychodrama & Sociometry, 39,* 31-39.
      Describes the success of sociodrama in reducing stress among Black Vietnam
      veterans with post-traumatic stress disorder.

669. Beal, D., Duckro, P., Elias, J., & Hecht, E. (1977). Increased verbal
      interaction via group techniques with regressed schizophrenics. *Psychological
      Reports, 40,* 319-325.
      Verbal interaction was higher in male chronic schizophrenics who received
      remotivation therapy than in the control condition.

670. Beal, D., Duckro, P., Elias, J., & Hecht, E. (1977). Graded group procedures
      for long-term regressed schizophrenics. *Journal of Nervous and Mental Disease,
      164,* 102-106.

671. Beales, J. N. (1986). The effects of in-service training in group counseling on
      educational and pastoral counselors. *Dissertation Abstracts International, 46*(11),
      3288. (University Microfilm No. AAC86-01456)

672. Bear, T. J. (1990). Evaluation of change in anger expression by women
      survivors of incest as a result of group therapy. *Dissertation Abstracts
      International, 51*(06), 3120. (University Microfilm No. AAC90-29122)

673. Beard, M. T., & Scott, P. Y. (1975). The efficacy of group therapy by nurses
      for hospitalized patients. *Nursing Research, 24,* 120-124.
      Describes the usefulness of group therapy with 100 chronic regressed psychiatric
      inpatients. Topics most frequently mentioned within the group were delusional
      systems and interpersonal relationships.

674. Beidleman, W. B. (1981). Group assertive training in correctional settings: A
      review and methodological critique. *Journal of Offender Counseling, Services
      and Rehabilitation, 6,* 69-87.
      Discusses beneficial results associated with group assertiveness training in
      correctional settings and examines studies' weaknesses.

675. Bell, W. J., Charping, J. W., & Strecker, J. B. (1989). Client perceptions of
      the effectiveness of divorce adjustment groups. Special issue: Advances in group
      work research. *Journal of Social Service Research, 13*(2), 9-32.
      Conducted a follow-up study assessing client perceptions of factors that
      influenced the effectiveness of short-term divorce adjustment groups. More than
      95% of the clients reported that they had found the short-term group experience
      helpful or very helpful overall. Findings are reviewed in terms of the
      supportive, therapeutic, and after-group adjustment value of the group
      experience. Discusses strengths and limitations of a retrospective study design.

676. Belsham, R. L. (1989). Examination of verbal interaction during group
      psychotherapy using sequential analysis. *Dissertation Abstracts International,
      49*(11), 5014. (University Microfilm No. AAC89-03912)

677.   Ben-David, S. (1992). Influence, leadership, and social desirability in psychotherapeutic groups. *Journal of Group Psychotherapy, Psychodrama & Sociometry, 45,* 17-23.

678.   Benfari, R. C., & Eaker, E. (1984). Cigarette smoking outcomes at four years of follow-up, psychosocial factors, and reactions to group intervention. *Journal of Clinical Psychology, 40,* 1089-1097.
        Examined the variables related to successful cigarette cessation with 182 male smokers who participated in group therapy. Baseline level of smoking, personal security, life events, and group process variables were predictive of treatment outcome.

679.   Benjafield, J., Pomeroy, E., & Jordan, D. (1976). Encounter groups: A return to the fundamental. *Psychotherapy: Theory, Research and Practice, 13*(4), 387-389.
        Investigated whether encounter groups increase the assimilative projection (AP), the degree to which people see others as like themselves. Measured AP using a modification of the role repertory grid task, which was administered to 12 subjects, at three intervals during a weekend basic encounter group marathon. Results are consistent with the notion that group experience gives its members access to universal features of personality.

680.   Bennun, I. (1985). Behavioral marital therapy: An outcome evaluation of conjoint, group and one spouse treatment. *Behavioural Psychotherapy, 13*(3), 186-201.
        Compared three marital therapy treatment modalities: conjoint, conjoint group, and treating one partner alone. Although the modalities did not significantly differ with regard to treatment outcome, conjoint treatment couples resolved their target problems more rapidly. Discusses the results and related issues.

681.   Benson, R. L. (1984). The comparison of the effect of two sex education models for families upon sex knowledge, general communication, and sexual communication. *Dissertation Abstracts International, 45*(03), 748A.

682.   Benyaker, M., Dasberg, H., & Plotkin, I. (1982). The influence of various therapeutic milieus on the course of group treatments in two groups of soldiers with combat reaction. *Series in Clinical and Community Psychology Stress and Anxiety, 8,* 151-155.
        Compared the use of a group dynamic model and a pharmacotherapeutic model in treating two groups of Israeli soldiers suffering from combat reactions. Noted between group differences in attitudes toward the group leader and in perceptions of the cause of illnesses.

683.   Berberich, R. R., Gabel, H., Anchor, K. N. (1979). Self-disclosure in reflective, behavioral and discussion parent-counseling groups. *Journal of Community Psychology, 7*(3), 259-263.
        Trained 1 father and 44 mothers in childrearing using small groups with behavioral, reflective, and discussion formats. The groups differed in the amounts of, and patterns of self-disclosure across time: The discussion group made significantly more self-disclosing statements (SDSs) than the reflective group, and these groups made significantly more SDSs than the behavioral

group.   Discusses the significance of these differences, as they relate to behavioral change.

684.   Berger, A. (1988). Differential effectiveness of nondirective-directive alcoholism group counseling as a function of the patients' internal-external health locus-of-control. *Dissertation Abstracts International, 49*(04), 1378B.
Randomly assigned 59 participants, categorized as internals or externals, to nondirective or directive groups.   The main hypothesis, that a nondirective group therapy procedure would be more effective with subjects showing an internal health locus of control, was not verified.

685.   Bernard, H. S. (1991). Patterns and determinants of attitudes of psychiatric residents toward group therapy. Special Issue: Group methods for enhancing the training of mental health professionals. *Group, 15,* 131-140.
Examined the attitudes of 10 psychiatric residents toward group therapy possibilities and limitations, as well as efficacy and dangers.   Found tremendous variability among the residents.

686.   Bernard, H. S., & Klein, R. H. (1979). Time-limited group psychotherapy: A case report. *Journal of Group Psychotherapy, Psychodrama & Sociometry, 32,* 31-37.
Examined the effectiveness of time-limited group therapy with five patients. Patients' perceptions of self-improvement were supported by significant others. Findings suggest that instant improvement can be achieved through participation in time-limited group psychotherapy.

687.   Berne, K. H. (1990). Chronic fatigue and immune dysfunction syndrome: A comprehensive analysis with emphasis on psychosocial aspects. *Dissertation Abstracts International, 50*(12), 5917B.

688.   Bernette, C., Williams, R. L., & Law, J. G. (1987). Therapeutic and lifestyle reduction of aggressiveness in Vietnam veterans. *Group, 11*(1), 3-14.
Assessed pre- and post-treatment levels of aggressiveness and self-management in sixty-six veterans who: were attending rap groups at a local outreach center, had attended during the previous year, or had never attended.   Veterans who had participated in rap groups had significantly lower anger scores.   As aggressiveness decreased across veterans, self-management scores increased. For the returning veterans, self-reported aggressiveness and level of support were negatively correlated.

689.   Bess, B. E., & Marlin, R. L. (1984). A pilot study of medication and group therapy for obesity in a group of physicians. *Hillside Journal of Clinical Psychiatry, 6*(2), 171-180.
Examined the effectiveness of group therapy, which included weekly group discussions and a behavior modification program, combined with phenylpropanolamine and caffeine administration, in reducing the weight of 12 obese physicians.   After treatment completion at 22 weeks, five participants lost an average of 33.2 pounds; others also lost weight during the treatment period. Discusses the benefits of this program.

690. Beutler, L. E. (1984). Comparative effects of group psychotherapies in a short-term inpatient setting: An experience with deterioration effects. *Psychiatry, 47,* 66-76.
Compared the use of an interactive, process oriented group (POG); an expressive, experientially oriented group (EOG); and a behaviorally oriented group (BOG) treating 176 psychiatric inpatients. The POG produced the best results, while systematic deterioration was noted in the EOG.

691. Beutler, L. E., Engle, D., Mohr, D., & Daldrup, R. J. (1991). Predictors of differential response to cognitive, experiential, and self-directed psychotherapeutic procedures. *Journal of Consulting and Clinical Psychology, 59,* 333-340.
Compared the use of group cognitive therapy (GCT), focused expressive psychotherapy (FEP), and self-directed therapy (SD) in treating 63 major depressive disorder patients. Found an interaction between subjects' coping styles and defensiveness and the treatment modality that worked best.

692. Beutler, L. E., Jobe, A. M., & Elkins, D. (1974). Outcomes of group psychotherapy: Using persuasion theory to increase treatment efficiency. *Journal of Consulting and Clinical Psychology, 42,* 547-553.
Examined the relationship between patient and therapist attitude and group psychotherapy outcome. Initial patient-therapist attitude similarity was related to patient rated improvement. Initial patient-therapist attitude difference was related to more attitude change.

693. Beutler, L. E., Machado, P. P., Engle, D., & Mohr, D. (1993). Differential patient treatment maintenance among cognitive, experiential and self-directed psychotherapies. *Journal of Psychotherapy Integration, 3,* 15-31.
Examined the long-term utility of matching patient indicators to therapy style with 49 patients suffering from major depressive disorder. Findings support assigning patients with externalizing coping styles and low resistance to group cognitive therapy, and assigning patients with internalizing coping styles and high resistance to self-directed therapy.

694. Biasco, F., & Redfering, D. (1981). Increasing appreciation of authority figures among Naval confines through group counseling. *Corrective and Social Psychiatry and Journal of Behavior Technology, Methods and Therapy, 27,* 96-98.
Naval men in a Navy correctional facility received either group counseling or no treatment. Those in the treatment group had a less negative view of authority than those with no treatment, indicating that treatment helped.

695. Billings, J. H., Rosen, D. H., Asimos, C., & Motto, J. A. (1974). Observations on long-term group therapy with suicidal and depressed persons. *Life Threatening Behavior, 4,* 160-170.
Describes the effectiveness of long-term, open-ended group therapy with 200 depressed and suicidal patients. Presents recommendations for starting such groups.

696. Binley, E. C. (1979). Group psychotherapy with persons on probation who have had alcohol related offenses. *Dissertation Abstracts International, 39*(11), 5537B.

697.   Birashi-Schnackel, M. (1982). Influence of a critical incident techniques
       workshop on perceptions of group leadership behaviors. *Dissertation Abstracts
       International, 43*(03), 724. (University Microfilm No. AAC82-18430).

698.   Bitter, J. A. (1987). The effects of group therapy on systemic lupus
       erythematosus patients. *Dissertation Abstracts International, 47*(10), 4294B.
       Examined 10-week group therapy which focused on reducing anxiety,
       depression, and physiological symptoms in systemic lupus erythematosus (SLE)
       patients. Data supported the hypothesis that group therapy would result in
       decreased depression and anxiety, and improved general well-being and
       sedimentation rates. Discusses clinical implications, limitations of the study and
       further research.

699.   Black, J. E. (1980). The effects of group counseling on job performance of
       attendant staff in a residential treatment facility. *Dissertation Abstracts
       International, 41*(06), 2445. (University Microfilm No. AAC80-18288)

700.   Blankenship, J. C. (1993). A field study of a social cognition training program
       for deaf adults in vocational rehabilitation. *Dissertation Abstracts International,
       54*(05), 1674. (University Microfilms No. AAC93-27015)
       Describes a treatment program, which combined an educational approach with
       group therapy techniques, used with 16 deaf adults experiencing difficulties in
       social functioning. Compared to the control group, the treatment group showed
       significant gains in social cognition levels.

701.   Bloch, G. R., & Bloch, N. H. (1976). Analytic group psychotherapy of post-
       traumatic psychoses. *International Journal of Group Psychotherapy, 26,* 49-57.
       Examined group behavior of people with post-traumatic psychopathology due to
       adulthood traumatic events of industrial injuries and long-lasting stress situations.
       The subjects participated in analytic group therapy, which concentrated on
       supporting and creating coping mechanisms.

702.   Bloch, S. (1976). Patients' expectations of therapeutic improvement and their
       outcomes. *American Journal of Psychiatry, 133,* 1457-1460.
       Examined the relationship between 27 neurotic patients' therapeutic expectations
       and their actual improvement. There was a positive relationship between
       expectations and outcome, but only when the patients assessed the outcomes.

703.   Bloch, S., & Reibstein, J. (1980). Perceptions by patients and therapists of
       therapeutic factors in group psychotherapy. *British Journal of Psychiatry, 137,*
       274-278.
       Questionnaire responses by patients and therapists of long-term therapy groups
       demonstrated that, when addressing therapeutic factors, therapists emphasized
       behavioral factors while patients stressed cognitive factors.

704.   Bly, L. N. (1988). Self-help and child-abuse: Victims, victimizers, and the
       development of self-control. Groves conference on marriage and the Family.
       Contemporary Family Therapy, an International Journal, 10(4), 243-255.

705.   Bodensieck, R. A. (1993). A model for differentiating types of change-oriented groups: Discussion, application, and empirical analysis. *Dissertation Abstracts International, 54*(05), 2740. (University Microfilm No. AAC93-18971)

706.   Bohanon, L. M. (1982). Personality differences in the curative experience of group therapy. *Dissertation Abstracts International, 43*(05), 1606. (University Microfilm No. AAC82-21919)

707.   Bollinger, R. L., Musson, N. D., & Holland, A. L. (1993). A study of group communication intervention with chronically aphasic persons. *Aphasiology, 7,* 301-313.
       Describes the successful use of a structured group program on the communication ability of 10 chronically aphasic patients.

708.   Bond, G., Bloch, S., & Yalom, I. D. (1979). The evaluation of a "target problem" approach to outcome measurement. *Psychotherapy: Theory, Research and Practice, 16,* 48-54.
       Examined the agreement of therapists, patients, and independent judges on the psychotherapeutic improvement of 25 subjects participating in group therapy. There was much disagreement on the content of the subjects' problems, and on subject improvement.

709.   Bond, G. R. (1984). Positive and negative norm regulation and their relationship to therapy group size. *Group, 8,* 35-44.
       Examined the relationship of group size and degree of norm regulation in group therapy. Small groups were found to have the least positive regulation, while very small groups had the most. Smaller groups were also found to have greater negative regulation than larger groups.

710.   Bond, G. R., McDonel, E. C., Miller, L. D., & Pensec, M. (1991). Assertive community treatment and reference groups: An evaluation of their effectiveness for young adults with serious mental illness and substance abuse problems. Special Issue: Serving persons with dual disorders of mental illness and substance use. *Psychosocial Rehabilitation Journal, 15,* 31-43.

711.   Bonnet, P. J. (1984). Group therapy with the disabled: An interactional study. *Masters Abstracts International, 22*(02), 178.

712.   Borden, J. W. (1989). The role of cognitions in panic: A self-efficacy analysis. *Dissertation Abstracts International, 49*(10), 4528. (University Microfilm No. AAC88-11981)

713.   Borkovec, T. D., Steinmark, S. W., & Nau, S. D. (1973). Relaxation training and single-item desensitization in the group treatment of insomnia. *Journal of Behavior Therapy and Experimental Psychiatry, 4,* 401-403.
       Compared the use of relaxation alone, desensitization with relaxation, and desensitization without relaxation with 24 sleep-disturbed subjects. All subjects improved in the areas of latency of sleep onset, difficulty in falling asleep, and number of awakenings during the night.

714. Bornstein, P. H., & Sipprelle, C. N. (1973). Group treatment of obesity by induced anxiety. *Behavior Research and Therapy, 11,* 339-341.
      Compared the effectiveness of nonspecific group therapy, relaxation group therapy, and induced anxiety therapy with 40 obese participants. Found no immediate differences among the groups, but at three and six month follow-up, there were significant differences in weight loss.

715. Bos-Branolte, G. (1991). Gynaecological cancer: A psychotherapy group. In M. Watson (Ed.), *Cancer patient care: Psychosocial treatment methods.* (pp. 260-280). Cambridge: Cambridge University Press.
      Ninety patients in remission from cancer completed the Basic Oncology Scale, which focuses on anxiety, depression, body image, self-esteem, partner relationships, and general well-being. Thirty percent (27 patients) of the patients accepted the offer of psychotherapy; six chose individual and 21 chose group psychotherapy. Treated patients had significantly higher anxiety and depression pre-treatment scores; at nine month follow-up, both individual and group patients showed psychological gains compared to untreated patients.

716. Bostwick, G. J. (1987). "Where's Mary" A review of the group treatment dropout literature. *Social Work with Groups, 10,* 117-132.
      Reviews 37 studies on dropout in group treatment and discusses various methodological issues.

717. Bovill, D. (1977). An outcome study of group psychotherapy. *British Journal of Psychiatry, 131,* 95-98.

718. Bovilsky, D. M., & Singer, D. L. (1977). Confrontational group treatment of smoking: A report of three comparative studies. *International Journal of Group Psychotherapy, 27*(4), 481-498.
      Presents three studies which contrasted the effects of confrontational group treatment for smoking versus nondirective group treatment. Taken together, results provide considerable support for the relative effectiveness of confrontational group treatment. Both at the end of treatment and at the two to three month follow-up, there was a significantly higher proportion of quitters in the confrontation condition than in either the nondirective or control conditions.

719. Bowen, D. J., Spring, B., & Fox, E. (1991). Tryptophan and high-carbohydrate diets as adjuncts to smoking cessation therapy. *Journal of Behavioral Medicine, 14,* 97-110.
      Describes a multicomponent group therapy approach to smoking cessation which included use of tryptophan (TRY) and high carbohydrate diets. The number of cigarettes smoked, anxiety, and other withdrawal symptoms were reduced.

720. Bowes, P. J. (1985). Differential treatment effects of structured goals in small group counseling. *Dissertation Abstracts International, 45*(10), 3070. (University Microfilm No. AAC84-29353)

721. Bowman, D. R. (1985). A comparison of counterconditioning and role-playing strategies in the hypnotic treatment for cigarette smoking. *Dissertation Abstracts International, 45*(11), 3612. (University Microfilm No. AAC85-01486)

722. Bowman, M. K. (1994). Wounded women. Healing journeys: The psychological experience of healing from childhood sexual abuse. *Dissertation Abstracts International, 55*(02), 584. (University Microfilm No. AAC94-17655)
This heuristic, qualitative research identified factors that help women heal from childhood sexual abuse, and the recurrent themes of healing. Women's stories of the healing process, expressed in various art forms, were part of the data. Included are the women's transcribed interviews and creative written work.

723. Bowman, V. E. (1990). Preparation for group therapy: The effects of preparer and modality of group process and individual functioning. *Dissertation Abstracts International, 52*(01), 80. (University Microfilm No. AAC91-04608)

724. Bowman, V. E., & DeLucia, J. L. (1993). Preparation for group therapy: The effects of preparer and modality on group process and individual functioning. *Journal for Specialists in Group Work, 18*(2), 67-79.

725. Boy, A. V., & Pine, G. J. (1990). *A person-centered foundation for counseling and psychotherapy.* Springfield, IL: Charles C. Thomas.
Discusses general aspects of counseling evaluation research, and makes suggestions about research design and evaluation instruments.

726. Boyle, T. J. (1977). Effects of group counseling on the self-concept of students identified as deviant. *Dissertation Abstracts International, 38*(04), 1884A.

727. Brabender, V., & Fallon, A. (1993). *Models of inpatient group psychotherapy.* Washington, DC: American Psychological Association.
Discusses the status of the research for each of the following models of inpatient group psychotherapy: the educative model, the interpersonal model, the object relations/systems model, the developmental model, the cognitive-behavioral model, the problem-solving model, and the behavioral-social skills training model.

728. Brady, J. (1985). A longitudinal study of patient perspective of the curative factors in group psychotherapy. *Dissertation Abstracts International, 46*(02), 519. (University Microfilm No. AAC85-08668)

729. Brady, J. P. (1977). An empirical study of behavioral marital therapy in groups. *Behavior Therapy, 8*(3), 512-513.
Briefly reports a comparative evaluation of behavioral and interactional group marital counseling treatments. Found few between group differences on self-report measures of marital satisfaction, although both groups significantly improved on these measures at six month follow-up. Direct observations indicated that, as a result of treatment, the behavioral group exhibited significantly more positive and mutually supportive verbal and nonverbal behaviors.

730. Brammer, L. M., Shostrom, E. L., & Abrego, P. J. (1989). *Therapeutic psychology: Fundamentals of counseling and psychotherapy* (5th ed.). Englewood Cliffs, NJ: Prentice Hall.
Reviews research on group counseling, and attempt to account for conflicting results. Important factors seem to be: differences in types of subjects,

leadership style, length of therapy as well as research design. More research is recommended on comparative outcomes of different approaches.

731. Brandel, I. W. (1975). The relationship between the quantity of verbal performance and selected variables in the group counseling process. *Dissertation Abstracts International, 36*(05), 2623. (University Microfilm No. AAC75-23957)

732. Brantley, R. C. (1991). The effect of inpatient family-of-origin therapy on the self-concept and sobriety rates of adult male alcoholics. *Dissertation Abstracts International, 51*(11), 5565.

733. Brennan, A. F. M. (1982). Brief skills enhancement counseling with renal dialysis patients. *Dissertation Abstracts International, 42*(11), 4569B.

734. Brinegar, J. R. (1978). A behavioral study of group counseling process: Member self-disclosure and leader social reinforcement. *Dissertation Abstracts International, 39*(09), 5320. (University Microfilm No. AAC79-05987)

735. Brinkerhoff, L. J. (1989). Symbolic interactionist perspective on negative outcomes in psychotherapy. *Dissertation Abstracts International, 50*(03), 794. (University Microfilm No. AAC89-11126)

736. Brown, B. S., Jackson, C. S., & Bass, U. F. (1973). Methadone and abstinent clients in group counseling sessions. *International Journal of the Addictions, 8,* 309-316.
Studied group counseling behavior of 23 methadone versus 33 abstinent clients and three ex-addict versus three nonaddict counselors. The methadone clients made more contributions and were more likely to support self-disclosure than abstinent clients, who expressed more antagonism. Ex-addict counselors were more active and more likely to express their feelings than were nonaddict counselors, who showed more support of others.

737. Brown, S., & Yalom, I. D. (1977). Interactional group therapy with alcoholics. *Journal of Studies on Alcohol, 38*(3), 426-456.
Discusses the techniques used and problems encountered when using interactional group therapy with alcoholics. Results indicate that long-term interactional group therapy may effectively treat alcoholics. When compared with a contrast sample of neurotic patients in group therapy, the alcoholics subjects had outcomes which were in every way equivalent.

738. Brown, S. D. (1980). Coping skills training: An evaluation of a psychoeducational program in a community mental health setting. *Journal of Counseling Psychology, 27*(4), 340-345.
Randomly assigned 40 adult clients at a community mental health center either to a coping skills training program based solely on a psychoeducational model, or to a group counseling control condition, which analyzed personal problems with anxiety and interpersonal relations, but included no direct skills training. Discusses significant differences between the two groups.

739. Brownell, K. D., Heckerman, C. L., & Westlake, R. J. (1978). Therapist and group contact as variables in the behavioral treatment of obesity. *Journal of Consulting and Clinical Psychology, 46,* 593-594.
      Compared three approaches to obesity treatment of women: manual plus behavioral treatment group therapy (BT); manual with minimal professional contact (MPC); waiting list, no treatment control. At post-treatment, women in the BT and MPC groups attained results superior to the those in the control group. At post-treatment, those in BT did significantly better than those in MPC, but at six month follow-up, this difference was not sustained.

740. Bruch, M. A., Heimberg, R. G., & Hope, D. A. (1991). States of mind model and cognitive change in treated social phobics. *Cognitive Therapy and Research, 15,* 429-441.

741. Brykczynska, C. (1990). Changes in the patients' perception of his therapist in the process of group and individual psychotherapy. *Psychotherapy and Psychosomatics, 53,* 179-184.

742. Buchanan, D. R., & Bandy, C. (1984). Jungian typology of prospective psycho-dramatists: Myers-Briggs Type Indicator analysis of applicants for psychodrama training. *Psychological Reports, 55,* 599-606.
      Evaluated 37 applicants of a psychodrama training program using the Myers-Briggs Type Indicator scale. Those applicants accepted for training tended to be extraverted, intuitive, feeling and perceiving.

743. Buchanan, D. R., & Taylor, J. A. (1986). Jungian typology of professional psychodramatists: Myers-Briggs Type Indicator analysis of certified psychodramatists. *Psychological Reports, 58*(2), 391-400.

744. Buchanan, J. R., & Rubin, T. I. (1973). Five year psychoanalytic study of obesity. *American Journal of Psychoanalysis, 33,* 30-41.

745. Bucher, J., Smith, E,., & Gillespie, C. (1984). Short-term group therapy for stroke patients in a rehabilitation centre. *British Journal of Medical Psychology, 57*(3), 283-290.
      Evaluated short-term group psychotherapy for three groups of eight stroke patients. Discusses the feasibility of this approach and how such groups may be beneficial.

746. Budman, S. H., Demby, A., Feldstein, M., & Gold, M. (1984). The effects of time-limited group psychotherapy: A controlled study. *International Journal of Group Psychotherapy, 34,* 587-603.
      Examined the time-limited effects of group therapy with 36 short-term therapy participants. Participants described important gains in their problem areas.

747. Budman, S. H., Demby, A., Feldstein, M., & Redondo, J. (1987). Preliminary findings on a new instrument to measure cohesion in group psychotherapy. Special Issue: Integration of research and practice in the field of group psychotherapy. *International Journal of Group Psychotherapy, 37,* 75-94.

748. Budman, S. H., Demby, A., Redondo, J. P., & Hannan, M. (1988). Comparative outcome in time-limited individual and group psychotherapy. *International Journal of Group Psychotherapy, 38,* 63-86.

749. Budman, S. H., & Gurman, A. S. (1988). *Theory and practice of brief therapy.* New York: Guilford Press.
      In the course of an exposition on time-limited group psychotherapy, previous research on length of treatment, central aspects of short-term group therapy, pregroup preparation and screening, important factors in early sessions, importance of cohesion in short-term groups, and phasic development are presented.

750. Budman, S. H., Soldz, S, Demby, A., & Davis, M. (1993). What is cohesiveness? An empirical examination. *Small Group Research, 24,* 199-216.

751. Budman, S. H., Soldz, S., Demby, A., & Feldstein, M. (1989). Cohesion, alliance and outcome in group psychotherapy. *Psychiatry, 52,* 339-350.

752. Budman, S. H., & Springer, T. (1987). Treatment delay, outcome, and satisfaction in time-limited group and individual psychotherapy. *Professional Psychology: Research and Practice, 18,* 647-649.
      Compared time-limited individual and group therapies. Participants in individual therapy reported a highly significant relationship between the delay and treatment satisfaction, as compared to those participating in group therapy.

753. Bugen, L. A. (1977). Composition and orientation effects on group cohesion. *Psychological Reports, 40*(1), 175-181.

754. Burns, J. M. (1981). The efficacy of group submaximal aerobic exercise as an adjunct to integrity therapy. *Dissertation Abstracts International, 43*(02), 518.

755. Butler, T., & Fuhriman, A. (1983). Curative factors in group therapy: A review of the recent literature. *Small Group Behavior, 14,* 131-142.

756. Butler, T., & Fuhriman, A. (1983). Level of functioning and length of time in treatment variables influencing patients' therapeutic experience in group psychotherapy. *International Journal of Group Psychotherapy, 33,* 489-505.
      Compared low and high functioning members of 23 psychotherapy groups. Cohesiveness, self-understanding, and interpersonal learning were correlated with length of time in treatment. High functioning patients valued the group therapy significantly more, relative to low functioning patients.

757. Butler, T., & Fuhriman, A. (1986). Professional psychologists as group treatment providers: Utilization, training, and trends. *Professional Psychology: Research and Practice, 17*(3), 273-275.

758. Butter, H. J., & Dutil, C. (1985). The assessment of a psychosocial treatment with chronic schizophrenic patients using neuropsychopharmacological indices. *Progress in Neuropsychopharmacology and Biological Psychiatry, 9,* 593-597.

759. Byrne, R. C., & Overline, H. M. (1991). A study of divorce adjustment among paraprofessional group leaders and group participants. *Journal of Divorce and Remarriage, 17*(1-2), 171-192.

760. Bywater, E. M. (1984). Coping with a life-threatening illness: An experiment in parents' groups. *British Journal of Social Work, 14*(2), 117-127.

761. Cabral, R., & Paton, A. (1975). Evaluation of group therapy: Correlations between clients' and observers' assessments. *British Journal of Psychiatry, 126,* 475-477.

762. Cabral, R. J., Best, J., & Paton, A. (1975). Patients' and observers' assessments of process and outcome in group therapy: A follow-up study. *American Journal of Psychiatry, 132,* 1052-1054.
Examined the process and outcome of two therapy groups. Recognized discrete stages within the therapeutic sequence.

763. Caddy, G. R., & Kretchmer, R. S. (1980). Evaluation of the alternate leaderless group in a military psychiatric hospital. *Journal of Group Psychotherapy, Psychodrama & Sociometry, 33,* 33-36.
Compared the use of a standard leader-led group (LLG) with an alternate leaderless group (ALG) with 30 personality-disordered males. Those in the ALG showed greater improvement in behavioral adjustment.

764. Cadogan, D. A. (1973). Marital group therapy in the treatment of alcoholism. *Quarterly Journal of Studies on Alcohol, 34*(4-A), 1187-1194.
Subjects treated for alcoholism and discharged from the hospital either participated with their spouses in outpatient marital group therapy (OMGT), which emphasized problem-solving techniques, or were placed on a waiting list control group (WLCG). At six month follow-up, nine subjects in the OMGT and two subjects in the WLCG were abstinent. OMGT spouses of the drinking subjects scored significantly lower on Ely's Conjugal Life Questionnaire, indicating that they had more difficulty with acceptance and trust than did the OMGT spouses of abstinent subjects. Relapses tended to occur within three months after hospital discharge. Case histories illustrate what type of couples benefits from marital group therapy.

765. Cahoon, E. P. (1984). An examination of relationships between post-traumatic stress disorder, marital distress, and response to therapy by Vietnam veterans. *Dissertation Abstracts International, 45*(04), 1279.

766. Caine, T. M., & Wijesinghe, B. (1976). Personality, expectancies and group psychotherapy. *British Journal of Psychiatry, 129,* 384-387.

767. Caldwell, H. S., Leveque, K. L., & Lane, D. M. (1974). Group psychotherapy in the management of hemophilia. *Psychological Reports, 35*(1, Pt 1), 339-342.
Three hemophiliacs and their wives and two couples who were parents of hemophiliacs participated in an eight month group psychotherapy program. Results from clinical observations and data from the Tennessee Self-Concept Scale indicated that intensive group psychotherapy positively affected members' feelings and self-concepts. Group members showed an increased personal

awareness, self-satisfaction, and positive feelings as family members, with an accompanying decrease in generalized maladjustment.

768.   Campbell, D. R., & Sinha, B. K. (1983). Psychotherapy and chronic hemodialysis. *International Journal for the Advancement of Counseling, 6*(1), 47-60.
Assessed psychopathology in 18 hemodialysis patients who required psychiatric consultation and 21 who were judged not suitable for consultation. Patients were entered into three conditions: group therapy, individual therapy, and no treatment control. Psychometric measures indicate the importance of psychiatric treatment for this population. Discusses the criteria used for treatment, and those found to be valid in terms of outcomes. More patients benefited from group rather than individual therapy.

769.   Campbell, L., & Page, R. (1993). The therapeutic effects of group process on the behavioral patterns of a drug-addicted group. *Journal of Addictions and Offender Counseling, 13,* 34-45.

770.   Carew, J. L. (1984). Physical exercise and counseling group behavior. *Dissertation Abstracts International, 45*(03), 1007. (University Microfilm No. AAC84-12605)

771.   Carlson, C. R. (1976). The relationship of anxiety, openness and group psychotherapy experience with perceptions of therapist self-disclosure among psychiatric patients. *Dissertation Abstracts International, 37*(01), 453. (University Microfilm No. AAC76-14420).

772.   Carlson-Sabelli, L. (1989). Role reversal: A concept analysis and reinterpretation of the research literature. *Journal of Group Psychotherapy, Psychodrama & Sociometry, 41,* 139-152.

773.   Carnie, M. A. (1986). Group psychotherapy with unmarried mothers. *Masters Abstracts International, 24*(02), 160.

774.   Carter, A. L. (1975). An analysis of the use of contemporary Black literature and music and its effects upon self-concept in group counseling procedures. *Dissertation Abstracts International, 35*(11), 7052A.

775.   Carter, M. P. L. (1993). A comparison of cognitive self-control therapy and interpersonal skills training for the treatment of sociotropic and autonomous depressions. *Dissertation Abstracts International, 53*(07), 3764B.

776.   Cartwright, M. H. (1976). A preparatory method for group counseling. *Journal of Counseling Psychology, 23,* 75-77.
Describes a film directed at clarifying expectations before group counseling begins. The film effectively reduced unclarified expectations with 85 subjects.

777.   Caruso, M. F. (1981). The effects of group assertiveness training on assertiveness, dyadic adjustment, and parenting attitudes of parents of incestuous families. *Dissertation Abstracts International, 41*(10), 4286. (University Microfilm No. AAC81-07169)

778. Caruthers, J. D. (1975). The effects of small group counseling on the self-concept of disadvantaged students. *Dissertation Abstracts International, 36*(04), 2017A.

779. Cates, C. W. (1980). An evaluation of individual vocational counseling and systematic group counseling with vocational rehabilitation clients. *Dissertation Abstracts International, 40*(10), 5319. (University Microfilm No. AAC80-07912)

780. Catina, A., & Tschuschke, V. (1993). A summary of empirical data from the investigation of two psychoanalytic groups by means of repertory grid technique. *Group Analysis, 26,* 433-447.
       Discusses changes within two psychoanalytic therapy groups in construing the self relative to significant others, and interactive behavior within the group.

781. Caughlin-Carver, J. L. (1986). Member and facilitator expectations and their relationship to attraction to group. *Dissertation Abstracts International, 47*(02), 780. (University Microfilm No. AAC86-07895)

782. Causey, A. R. (1986). Preparation for group psychotherapy using a modeling/instructional videotape with a female inpatient population. *Dissertation Abstracts International, 47*(01), 367. (University Microfilm No. AAC86-06113)

783. Cerbone, M. J., Mayo, J. A., Cuthbertson, B. A., & O'Connell, R. A. (1992). Group therapy as an adjunct to medication in the management of bipolar affective disorder. *Group, 16,* 174-187.
       Examined the success of a combination of group therapy and medication with 43 bipolar subjects. Noted significant improvements in symptom relief, and vocational and interpersonal functioning.

784. Chaffin, M. (1992). Factors associated with treatment completion and progress among intrafamilial sexual abusers. *Child Abuse and Neglect, 16,* 251-264.

785. Chance, G. R. (1981). The effects of group psychotherapy on the self-actualization of male inmates in a federal penitentiary. *Dissertation Abstracts International, 42*(06), 2499. (University Microfilm No. AAC81-26568)
       Randomly assigned inmates in a federal penitentiary to one of four types of group therapy (GT) - rational behavior therapy, psychodrama, transactional analysis, discussion - or to a testing group. Test scores of participants in GT conditions showed no change in self-actualization or behavior.

786. Charlesworth, E. A., & Dempsey, G. (1982). Trait anxiety reductions in a substance abuse population trained in stress management. *Journal of Clinical Psychology, 38,* 764-768.
       Hospitalized poly-drug abusing males who were given stress management training therapy showed significantly reduced trait anxiety; there was a significant difference between the trained and the untrained control group.

787. Charm, H. (1993). The issues and concerns of school counselors: A comparative analysis of the impact of gender and ethnicity on counselor activities and interactions. *Dissertation Abstracts International, 54*(03), 812A.

788. Chester, M. A., Barbarin, O. A., & Lebo-Stein, J. (1984). Patterns of participation in a self-help group for parents of children with cancer. *Journal of Psychosocial Oncology, 2*(3-4), 41-64.

789. Clabby, J. F., & Belz, E. J. (1985). Psychological barriers to learning: An approach using group treatment. *Small Group Behavior, 16,* 525-533.
      Describes an intervention method in which 22 adults, who functioned on or below the literacy level, were provided psycho-educational counseling. Treatment subjects took a more active role in their work place, families, and in their own education.

790. Claghorn, J. L., Johnstone, E. E., Cook, T. H., & Itschner, L. (1974). Group therapy and maintenance treatment of schizophrenics. *Archives of General Psychiatry, 31,* 361-365.
      Examined symptoms of schizophrenics who took antipsychotic drugs, thiothixene and chlorpromazine. Further divided each of these drug conditions into group versus nongroup therapy. Schizophrenic symptomology improved in both drug conditions but was unaffected by group therapy; schizophrenics acquired, through group therapy, an increased awareness and understanding of their own behavior.

791. Clarke, D. L., Kramer, E., Lipiec, K., & Klein, S. (1982). Group psychotherapy with mastectomy patients. *Psychotherapy: Theory, Research and Practice, 19*(3), 331-334.

792. Coche, E., Cooper, J. B., & Petermann, K. J. (1984). Differential outcomes of cognitive and interactional group therapies. *Small Group Behavior, 15,* 497-509.
      Compared the use of cognitively oriented problem-solving training (PST) with interactive group therapy (IGT) for adult psychiatric patients. While participants in both groups made significant gains overall, females gained more from IGT and males gained more from PST.

793. Coche, E., Dies, R. R., & Goettelmann, K. (1991). Process variables mediating change in intensive group therapy training. *International Journal of Group Psychotherapy, 41*(3), 379-397.
      In follow-up after a two day training experience in intensive groups, subjects reported that successful outcomes were related to self-disclosure, feedback, interpersonal support, personal qualities, and technical expertise modeled by group leaders. The groups were regarded as impacting clinical practices.

794. Coche, E., & Spector, J. (1978). TAT-derived affiliation scores and social behavior in therapy groups. *Psychological Reports, 42,*(3, Pt 1) 739-744.
      Men and women completed the TAT, scored for need affiliation, and were observed in eight group therapy sessions for affiliative behaviors. In the first three sessions, there were no significant correlations between need affiliation (thought) and affiliative behaviors (action), but in the last three, there was a significant direct correlation for men which was positive, and a more complicated significant relationship for women, which was curvilinear.

795. Coche, J., & Coche, E. (1990). *Couples group psychotherapy: A clinical practice model.* New York: Brunner/Mazel.

Presents and summarizes research on a project that compares process and outcome of a person-centered approach, a couple centered, an interpersonal, or a group-as-a-whole approach.

796.   Cohen, D. (1982). A group therapy outcome study and validation of Yalom's theory of curative factors. *Dissertation Abstracts International, 42*(07), 2981. (University Microfilm No. AAC81-29963)

797.   Cole, C. F. (1981). Treatment of pre-orgasmic women utilizing group therapy and home-based training. *Masters Abstracts International, 19*(01), 85. (University Microfilm No. AAC13-14960)

798.   Coller, C. F. (1978). The effective personal integration model and its impact upon locus-of-control with clients in group counseling. *Dissertation Abstracts International, 38*(07), 3386. (University Microfilm No. AAC77-29540)

799.   Collinge, W. B. (1989). Effects of a complementary cancer therapy program on coping and quality of life. *Dissertation Abstracts International, 49*(09), 3997B.

800.   Collins, J. H. (1985). The assessment of pre- post-test changes in selected personality variables among incarcerated felons participating in a therapeutic community at a maximum security federal penitentiary. *Dissertation Abstracts International, 46*(06), 1588. (University Microfilm No. AAC85-16221)

801.   Colson, D. B., & Horwitz, L. (1983). Research in group psychotherapy. In H. I. Kaplan & B. J. Sadock (Eds.), *Comprehensive group psychotherapy* (2nd ed., pp. 304-311). Baltimore: Williams & Wilkins.
       Lack of sufficiently specific questions in research on the appropriateness of special techniques with specific patient groups, the complexity of the research enterprise on group therapy, and unrealistic expectations of the type of answers to be gained from research on group therapy are presented as some of the reasons for the apparent inutility of group therapy research for clinicians. Research is reviewed under the following headings: therapeutic benefits, harmful effects, premature termination, therapeutic factors, therapists, patients, groups, the process, and methodology and instrumentation.

802.   Comas-Diaz, L. (1981). Effects of cognitive and behavioral group treatment on the depressive symptomatology of Puerto Rican women. *Journal of Consulting and Clinical Psychology, 49*, 627-632.
       Compared the use of cognitive and behavior group therapies with 26 low income Puerto Rican women identified as depressed. Both therapies reduced depression, and at five week follow-up, the behavioral group participants maintained positive gains.

803.   Compton, A. B., & Puviance, M. (1992). Emotional distress in chronic medical illness: Treatment with time-limited group psychotherapy. *Military Medicine, 157*(10), 533-535.
       Provided time-limited (12 sessions) group psychotherapy, which emphasized validation of feelings, interpersonal understanding, and problem solving, to 14 patients with neurological, cardiovascular, rheumatic or other diagnoses. Although the patients reported an increased sense of well-being, the Millon

Behavioral Health Inventory results indicated generally sustained somatic concern. There was a moderate reduction in the number of visits to other clinics during treatment. Despite incomplete outcome data, this appears to be a useful and cost-effective treatment for mixed groups of emotionally distressed medical patients.

804.   Comstock, B. S., & Jones, M. A. (1975). Group therapy as a treatment technique for severely disturbed patients. *Hospital and Community Psychiatry, 26,* 677-679.
        Describes an outpatient therapy program consisting of group treatment, occupational therapy, vocational rehabilitation counseling, and community activities.

805.   Comstock, B. S., & McDermott, M. (1975). Group therapy of patients who attempt suicide. *International Journal of Group Psychotherapy, 25,* 44-49.
        Describes the use of group treatment in the form of crisis intervention and long-term therapy with 105 suicide attempters.

806.   Connelly, J. L., Piper, W. E., deCarufel, F. L., & Debbane, E. G. (1986). Premature termination in group psychotherapy: Pre-therapy and early therapy predictors. *International Journal of Group Psychotherapy, 36,* 145-152.
        Explored the relationship between pre-therapy patient characteristics, early therapy experiences, and drop out rates of 66 neurotic participants. Dropouts were likely to have a primary diagnosis of personality disorder, no experience with therapy, negative expectations, and lower interpersonal functioning.

807.   Conners, M. E., Johnson, C. L., & Stuckey, M. K. (1984). Treatment of bulimia with brief psycho-educational group therapy. *American Journal of Psychiatry, 141,* 1512-1516.
        Describes a multifaceted treatment approach for women with bulimia, which included short-term, structured group therapy. Reports a 70% reduction in binge/purge episodes, and improvements in depression, self-esteem, assertiveness, and psychological functioning.

808.   Conyne, R. K., Lamb, D. H., & Strand, K. H. (1975). Group experiences in counseling centers: A national survey. *Journal of College Student Personnel, 16*(3), 196-200.
        Reports that large public institutions provide the greatest number and variety of groups, that most groups are of an "adequacy enhancing" rather than of a "problem education" nature, and that centers subscribe to a developmental rather than a remedial model.

809.   Conyne, R. K., & Rapin, L. S. (1977). Facilitator and self-directed groups: A statement by statement interaction study. *Small Group Behavior, 8,* 341-350.
        Compared the impact of facilitator-directed (FD) and self-directed (SD) personal growth group treatments on verbal interaction. FD group interaction was found to be more task oriented, more continuous, and more relevant than SD group interaction.

810. Conyne, R. K., & Rapin, L. S. (1977). A HIM-G interaction process analysis study of facilitator- and self-directed groups. *Small Group Behavior, 8*(3), 333-340.
Compared the effects of facilitator-directed (FD) and self-directed (SD) personal growth group treatments on group member interaction, using the Hill Interaction Matrix Group to assess treatment effectiveness. Results indicate that the FD treatment induced interaction among group members which was more therapeutic, more consistent, and higher in quality than that induced by the SD treatment.

811. Cook, D. A., Fox, C. A., Weaver, C. M., & Rooth, F. G. (1991). The Berkeley Group: Ten years experience of a group for non-violent sex offenders. *British Journal of Psychiatry, 158,* 238-243.
Evaluated long-term group therapy with nonviolent sex offenders, finding that 36 of 55 former group participants had not had any further convictions.

812. Cooper, A., & McCormack, W. A. (1992). Short-term group treatment for adult children of alcoholics. *Journal of Counseling Psychology, 39*(3), 350-355.

813. Corkum, J. A. (1984). A study of the effects of short-term group therapy with an adult inpatient psychiatric population. *Dissertation Abstracts International, 44*(10), 3188. (University Microfilm No. AAC84-02722)

814. Cotten, H., Annie, L., & Katherine, A. (1983). Preorgasmic group treatments: Assertiveness, marital adjustment, and sexual function in women. *Journal of Sex and Marital Therapy, 9*(4), 296-302.

815. Coursol, D. H. (1991). The relationship of counseling expectations to selected outcome measures for more and less structured groups. *Dissertation Abstracts International, 51*(08), 4044. (University Microfilm No. AAC90-26883)

816. Courtney, D. J. (1993). Transference tests of unconscious pathogenic beliefs in therapy: The application of the San Francisco Psychotherapy Research Group's plan formulation method. *Dissertation Abstracts International, 53*(10), 3674. (University Microfilm No. AAC93-05444)
Examined the reliability of the Control-Mastery Theory's Plan Formulation Method (PFM). Findings suggest that the PFM is a useful tool in predicting how group members will test within groups.

817. Covert, A. H. (1981). The effects of group therapy on anxiety, somatic symptoms, and marital communication among primiparous married couples. *Dissertation Abstracts International, 41*(12), 5028A.

818. Covi, L. (1974). Drugs and group psychotherapy in neurotic depression. *American Journal of Psychiatry, 131,* 191-198.
Examined the effects of imipramine and group psychotherapy with 149 chronically depressed neurotic women. Imipramine had therapeutic advantages, but group therapy had no observable advantages.

819.   Covi, L., Lipman, R. S., Alarcon, R. D., & Smith, V. K. (1976). Drug and psychotherapy interactions in depression. *American Journal of Psychiatry, 133,* 502-508.
        Examined factors that affected treatment response of 149 non-psychotic depressed females. Identified eight factors: initial level of distress, imipramine treatment, attitude toward group therapy, employment history, estrogen treatment, intelligence, initial level of interpersonal sensitivity, and significant others' attitude toward therapy.

820.   Cox, G. L., & Merkel, W. T. (1989). A qualitative review of psychosocial treatment for bulimia. *Journal of Nervous and Mental Disease, 177,* 77-84.
        Uses 14 criteria to evaluate adequacy of research methodology in 32 individual and group therapy investigations of psychosocial treatment of bulimia. Judged more than one-third of the studies to be inadequate and not comparable.

821.   Cox, J. W., & Stoltenberg, C. D. (1991). Evaluation of a treatment program for battered wives. *Journal of Family Violence, 6*(4), 395-413.

822.   Craigie, F. C. (1992). Evaluation and six-year follow-up of a community-based Christian cognitive-behavioral stress management program. *Journal of Psychology and Christianity, 11*(3), 269-276.
        Discusses a Christian cognitive-behavioral group stress management program which was presented in a community setting over an eight week period in 1985. Data from seven participants revealed strong changes at the conclusion of the program; several measures suggested that changes were sustained at six year follow-up. Particularly noteworthy were beneficial changes in measures of cognitive/evaluative processes.

823.   Crosby, R. D., Mitchell, J. E., Raymond, N., & Specker, S. (1993). Survival analysis of response to group psychotherapy in bulimia nervosa. *International Journal of Eating Disorders, 13*(4), 359-368.

824.   Cryer, L., & Beutler, L. (1980). Group therapy: An alternative treatment approach for rape victims. *Journal of Sex and Marital Therapy, 6,* 40-46.
        Pre- and post-tests of nine rape victims who participated in 10 weeks of group therapy demonstrated great decreases in hostility, fear and anxiety. Some subjects showed no gains, and may have even worsened.

825.   Cumbia, G. G. (1986). Therapeutic intervention in the treatment of adult patients with metastatic cancer: A comparative study of two group counseling approaches. *Dissertation Abstracts International, 46*(12), 4180B.
        Examined two group counseling approaches, nondirective or stress management, on five personality characteristics. Analyses of data revealed no significant differences among the nondirective, stress management, and control groups on any of the post-test measures. While the follow-up interviews at two weeks supported this quantitative finding, the interviews indicated a qualitative difference between groups.

826.   Cunningham, A. J., Lockwood, G. A., & Cunningham, J. A. (1991). A relationship between perceived self-efficacy and quality of life in cancer patients. *Patient Education and Counseling, 17*(1), 71-78.

Adults

105

Examined the role of the perceived amount of control patients feel they can exert over stressful situations arising from the disease. Found a strong positive correlation between self-efficacy and quality of life, and between self-efficacy and mood. Improvements in all three measures brought about by a brief group program teaching coping skills were also highly correlated. Found no significant association between improvement in mood or quality of life and amount of home practice of coping.

827. Cutter, H. S. (1974). Emotional openness and mood change in marathon group psychotherapy. *International Journal of the Addictions, 9,* 741-748.

828. Cutter, H. S., Boyatzis, R. E., & Clancy, D. D. (1977). Effectiveness of power motivation training in rehabilitating alcoholics. *Journal of Studies on Alcohol, 38*(1), 131-141.
Compared Power Motivation Training (PMT) and standard treatment (ST) in rehabilitating alcoholics. Exposed all subjects to the regular treatment program, which included disulfiram, weekly group therapy meetings, individual counseling, exposure to Alcoholics Anonymous (AA), and encouragement to join an active AA group. Follow-up 6 to 12 months after the program revealed that the PMT treatment decreased the frequency of intoxication in the nonauthoritarian subjects, while authoritarian subjects were more successful in ST.

829. D'Artenay, J. F. (1984). Effects of large group techniques on couples' sexual satisfaction. *Dissertation Abstracts International, 44*(11), 3522B.

830. Daley, P. C., Bloom, L. J., Deffenbacher, J. L., & Stewart, R. (1983). Treatment effectiveness of anxiety management training in small and large group formats. *Journal of Counseling Psychology, 30*(1), 104-107.
Divided participants into three groups: small group anxiety management training (AMT), large group AMT, or a waiting list control group. Immediately following treatment, small group AMT participants reported significantly less general anxiety than control participants, which was maintained at the seven month follow-up. Large group AMT did not differ significantly from the other groups in any comparisons.

831. Daniel, D. A. (1984). Effects of extensive group therapy on incarcerated young men's attitudes toward themselves and prison staff. *Journal of Offender Counseling, Services and Rehabilitation, 8,* 27-39.
Evaluated whether extensive group therapy for drug abusers would change the incarcerated young men's attitude toward themselves and others. There were no significant changes in the subjects' attitudes, but there was a more positive attitude change in those convicted of crimes against persons than those convicted of crimes against property.

832. Davenport, Y. B., Ebert, M. H., Adland, M. L., & Goodwin, F. K. (1977). Couples group therapy as an adjunct to lithium maintenance of the manic patient. *American Journal of Orthopsychiatry, 47*(3), 495-502.

833. Davies, D. R. (1991). A comparison of hypnotic and non-hypnotic users in the group therapy of insomnia. *Behavioral Psychotherapy, 19,* 193-204.

Describes the success of a group therapy approach involving cognitive and behavioral strategies, stimulus control, muscle relaxation, self-monitoring, and sleep education in treating insomniac patients.

834.   Davis, E. L. (1983). Uncensored versus measured communication treatments in therapy for marital adjustment. *Dissertation Abstracts International, 44*(04), 988A.
An uncensored communication therapy group (UCTG) and a measured communication therapy group (MCTG), each with 10 subjects, were given six weeks of treatment for marital adjustment, while a control group (CG) received no treatment. Found a significant difference between each treatment, with the MCTG showing a significant difference in a positive direction over the UCTG. The CG, however, scored significantly higher on marital adjustment than either treatment group.

835.   Davis, G. L., & Hoffman, R. G. (1991). MMPI and CPI scores of child molesters before and after incarceration-for-treatment. *Journal of Offender Rehabilitation, 17,* 77-85.
Evaluated a group treatment program of incarcerated males convicted of child molestation, using the Minnesota Multiphasic Personality Inventory (MMPI) and the California Psychological Inventory (CPI). Each inventory reflected significant pre- and post-test differences.

836.   Davis, J. M., & Hartsough, C. S. (1992). Assessing psychosocial environment in mental health consultation groups. *Psychology in the Schools, 29*(3), 224-229.
Examined whether there are any similarities in the psychosocial environments of consultee-centered consultant groups and task oriented, social-recreational, psychotherapy and mutual support groups. Analyses reveal that the profiles of the consultation and the psychotherapy/mutual support groups are similar.

837.   Davis, M. (1972). A self-confrontation technique in alcoholism treatment. *Quarterly Journal of Studies on Alcohol, 33*(1-A), 191-192.

838.   Davis, R., Olmsted, M. P., & Rockert, W. (1992). Brief group psycho-education for bulimia nervosa: II. Prediction of clinical outcome. *International Journal of Eating Disorders, 11,* 205-211.
Describes the pre treatment variables associated with poor outcome in 41 bulimia nervosa patients. Greater self-reported depression, higher frequency of vomiting, and a history of low adult body weight all correlated with poorer outcome.

839.   Davis-Karlosky, P. L. (1986). Effectiveness of self-evaluation training and group counseling in enhancing self-efficacy and reducing anxiety. *Dissertation Abstracts International, 47*(04), 1704B.

840.   Dawley, H. H., & Wenrich, W. W. (1973). Massed group desensitization in reduction of test anxiety. *Psychological Reports, 33*(2), 359-363.

841.   Dawley, H. H., & Wenrich, W. W. (1973). Treatment of test anxiety by group implosive therapy. *Psychological Reports, 33*(2), 383-388.

Assigned subjects to either the no treatment control groups (CGs), placebo-attention groups (PAGs), or implosive therapy groups (ITGs). Results indicate significant differences between the CGs and ITGs, but no differences between the PAGs and ITGs on the post-test measure.

842. Deal, G. A. (1977). Existential group psychotherapy with mentally retarded adults. *Dissertation Abstracts International, 37*(07), 4128. (University Microfilm No. AAC77-00689)

843. Decarlo, J. J., & Mann, W. C. (1985). The effectiveness of verbal versus activity groups in improving self-perceptions of interpersonal communication skills. *American Journal of Occupational Therapy, 39,* 20-27.
Randomly assigned adult males, diagnosed with schizophrenia and depression, either to an activity group (AG), a verbal group (VG), or a control group (CG) for treatment of interpersonal communication deficiencies. Those in the AG achieved a significantly higher level of interpersonal communication skills; there were no significant differences between the control and experimental groups.

844. Decker, R. E. (1976). The effects of visual observation, videotape and audiotape recording on verbal and nonverbal behavior in group psychotherapy. *Dissertation Abstracts International, 37*(03), 1428. (University Microfilm No. AAC76-20561)

845. Decshner, J. P., & McNeil, J. S. (1986). Results of anger control training for battering couples. *Journal of Family Violence, 1*(2), 111-120.
Subjects participated in a 10-week structured group therapy program aimed at reducing family violence and facilitating anger control. Data collected from half of the subjects six to eight months following treatment indicated that 85% of the families were free from further violence; the couples who had reverted to violence were more likely to include a partner who had not attended sessions or who would not admit to contributing to the conflicts.

846. de Leon, G., & Biase, D. V. (1975). Encounter group: Measurement of systolic blood pressure. *Psychological Reports, 37,* 439-445.
Took systolic blood pressure readings of 32 male drug-free heroin addicts, who were residents in a therapeutic community, before and after encounter groups and general discussion meetings. There were significant elevations and decreases of pressure before and after the encounters only, respectively.

847. Deluca, A. V. (1980). The impact of a parent effectiveness training program on parents and the behavior of their problem school children. *Dissertation Abstracts International, 41*(01), 103A.

848. DeLucia, J. L., & Bowman, V. E. (1991). Internal consistency and factor structure of the Group Counselor Behavior Rating Form. *Journal for Specialists in Group Work, 16*(2), 109-114.
Analysis of data from 104 graduate students indicated a high reliability and internal consistency for the 30 item instrument, which assesses group leadership behavior and skills. Four factors were indicated by factor analysis: interventions, applications of theory, facilitative conditions, and professionalism.

849.   Denney, D. R., & Sullivan, B. F. (1976). Desensitization and modeling treatments of spider fear using two types of scenes. *Journal of Consulting and Clinical Psychology, 44*(4), 573-579.

850.   Denny, G. M., & Lee, L. J. (1984). Grief work with substance abusers. *Journal of Substance Abuse Treatment, 1,* 249-254.
        Reports on group therapy designed to decrease depression and to help resolve grief using 20 subjects with psychiatric, and drug and alcohol dependency diagnoses. Subjects showed decreases in depression, but no differences in feelings toward the loved one or self, relative to controls.

851.   Deouell, R. (1989). A case study in group therapy with male homosexuals in Israel. *Dissertation Abstracts International, 50*(02), 778. (University Microfilm No. AAC89-06568)

852.   Deter, H. C. (1986). Cost-benefit analysis of psychosomatic therapy in asthma. *Journal of Psychosomatic Research, 30,* 173-182.
        Describes the success of a psychosomatic coping group therapy in reducing lost working days with 22 asthmatic subjects.

853.   Deter, H. C., & Allert, G. (1983). Group therapy for asthma patients: A concept for the psychosomatic treatment of patients in a medical clinic: A controlled study. *Psychotherapy and Psychosomatics, 40*(1-4), 95-105.

854.   Devereaux, N. E. (1984). Psychodrama training: History, development, and a survey of current practices. *Dissertation Abstracts International, 44*(11), 3522B.
        Describes the history and development of psychodrama training; its trainers and their methods; and content of training. Presents evidence of consistency in training across trainers and compares psychodrama training to other group psychotherapy training programs.

855.   Diament, C., & Colletti, G. (1978). Evaluation of behavioral group counseling for parents of learning-disabled children. *Journal of Abnormal Child Psychology, 6*(3), 385-400.
        Treatment group mothers received a series of eight weekly sessions in which they were taught basic principles and procedures of behavior modification. Results indicate that treatment ratings of children's conduct and disruption, and postbehavioral observations of mother-child interactions showed improvement for the behavioral-counseling groups, while control group ratings and behavior observations remained the same. All treatment group changes were maintained at three month follow-up. Consistency of treatment group data across measures and over time suggests the effectiveness of this approach as a training method.

856.   Diamond, M. J., & Shapiro, J. L. (1973). Changes in locus of control as a function of encounter group experiences: A study and replication. *Journal of Abnormal Psychology, 82*(3), 514-518.
        Investigated the effects of encounter group experience on locus of control, and reports on two group phases. Significant increases in internal locus of control occurred as a result of encounter group experience, which is seen as a potent means for inducing cognitive behavioral change. Notes implications of the modification of generalized expectancies and considers future studies.

857. Dick, B. M. (1975). A ten-year study of out-patient analytic group therapy. *British Journal of Psychiatry, 127,* 365-375.

858. Dick, B. M., & Wooff, K. (1986). An evaluation of a time-limited programme of dynamic group psychotherapy. *British Journal of Psychiatry, 148,* 159-164. Reports on the success of a dynamic group psychotherapy program with 40 outpatients. Eighty-two percent of the outpatients reduced their dependence on psychiatric services and most improved their self-satisfaction.

859. Dies, R. R. (1973). Group therapist self-disclosure: An evaluation by clients. *Journal of Counseling Psychology, 20,* 344-348. Describes leader evaluations made by 24 group therapy members. Self-revealing therapists were judged as more friendly, disclosing, trusting, intimate, helpful, but less relaxed, strong, stable and sensitive.

860. Dies, R. R. (1973). Group therapist self-disclosure: Development and validation of a scale. *Journal of Consulting and Clinical Psychology, 41,* 97-103. Describes development of the Group Therapist Orientation Scale, designed to measure attitudes toward therapist self-disclosure in group therapy. The scale demonstrated internal consistency and validity. Scores on the scale were associated with years of experience, involvement in encounter groups and theoretical orientation.

861. Dies, R. R. (1974). Attitudes toward the training of group psychotherapists: Some interprofessional and experience-associated differences. *Small Group Behavior, 5*(1), 65-79. Surveyed 30 psychiatrists, 98 psychologists and 43 social workers and found that the therapist's own group training was unrelated to the type of training the therapist rated as important. Insight approaches were rated highest by social workers in general and by experienced psychiatrists. Behavioristic approached were rated highest by psychologists and experienced social workers.

862. Dies, R. R. (1980). Current practice in the training of group psychotherapists. *International Journal of Group Psychotherapy, 30*(2), 169-185. Results indicated that the preferred specialized training methods were experiential groups, workshops, and role playing. Overall, experiential and supervision groups were usually favored over academic and observational techniques.

863. Dies, R. R. (1992). Models of group psychotherapy: Sifting through confusion. *International Journal of Group Psychotherapy, 42*(1), 1-17. Results revealed significant differences in how 111 senior clinicians within the American Group Psychotherapy Association conceptualized therapeutic interventions, but a significant proportion of practitioners agreed on what were essential areas of knowledge.

864. Dies, R. R., & Dies, K. R. (1993). The role of evaluation in clinical practice: Overview and group treatment illustration. *International Journal of Group Psychotherapy, 43,* 77-105.

865.   Dies, R. R., & MacKenzie, K. R. (Eds.). (1983). *Advances in group psychotherapy: Integrating research and practice* (American Group Psychotherapy Association Monograph Series, Monograph No. 1). New York: International Universities Press.
        Senior chapter contributors include: Robert R. Dies (Bridging the gap between research and practice in group psychotherapy; also, Clinical implications of research on leadership in short-term group psychotherapy), Erich Coche (Change measures and clinical practice in group psychotherapy), K. Roy MacKenzie (A developmental model for brief group therapy; also, The clinical application of a group climate measure), W. John Livesley (Social roles in psychotherapy groups), Ariadne P. Beck (The participation of leaders in the structural development of therapy groups), Gary R. Bond (Norm regulation in therapy groups), and Morton A. Lieberman (Comparative analyses of change mechanisms in groups). Although some of these chapters seem to be superseded by the *Handbook of group psychotherapy: An empirical and clinical synthesis* (Fuhriman & Burlingame, Eds., 1994), others are still timely and of major importance.

866.   Dietz, P. E. (1984). Psychiatrists and their treatments: A study in the sociology of psychiatry. *Dissertation Abstracts International, 45*(03), 1059B.

867.   Dimmitt, J., & Davila, Y. R. (1995). Group psychotherapy for abused women: A survivor group prototype. *Applied Nursing Research, 8,* 3-7.
        Analyzes the major process and content themes from group therapy for abused women, based on Campbell's adaptation of Litton's survivor group prototype.

868.   Dinkmeyer, D. C., & Muro, J. J. (1971). *Group counseling: Theory and practice.* Itasca, IL: F. E. Peacock.
        Presents a comprehensive overview covering the following areas: recent history of group counseling research, reviews of group counseling research, evaluation studies of group counseling, variables in group counseling evaluation, directions for future research, conducting group counseling research, control and control groups, pre- and post-evaluation, follow-up, overall suggestions for conducting group counseling research, and experimental designs.

869.   Dixon, D. N., & Sciara, A. D. (1977). Effectiveness of group reciprocity counseling with married couples. *Journal of Marital and Family Therapy, 3*(3), 77-83.

870.   Dixon, K. N. (1986). Group therapy for bulimia. In S. C. Feinstein (Ed.), *Adolescent psychiatry: Developmental and clinical studies* (pp. 291-404). Chicago: University of Chicago Press.
        Before presenting a case study of group therapy for bulimic patients, findings of research from several studies on successful treatment of bulimia in groups are discussed.

871.   Dixon, K. N., & Kiecolt-Glaser, J. (1984). Group treatment for bulimia. *Hillside Journal of Clinical Psychiatry, 6,* 156-170.
        Determined therapy's effectiveness by comparing 19 noncompleters with 11 completers of a group therapy program for bulimic subjects. Completers

reported improvement in their symptoms and increases in internal locus of control, while noncompleters had higher social desirability scores.

872. Donahoe, P. M. (1978). A comparison of the effects of group assertiveness training and unstructured group counseling on changes in locus-of-control. *Dissertation Abstracts International, 38*(10), 5922. (University Microfilm No. AAC78-04209)

873. Dong, Y. L. (1977). Evaluation of a group counseling program designed to enhance social adjustment of mentally retarded adults. *Journal of Counseling Psychology, 24,* 318-323.
Evaluated a group counseling program's effectiveness in improving social adjustment skills of moderately retarded, institutionalized male and female adults. Results supported the use of group counseling, as the counseling group had higher mean scores than the control group.

874. Dongiovanni, V. J. (1989). An evaluation of an ongoing treatment program for the psychiatrically impaired substance abuser. *Dissertation Abstracts International, 49*(07), 2850. (University Microfilm No. AAC88-17876)
Evaluation of a multifaceted treatment program for those with dual diagnoses resulted in a recommendation to continue the program, which consisted of Alcoholics Anonymous (AA) meetings, Alpha Group therapy, a Drug/Alcohol class and medicine/antabuse.

875. Donlon, P. T., Rada, R. T., & Knight, S. W. (1973). A therapeutic aftercare setting for "refractory" chronic schizophrenic patients. *American Journal of Psychiatry, 130,* 682-684.
Compared nurturance in a social group (SG) setting to individual supportive psychotherapy (ISP) with 24 chronic "refractory" schizophrenics. SG participants responded more favorably than those in ISP, as reflected in cost efficiency, clinic attendance and socialization.

876. Donovan, J. M., Bennett, M. J., & McElroy, C. M. (1979). The crisis group: An outcome study. *American Journal of Psychiatry, 136,* 906-910.

877. Drescher, S. R. (1989). Therapeutic factors and verbal interaction style in group psychotherapy. *Dissertation Abstracts International, 49*(07), 2851. (University Microfilm No. AAC88-17313)

878. Drob, S., Bernard, H., Lifshutz, H., & Nierenberg, A. (1986). Brief group psychotherapy for herpes patients: A preliminary study. *Behavior Therapy, 17*(3), 229-238.
Compared three time-limited group psychotherapies for people with genital herpes: a self-help group, a dynamically oriented therapy group, and a cognitive-behavioral stress management group. Participants in the cognitive-behavioral group reported receiving the most benefits from therapy; benefits related to affect, sexuality, communication, interpersonal relationships, and self-confidence.

879. Droge, D., Arntson, P., & Norton, R. (1986). The social support function in epilepsy self-help groups. *Small Group Behavior, 17*(2), 139-163.

Presents the results of a national survey of 136 members of epilepsy self-help groups, which examined stigmatization effects, asserted curative factors, reasons for participation, and formal only versus informal participation in the self-help group process. Concludes that perceived subject control of his/her life is a mediator in resolving the major problems associated with stigmatization.

880. Duckert, F., Amundsen, A., & Johnson, J. (1992). What happens to drinking after therapeutic intervention? *British Journal of Addiction, 87*(10), 1457-1467. Studied 84 men and 51 women treated for alcohol problems with either brief counseling or short-term group therapy; all subjects were followed up after 3, 9, 15 and 21 months. Throughout the follow-up period, the sample as a whole maintained a significant reduction in alcohol consumption. The reductions took place mainly through less frequent drinking, fewer episodes of heavy drinking, and reduced consumption during weeks of moderate drinking.

881. Duckert, F., & Johnson, J. (1987). Behavioral use of disulfiram in the treatment of problem drinking. *International Journal of the Addictions, 22*(5), 445-454.

882. Duehn, W. D., & Mayada, N. S. (1976). A study of client content expectancies as related to interactional processes during short-term group sexual counseling. *Small Group Behavior, 7,* 457-472.

883. Duma, J. (1993). Termination from a psychiatric day treatment program: A process of a transformational versus restorational nature. *Dissertation Abstracts International, 53*(12), 4208. (University Microfilm No. AACNN-73811)

884. Duncombe, L. W., & Howe, M. C. (1985). Group work in occupational therapy: A survey of practice. *American Journal of Occupational Therapy, 39*(3), 163-170.

885. Durst, K. L. (1994). The effects of pre-training on incest-theme-oriented, time-limited group psychotherapy: A clinical trials study. *Dissertation Abstracts International, 54*(09), 4914. (University Microfilm No. AAC94-05043)

886. Dutton, D. G. (1986). The outcome of court-mandated treatment of wife assault: A quasi-experimental evaluation. *Violence and Victims, 1*(3), 163-175. Examined 50 treated and 50 untreated male perpetrators and their wives. Longitudinal pre- and post-treatment measures indicated a 4% recidivism rate for those treated versus 40% for untreated subjects; treated subjects reported significant declines in physical and verbal abuse.

887. Eastin, D. L. (1990). The treatment of adult female incest survivors by psychological forgiveness processes. *Dissertation Abstracts International, 50*(09), 4215B. (University Microfilm No. AAC89-15533)

888. Eastman, P. C. (1973). Consciousness-raising as a resocialization process for women. *Smith College Studies in Social Work, 43,* 153-183. Examined consciousness-raising group participation as a resocialization process for women, in this case, for educationally and economically advantaged women. Participants reported positive results in several life areas.

889. Eayers, C. B., Rowan, D., & Harvey, P. G. (1984). Behavioral group training for anxiety management. *Behavioral Psychotherapy, 12*(2), 117-129.
Describes three experiments with 31 subjects which evaluated a newly developed coping skills (CS) package against group relaxation training (GR). Results indicated equivocal treatment gains for experimental and control groups, but there was some evidence for the superiority of the CS package on the State-Trait Anxiety Inventory.

890. Ebenstein, N. (1976). The effect of a group counseling program on the self-concept and the sense of independence in women. *Dissertation Abstracts International, 37*(05), 2633A.

891. Eckman, B. K. (1980). Seating pattern and working in a Gestalt therapy group. *Gestalt Journal, 3,* 99-106.
Reports on typical seating patterns and their effects within group therapy. A higher degree of good work and greater self-initiation was more typical of members sitting nearer to the therapist than those sitting further away.

892. Edleson, J. L., Miller, D. M., Stone, G. W., & Chapman, D. G. (1985). Group treatment for men who batter. *Social Work Research and Abstracts, 21*(3), 18-21.

893. Edleson, J. L., & Syers, M. (1991). The effects of group treatment for men who batter: An 18-month follow-up study. *Research on Social Work Practice, 1*(3), 227-243.
Compared three types of brief treatment groups offered in two differing intensities to men who batter their women partners. Subjects completed 80% or more of the assigned sessions. Conducted an 18 month follow-up interview with about half of the subjects or their partners. Results indicate that short-term, relatively structured group treatment tended to produce the most consistent successful results.

894. Edmonstone, Y., & Freeman, C. (1992). Research in psychotherapy. In C. Freeman & P. Tyrer (Eds.), *Research methods in psychiatry: A beginner's guide* (2nd ed., pp. 208-232). London: Gaskell.
Discusses potential problems in conducting psychotherapy research under the following headings: defining psychotherapy treatments; controls in psychotherapy; power and sample size; measurements of outcome; generalization of results; outcome research; single-case research; process research; and meta-analysis.

895. Edwards, D. W., & Roundtree, G. A. (1981). Assessment of short-term treatment groups with adjudicated first offender shoplifters. *Journal of Offender Counseling, Services and Rehabilitation, 6,* 89-102.
Adjudicated first time offender shoplifters were assigned to either short-term group treatment or no treatment. The MMPI Ego Strength Scale showed no significant post-treatment differences between the two groups, and at a 90 day follow-up, there were no re-arrests.

896.   Edwards, J. D., & Dill, J. E. (1974). Alcoholism clinic in a military setting: A combined disulfiram and group therapy outpatient program. *Military Medicine, 139*(3), 206-209.
        Treated 38 subjects diagnosed as chronic alcoholics with a combination of disulfiram and group therapy for 10 months. The overall success rate, with success defined as complete abstinence during treatment, was 61%; fifteen subjects drank at least once while under treatment. All abstinent subjects improved in social functioning. Side effects of disulfiram alone, or in combination with drugs other than alcohol, were minor in degree.

897.   Elgort, A. C. (1992). Reducing teachers' levels of stress: A comparison of two counseling treatment models. *Dissertation Abstracts International, 53*(05), 1451A.

898.   Elizabeth, P. (1983). Comparison of psychoanalytic and a client-centered group treatment model on measures of anxiety and self-actualization. *Journal of Counseling Psychology, 30*(3), 425-428.
        Compared a psychoanalytic approach to a client-centered group treatment approach. Data from 19 subjects who completed both days of treatment indicated significant differences: The psychoanalytic group reported higher anxiety and the client-centered group showed greater gains on the Personal Orientation Inventory, maintained at follow-up. Sex of the leader did not differentiate between group treatment models.

899.   Ellinger-Dixon, P. S. (1990). An experimental study to determine the effects of structured group counseling on co-dependency in women. *Dissertation Abstracts International, 51*(06), 1954. (University Microfilm No. AAC90-22493)

900.   Ellis, E. M., & Nichols, M. P. (1979). A comparative study of feminist and traditional group assertiveness training with women. *Psychotherapy: Theory, Research and Practice, 16,* 467-474.
        Compared the effectiveness of traditional versus feminist group assertiveness training using all female groups and leaders. Both groups made significant gains, but neither group made more significant gains than the other.

901.   Ellis, H. R. (1991). Dream drama: Small group enactment of dreams. *Dissertation Abstracts International, 51*(08), 4045. (University Microfilm No. AAC90-33581)

902.   El-Mallakh, R. S., & Hair, C. S. (1993). Medication dynamics in group psychotherapy. *Group, 17,* 101-106.
        Examines the effects of anxiolytic buspirone on group cohesiveness, group dynamics, and group regression.

903.   Elmore, C. B. (1977). A study of the effects of a transactional analysis learning model in group counseling with couples experiencing marital maladjustments. *Dissertation Abstracts International, 37*(10), 5320B.

904.   Emerson, P. M. (1990). Application of life style assessment in married couples counseling. *Dissertation Abstracts International, 50*(07), 1943A.

905. Emory, L. E., Cole, C. M., & Meyer, W. J. (1992). The Texas experience with depoprovera: 1980-1990. Special Issue: Sex offender treatment: Psychological and medical approaches. *Journal of Offender Rehabilitation, 18,* 125-139.
Two groups of male sex offenders received group and individual therapy, and occasionally, family therapy, but one group took depoprovera (DP) while the other refused pharmacological treatment. Findings suggest that DP may facilitate certain carefully chosen men to deal with sexual behaviors in an outpatient program.

906. Engelman, S. R., Clance, P. R., & Imes, S. (1982). Self- and body-cathexis change in therapy and yoga groups. *Journal of the American Society of Psychosomatic Dentistry and Medicine, 29*(3), 77-88.
Conducted pre- and post-treatment comparisons of 45 subjects in non-body-oriented group therapy, 33 subjects in yoga, and 42 in a control condition. Yoga subjects changed significantly more on self-cathexis and body-cathexis than did control subjects. Compared to the control, the therapy groups showed significant positive self-cathexis change, but not body-cathexis change. Yoga and therapy groups did not significantly differ from each other.

907. Englander, T. R. (1990). The facilitating environment, cohesion, and the contract in group psychotherapy. *Dissertation Abstracts International, 50*(12), 5877. (University Microfilm No. AAC90-12230)

908. English, D. (1982). Effectiveness of a stress reduction training program for women. *Dissertation Abstracts International, 43*(03), 671A.
Divided 18 women were into three treatment groups: a stress-reduction training group, a support-counseling group, and a no-treatment control group. These groups met for two hours weekly for eight weeks. Found a significant positive correlation between anxiety proneness and perceived stress. At post-test, the three groups did not differ on level of perceived stress.

909. Enright, S. J. (1991). Group treatment for obsessive-compulsive disorder: An evaluation. *Behavioral Psychotherapy, 19,* 183-192.
Examined the effects of group cognitive-behavioral therapy with 24 patients with obsessive-compulsive disorder (OCD). Although reduction of specific OCD symptoms were small, nonspecific positive effects relating to mood, sense of control, hope and understanding were noted.

910. Erickson, J. R. (1994). Predicting attitudes about being seen in group counseling according to expectations about counseling, social anxiety, and perceived need for counselor expertness. *Dissertation Abstracts International, 54*(12), 6459. (University Microfilm No. AAC94-14273)

911. Ernst, J. M., & Heesacker, M. (1993). Application of the elaboration likelihood model of attitude change to assertion training. *Journal of Counseling Psychology, 40*(1), 37-45.

912. Evans, J. J., & Wilson, B. A. (1992). A memory group for individuals with brain injury. *Clinical Rehabilitation, 6*(1), 75-81.

Five patients with memory impairments resulting from brain injury attended a memory group which met weekly for 11 months. The group focused on using memory aids to help with everyday memory problems, and one of its goals was to facilitate social support among patients. Memory functioning as Measured by the Rivermead Behavioural Memory Test did not show any significant improvements. Some reduction in levels of general anxiety and depression over the course of the group were noted. Subjects' feedback indicated that being in a group with others with similar difficulties was helpful and enjoyable.

913.   Evans, R. L., & Jaureguy, B. M. (1981). Telephone counselling with visually impaired adults. *International Journal of Rehabilitation Research 4*, 550-552.
        Reports improvements in social involvement in 24 blind veterans who participated in eight telephone group counselling sessions; noted no change in depression or loneliness.

914.   Evans, R. L., Kleinman, L., Halar, E. M., & Herzer, K. (1984). Predicting change in life satisfaction as a function of group counseling. *Psychological Reports, 55*(1), 199-204.

915.   Evans, R. L., Kleinman, L., Halar, E. M., & Herzer, K. (1985). Predicting outcome of group counseling with severely disabled persons. *International Journal of Rehabilitation Research, 8*, 193-196.
        Examined group counseling by telephone for its effect on life satisfaction of 38 disabled individuals. Subjects reported higher and more frequent goal attainment than did same aged controls.

916.   Everaerd, W., Dekker, J., Dronkerse, J., van der Rhee, K., Staffelen, J., & Wiselins, G. (1982). Treatment of homosexual and heterosexual sexual dysfunction in male-only groups of mixed sexual orientation. *Archives of Sexual Behavior, 11*, 1-10.
        Gay and heterosexual males with erectile or ejaculatory dysfunction participated without their partners in structured group therapy groups, led by male therapists. Treatment was highly successful.

917.   Exner, J. E., & Andronikof, S. A. (1992). Rorschach changes following brief and short-term therapy. *Journal of Personality Assessment, 59*, 59-71.

918.   Fagerstrom, K. O., & Lisper, H. O. (1978). Sleepy drivers: Analysis and therapy of seven cases. *Accident Analysis and Prevention, 10*, 241-250.
        Examined the effectiveness of a behavioral treatment with seven car drivers who suffered from frequent difficulty staying awake while driving. Six subjects reported that sleepiness while driving had diminished considerably.

919.   Faillace, L. A., Flamer, R. N., Imber, S. D., & Ward, R. F. (1972). Giving alcohol to alcoholics: An evaluation. *Quarterly Journal of Studies on Alcohol, 33*(1-A), 85-90.

920.   Falloon, I. R. (1981). Interpersonal variables in behavioral group therapy. *British Journal of Medical Psychology, 54*, 133-141.
        Randomly assigned psychiatric outpatients lacking in certain interpersonal skills to one of two types of behavioral group therapy: role rehearsal and modeling,

or guided discussions. The role rehearsal group had higher levels of attraction, which were associated with enhanced self-esteem and, at post-treatment, decreased fear. Examined dropouts.

921.   Fals, S. W., Marks, A. P., & Schafer, J. (1993). A comparison of behavioral group therapy and individual behavior therapy in treating obsessive-compulsive disorder. *Journal of Nervous and Mental Disease, 181,* 189-193.
Randomly assigned obsessive-compulsive disordered (OCD) outpatients to either behavioral group therapy, individual behavior therapy, or progressive muscle relaxation. Subjects in individual therapy showed a speedier decrease in the severity of OCD symptoms, but by the end of treatment, subjects in the two behavioral therapy conditions showed equal decrease in the severity of OCD symptomology, anxiety, and depression; improvement was maintained at follow-up.

922.   Farenhorst, D. (1982). The comparative effectiveness of individual and group counseling modalities for post-divorce adjustment and self-esteem. *Dissertation Abstracts International, 42*(12), 5024A.

923.   Fassett, L. Y. (1993). Criminal history, use of alcohol, employment status, and demographic characteristics as factors which differentiate substance abusers who successfully complete treatment from those who do not. *Dissertation Abstracts International, 54*(06), 2062A.

924.   Faulkner, K., Stoltenberg, C. D., Cogen, R., & Nolder, M. (1992). Cognitive behavioral group treatment for male spouse abusers. *Journal of Family Violence, 7*(1), 37-55.

925.   Favret, J. V. (1991). Using the theory of reasoned action for the understanding, prediction, and control of premature termination behavior in group psychotherapy. *Dissertation Abstracts International, 51*(07), 3547. (University Microfilm No. AAC90-35077)

926.   Fawzy, F. I. (1984). Psychotherapy as an adjunct to supervised fasting for obesity. *Psychosomatics, 25*(11), 821-829.
Assigned subjects to one of three conditions: a control group, individual crisis-oriented therapy, or group crisis-oriented therapy. All subjects conjointly underwent medically supervised fasting. The individual therapy condition resulted in more successful completions of the program and a higher percentage of excess weight loss.

927.   Fawzy, F. I., Fawzy, N. W., Arndt, L. A., & Pasnau, R. O. (1995). Critical review of psychosocial interventions in cancer care. *Archives of General Psychiatry, 52,* 100-113.
Reviews the outcome literature on the four most frequently used psychological interventions in cancer care: group interventions, individual psychotherapy, education, and behavioral training.

928.   Fawzy, F. I., Fawzy, N. W., Hyun, C. S., & Elashoff, R. (1993). Malignant melanoma: Effects of an early structured psychiatric intervention, coping and

affective state on recurrence and survival six years later. *Archives of General Psychiatry, 50*(9), 681-689.

929. Federoff, J. P., Wisner-Carlson, R., Dean, S., & Berlin, F. S. (1992). Medroxy-progesterone acetate in the treatment of paraphiliac sexual disorders: Rate of relapse in paraphiliac men treated in long-term group psychotherapy with or without medroxy-progesterone acetate. Special Issue: Sex offender treatment: Psychological and medical approaches. *Journal of Offender Rehabilitation, 18*, 109-123.
Examines the combined effects of group psychotherapy and medroxy-progesterone acetate (MPA) in the treatment of 46 male paraphiliac patients. Males receiving group therapy alone had a relapse rate was 68%, versus 15% for those receiving a combination of group therapy and MPA.

930. Feeney, D. J., & Dranger, P. (1976). Alcoholics view group therapy: Process and goals. *Journal of Studies on Alcohol, 37*(5), 611-618.

931. Felde, R. (1973). Alcoholics before and after treatment: A study of self-concept changes. *Newsletter for Research in Mental Health and Behavioral Sciences, 15*(4), 32-34.
Assessed pre- and post-treatment self-concept changes in 1 female and 34 male alcoholic volunteer participants in a 90 day treatment program, which included group, attitude, and occupational therapy. The Tennessee Self-Concept Scale indicated no change in self-concept.

932. Feldman, R. A. (1986). Group work knowledge and research: A two-decade comparison. *Social Work with Groups, 9*, 7-14.
Compared more recent social group work research with that from 1956 to 1964 and found that, although systematic research and surveys on group work education has increased, there is a need to improve the quantity and quality of social group work research in the future.

933. Fellows, C. W. (1986). The effect of heterosexual group composition on outcome in a treatment program for spouse abuse. *Dissertation Abstracts International, 46*(10), 3591B.

934. Felton, G. S. (1973). Teaching internalization to middle-level mental health workers in training. *Psychological Reports, 32*, 1279-1282.
Describes the changes in locus of control for 13 subjects participating in intensive group counseling, which emphasized internalization and actuation of responsible behavior. The subjects' scores on Rotter's Scale and their behavior shifted in the direction of internality.

935. Fettes, P. A., & Peters, J. M. (1992). A meta-analysis of group treatments for bulimia nervosa. *International Journal of Eating Disorders, 11*, 97-110.
Describes the analysis of 40 outcome reports of group treatment with bulimia patients. More hours of therapy per week and the addition of other treatment components (i.e., individual therapy) were associated with larger post-treatment effect sizes.

936. Fiedler, J. M. (1994). The development of group cohesion and its relation to
      outcome in cognitive-behavioral and mutual support interventions for depression.
      Dissertation Abstracts International, 54(12), 6459. (University Microfilm No.
      AAC94-14956)

937. Fiegenbaum, W. (1981). A social training program for clients with facial
      disfigurations: A contribution to the rehabilitation of cancer patients.
      International Journal of Rehabilitation Research, 4(4), 501-509.

938. Field, H. L., & Shore, M. (1992). Living and dying with AIDS: Report of a
      three-year psychotherapy group. *Group, 16*(3), 156-164.
      Describes an ongoing psychotherapy group for persons with AIDS; the group
      combined educative, supportive, and intensive psychodynamic models. Although
      the education and discussion of reality issues may suggest a support group
      patterned on the self-help model, the group explored motivations and
      relationships, as well as reactions to the disease and its outcomes. At times,
      catharsis could be intense. Discusses population characteristics, psychological
      issues, problems, and advantages of this group.

939. Fielding, J. M. (1983). Verbal participation and group therapy outcome. *British
      Journal of Psychiatry, 142*, 524-528.
      Examined the relationship between patients' speaking out and outcomes for eight
      psychotherapy group members. Speaking out was associated with more chance
      of change and improvement, while the inverse was true of silence.

940. Figueroa, J. L. (1982). Group treatment of chronic tension headaches: A
      comparative treatment study. *Behavior Modification, 6*(2), 229-239.
      Compared three group treatments for tension headaches: a behavioral program
      (BG), traditional psychotherapy (TP), and self-monitoring (SM). Subjects
      monitored their frequency of headaches, type and amount of medication taken,
      severity and duration of the headaches, degree of pain disablement, and level of
      relaxation. Significant improvement occurred across all measures for the BG;
      neither the TP or the SM groups showed significant improvement.

941. Finando, S. J., Croteau, J. M., Sanz, D., & Woodson, R. (1977). The effects
      of group type on changes of self-concept. *Small Group Behavior, 8*(2), 123-134.

942. Finn, T., DiGiuseppe, R., & Culver, C. (1991). The effectiveness of rational-
      emotive therapy in the reduction of muscle contraction headaches. *Journal of
      Cognitive Psychotherapy, 5*(2), 93-103.

943. Fischer, J., & Coyle, B. (1977). A specialised treatment service for young
      problem drinkers (16-30 years): Treatment results obtained during the first six
      months of the treatment programme. *British Journal of Addiction, 72*(4), 317-
      319.
      Established a special bi-weekly group therapy program for young problem
      drinkers. Results obtained during the first six months of the program were
      encouraging, suggesting that separate treatment for young alcohol abusers merits
      further exploration.

944.   Fisher, D. E. (1991). Effects of support group intervention on psychological aspects linked to coronary heart disease. *Dissertation Abstracts International, 52*(03), 1715B.

945.   Fisher, P. M. (1993). Women survivors of childhood sexual abuse: Clinical sequelae and treatment. *Dissertation Abstracts International, 54*(04), 2197. (University Microfilm No. AACNN-78342)

946.   Fisk, N. B. (1990). A role for nursing in teaching and counseling wives of alcoholics: A comparison of two group approaches. *Dissertation Abstracts International, 51*(02), 414A.
        Compared the behavioral outcomes for wives of alcoholics who were treated by two psychoeducational approaches, which combined didactic teaching and group counseling techniques; groups met for six, two-hour sessions. Group A wives received a program based on a family-systems perspective while Group B received a more person-focused approach with a more conventional program stressing the disease concept of alcoholism.

947.   Flammang, M. R., & Wilson, G. L. (1992). Marital therapy formats: An analysis of acceptability ratings with married couples. *Journal of Sex and Marital Therapy, 18*(3), 159-172.

948.   Fleming, S. D. (1989). A comparison of levels of denial between mothers of victims of father-daughter incest and nonincest mothers. *Dissertation Abstracts International, 50*(03), 1144. (University Microfilm No. AAC89-08507)
        Studied levels of denial between mothers of victims of father-daughter incest (incest mothers) and nonincest mothers. Incest mothers had higher levels of denial than nonincest mothers, which supports clinical studies. A comparison of incest mothers showed that, upon discovering the incest, mothers who seemed not to know about the incest acted quickly to protect the daughter, whereas mothers who seemed to deny the incest, in whole or in part, used more denial upon disclosure.

949.   Flora-Tostado, J. (1981). Patient and therapist agreement on curative factors in group psychotherapy. *Dissertation Abstracts International, 42*(01), 371B.

950.   Flowers, J. V. (1978). The effect of therapist support and encounter on the percentage of client-client interactions in group therapy. *Journal of Community Psychology, 6*(1), 69-73.

951.   Flowers, J. V. (1978). Goal clarity as a component of assertive behavior and a result of assertion training. *Journal of Clinical Psychology, 34*(3), 744-747.
        In an initial study, found a direct relationship between assertion and goal clarity scores: More assertive subjects had greater goal clarity. After this assessment, 24 subjects were assigned to either 10 sessions of assertion training (AT) or an insight therapy group (IT). While there was no difference between the two groups prior to treatment, after treatment, the AT group demonstrated significantly greater goal clarity than did the IT group.

952.   Flowers, J. V. (1987). Client outcome as a function of agreement or disagreement with the modal group perception of curative factors in short-term,

structured, group psychotherapy. Special Issue: Integration of research and practice in the field of group psychotherapy. *International Journal of Group Psychotherapy, 37*, 113-118.
Compared 24 subjects' perceptions of curative factors; subjects either had improved or not improved after participating in group therapy. Subjects who improved, substantially agreed upon the rank ordering of curative factors, while those who did not improve disagreed with one another and with the improved subjects on the rank ordering.

953.   Flowers, J. V. (1993). Group therapy client outcome and satisfaction as a function of the therapists' use of rapid assessment instruments. *Small Group Research, 24*, 116-126.

954.   Flowers, J. V., & Booraem, C. D. (1991). Focusing on emotion in group therapy: What clients, what problems, and what for. *Psychological Reports, 69*, 369-370.
Examined the problems discussed by clients in three cognitive-behavioral therapy groups. Classified problems as inadequate or inappropriate emotional experience, inadequate or inappropriate emotional expression, and other.

955.   Flowers, J. V., & Booraem, C. D. (1991). A psycho-educational group for clients with heterogenous problems: Process and outcome. *Small Group Research, 22*, 258-273.
Compared a structured therapy (ST) group to an unstructured therapy (UT) group for clients with psychological problems. Participants in ST improved significantly more in goal attainment than those in UT.

956.   Flowers, J. V., Booraem, C. D., Brown, T. R., & Harris, D. E. (1974). An investigation of a technique for facilitating patient to patient therapeutic interactions in group therapy. *Journal of Community Psychology, 2*, 39-42.
Examined the use of tokens in group therapy with six severely disturbed outpatients. Tokens provided a tool to record verbal behavior accurately, and to facilitate patient verbal interaction.

957.   Follette, V. M., Alexander, P. C., & Follette, W. C. (1991). Individual predictors of outcome in group treatment for incest survivors. *Journal of Consulting and Clinical Psychology, 59*, 150-155.
Identified factors that seem to predict response to group treatment by women incest survivors. These were education, marital status, type of sexual contact, and initial levels of distress and depression.

958.   Follingstad, D. R., Kilmann, P. R., & Robinson, E. A. (1976). Prediction of self-actualization in male participants in a group conducted by female leaders. *Journal of Clinical Psychology, 32*(3), 706-712.

959.   Fontana, A. F., Dowds, B. N., & Bethel, M. H. (1976). A. A. and group therapy for alcoholics: An application of the world hypothesis scale. *Journal of Studies on Alcohol, 37*(5), 675-682.
Administered Pepper's World Hypothesis Scale (WHS) to 30 hospitalized alcoholics and to 17 members of Alcoholics Anonymous (AA). Results suggest

that alcoholics with a preference for formistic thinking are more likely to benefit from AA than from group therapy.

960.   Forester, B., Kornfeld, D. S., Fleiss, J. L., & Thompson, S. (1993). Group psychotherapy during radiotherapy: Effects on emotional and physical distress. *American Journal of Psychiatry, 150*(11), 1700-1706.

961.   Forrest, A. W. (1990). Therapeutic intervention in the treatment of substance abuser's unresolved grief reactions in an inpatient hospital setting: A study of two group approaches. *Dissertation Abstracts International, 51*(05), 1507. (University Microfilm No. AAC90-24573)

962.   Foster, T. (1978). Inpatient group therapy with observer feedback: A pilot study. *Psychiatric Forum, 7,* 23-27.

963.   Fraggetti, G. (1990). An investigation into the effects of assertion training on parents' behavior and the assessment of assertive and aggressive responses in parent-adolescent relationships. *Dissertation Abstracts International, 51*(05), 2618B.

964.   France, D. G., & Dugo, J. M. (1985). Pre-therapy orientation for open psychotherapy groups. *Psychotherapy, 22,* 256-261.
       Describes the success of pre-therapy training in improving attendance rates.

965.   Frank, M. (1986). Group therapy effects on psychiatric inpatients who possess character styles that employ externalizing defenses. *Dissertation Abstracts International, 47*(05), 2161. (University Microfilm No. AAC86-16326)

966.   Frank, R. (1973). Rotating leadership in a group therapy setting. *Psychotherapy: Theory, Research, and Practice, 10,* 337-338.

967.   Frank, R. A. (1993). Structured group psychotherapy for individuals with spinal cord injury. *Dissertation Abstracts International, 53*(09), 4952B.

968.   Frank, W. F. (1986). Length of sobriety and affiliative attributes of recovering alcoholic women. *Dissertation Abstracts International, 46*(12), 4183B.

969.   Frankel, A. J. (1992). Groupwork with recovering families in concurrent parent and children's group. *Alcoholism Treatment Quarterly, 9*(3-4), 23-37.
       Presents a concurrent parent training-children's groupwork model (PTCGM) that improved parenting skills, opened up communication in recovering families, gave more support for the expression of feelings, and helped families gain insight into the effects of prior addictions on children. Results suggest that there was value in conducting parallel parent training and children's groups for recovering families. Most parents demonstrated the ability to apply effectively the parent training skills they learned in group with their children at home.

970.   Frankel-Fein, R. (1991). Defense style, social support appraisal, response to a counseling sessions, and stress perception in women undergoing abortion. *Dissertation Abstracts International, 52*(06), 2071A.

971. Franklin, M. S. (1988). Changes in concepts of self and parent figures in self-reparenting groups. *Dissertation Abstracts International, 49*(06), 2377. (University Microfilm No. AAC88-09257)

972. Frederiksen, L. W., & Miller, P. M. (1976). Peer-determined and self-determined reinforcement in group therapy with alcoholics. *Behaviour Research and Therapy, 14*(5), 385-388.
      Compared the effectiveness of a self-determined (SD) reinforcement procedure with a peer-determined (PD) reinforcement system, using 13 male participants in a token economy program. The two reinforcement procedures show striking differences in the reward patterns. In the initial SD sessions, participants tended to under-reward their own performance, while in the PD system, they initially over-rewarded individual performance, but this trend was transitory.

973. Freedman, R. J. (1976). The effects of extra-group socializing and alternate sessions on group psychotherapy outcome. *Dissertation Abstracts International, 37*(04), 1896. (University Microfilm No. AAC76-22041)

974. Freeman, C., Sinclair, F., Turnbull, J., & Annandale, A. (1985). Psychotherapy for bulimia: A controlled study: Conference on Anorexia Nervosa and Related Disorders. *Journal of Psychiatric Research, 19*, 473-478.
      Compared the use of cognitive behavior therapy, behavior therapy, and group psychotherapy in the treatment of 60 bulimic females. Cognitive therapy had a greater effect on self-esteem and depression; all treatments effectively reduced the behavioral symptoms of bulimia.

975. Fretz, R. K. (1981). The effects of psychodrama and group therapy on emotional state. *Dissertation Abstracts International, 42*(03), 1171. (University Microfilm No. AAC81-18196)

976. Frey, D. H., Motto, J. A., & Ritholz, M. D. (1983). Group therapy for persons at risk for suicide: An evaluation using the intensive design. *Psychotherapy: Theory, Research and Practice, 20*, 281-291.
      Describes the success of a crisis intervention group therapy designed for individuals who are at high risk for suicide.

977. Friedlander, M. L. (1985). Introducing semantic cohesion analysis: A study of group talk. *Small Group Behavior, 16*, 285-302.
      Used semantic cohesion analysis in the examination of the conversational involvement of 31 participants in time-limited group counseling. Findings indicated that groups with nondisclosing therapists are significantly more cohesive throughout the life of the group.

978. Friedman, S. B., Ellenhorn, L. J., & Snortum, J. R. (1976). A comparison of four warm-up techniques for initiating encounter groups. *Journal of Counseling Psychology, 23*(6), 514-519.
      Compared the following four warm-up techniques: nonverbal exercises, modeling of intensive group interaction using an edited tape recording of an encounter group, autobiographical information exchange among group members, or no warm-up. The nonverbal exercises seemed to promote the largest increases in self-ratings of extraversion. The modeling condition was most

effective in fostering a group atmosphere rated as "active" and in stimulating intentions for further self-disclosures to the group. A correlational analysis of the dependent variables provided clues to the process components of the successful encounter group.

979.   Froehlich, R. A. (1987). A descriptive study of general procrastination in a group oriented treatment setting. *Dissertation Abstracts International, 48*(04), 1151. (University Microfilm No. AAC87-14641)

980.   Fromme, D. K., Dickey, G. V., & Schaefer, J. P. (1983). Group modification of affective verbalizations: Reinforcement and therapist style effects. *Journal of Clinical Psychology, 39*(6), 893-900.
        Examined the effects of reinforcement, combined with differing therapist styles, on affective verbalizations within an operant group paradigm. Groups received feedback or no feedback under three therapist conditions: role modeling, direct elicitation, or no facilitator. Observed subjects' discussion of specific topics. Direct questioning was quantitatively superior to either role modeling or no therapist in eliciting the subjects' affective verbalizations. However, evidence indicated that subjects in reinforced role modeling conditions were significantly better than direct elicitation subjects in predicting other group members' self-descriptions. The reverse was true for non-reinforced subjects.

981.   Frost, B. E. (1983). The effect of women's group counseling, marital group counseling and no group counseling on the self-images of women who have experienced a modified mastectomy. *Dissertation Abstracts International, 44*(03), 673A.

982.   Fuchs, C. Z., & Rehm, L. P. (1977). A self-control behavior therapy program for depression. *Journal of Consulting and Clinical Psychology, 45,* 206-215.
        Examined the effectiveness of a behavior therapy program based on a self-control model of depression. Subjects showed significantly greater reduction in depression and greater improvement in overall pathology relative to a nonspecific therapy group and a control group.

983.   Fuhriman, A., & Burlingame, G. M. (Eds.). (1994). *Handbook of group psychotherapy: An empirical and clinical synthesis.* New York: Wiley.
        Divided into four sections (Conceptual and methodological foundations; Structural entities in group psychotherapy; Therapeutic components of the group ecosystem, and Special applications and populations), senior contributors for each chapter within the four sections include: Addie Fuhriman, Gary M. Burlingame, Robert R. Dies, Theodore J. Kaul, K. Roy MacKenzie, Erick C. Crouch, Simon H. Budman, John C. Dagley, Robert H. Klein, J. Kelly Moreno, Randy Stinchfield, Gerald Goodman, and Morton A. Lieberman. This is an excellent comprehensive handbook on the scientific status of group psychotherapy with each chapter providing a good literature review, a thorough discussion of research issues, and suggestions regarding needed investigations.

984.   Fuhriman, A., Drescher, S., Hanson, E., & Henrie, R. (1986). Refining the measurement of curativeness: An empirical approach. *Small Group Behavior, 17,* 186-201.

Examined the curative factors valued by four different types of therapy groups: community mental health, Veterans Administration, university counseling center, and group behavior class. All groups valued catharsis, cohesion, and insight.

985.   Gagerman, J. R. (1991). An examination of gender-related themes and affective states in the social group work treatment setting. *Dissertation Abstracts International, 52*(02), 683. (University Microfilm No. AAC91-19815)
Compared men's and women's treatment groups using a sample of convenience. Divided 18 "themes discussed," 24 "feelings felt," and 24 "feelings discussed" into hypothesized male, female, and neutral categories. Results, measured with a self-reporting instrument, confirmed the hypothesis that the women's groups would score higher on female items, and disconfirmed the hypothesis that the men's groups would score higher on the male items. Women scored higher than men on all but one theme, and women scored significantly higher on "feelings discussed."

986.   Galanter, M. (1984). Self-help large group therapy for alcoholism: A controlled study. *Alcoholism: Clinical and Experimental Research, 8*(1), 16-23.
Evaluated a new approach to ambulatory treatment that adapts a self-help modality to the institutional clinical setting in the treatment of alcoholism. Results indicated that over a one-year period, retention and visit rates did not differ between the control and experimental groups. For experimental groups, the engagement of inpatients into ambulatory care was more effective.

987.   Galassi, J. P., Galassi, M. D., & Litz, M. C. (1974). Assertive training in groups using video feedback. *Journal of Counseling Psychology, 21*(5), 390-394.

988.   Galinsky, M., Schopler, J. H. (1985). Patterns of entry and exit in open-ended groups. Special Issue: Time as a factor in groupwork: Time-limited group experience. *Social Work With Groups, 8*(2), 67-80.

989.   Gallagher, G. G. (1984). A study of the effect of an expanded intake process on therapy group member retention. *Dissertation Abstracts International, 44*(12), 3931.

990.   Gallen, M. (1976). Prediction of improvement in two contrasting alcoholism treatment programs. *Newsletter for Research in Mental Health and Behavioral Sciences, 18*(2), 31-32.

991.   Galliford, J. E. (1982). Eliminating self-defeating behavior: The effects of ESDB Bibliotherapy compared to ESDB Group therapy on weight control in women. *Dissertation Abstracts International, 43*(06), 1978. (University Microfilm No. AAC82-24784)
Describes use of the Eliminating Self-Defeating Behavior (ESDB) method in bibliotherapy during a workshop for weight control and state and trait anxiety.

992.   Gallo-Silver, L., Raveis, V. H., & Moynihan, R. T. (1993). Psychosocial issues in adults with transfusion-related HIV infection and their families. *Social Work in Health Care, 18*(2), 63-74.
Gathered information about 20 hemophiliac adults with transfusion-related HIV infection through individual, family, and group counseling sessions; outpatient

clinic review meetings with physicians; and, multidisciplinary inpatient rounds. Psychosocial issues raised included: coping with personal feelings of victimization, sadness, anger and isolation, decision-making concerning medical treatment, and rebuilding trust in relationships with medical care professionals.

993. Gamble, E. H., Elder, S. T., & Lashley, J. K. (1989). Group behavior therapy: A selective review of the literature. *Medical Psychotherapy: An International Journal, 2,* 193-204.

994. Gamble, R. E. (1984). The effects of short-term group counseling on custodial parents and their minor children experiencing a family separation/divorce. *Dissertation Abstracts International, 45*(05), 1298A.
      Offered short-term, structured group counseling to custodial parents and their minor children immediately after the parents' separation; a matched control group was provided no treatment. Results demonstrated that subjects from both groups were functioning within the "average" or normal ranges established by specific tests. The lowest functional area (non-clinical) was income management for adults. The experimental groups improved significantly over the control groups in only one area for adults and one area for children, physical symptoms and dependency, respectively. In all other clinical areas, the experimental and control groups showed no significant between group differences.

995. Gardner, G. T. (1975). The effects of group counseling of counselors upon counselor-client congruence and client congruence. *Dissertation Abstracts International, 35*(10), 6454. (University Microfilm No. AAC75-09586)

996. Garrison, J. E. (1978). Written vs verbal preparation of patients for group psychotherapy. *Psychotherapy: Theory, Research, and Practice, 15,* 130-134.
      Describes the effects of two preparatory introductions, verbal and written, designed to foster realistic expectations and to encourage appropriate role behavior in group psychotherapy. Prepared patients had better attendance records and were judged to manifest better role behavior relative to controls.

997. Gary, A. L., Davis, L., & Howell, T. (1977). Melanin distribution and sensitivity to group therapy. *Journal of Psychology, 96*(2), 315-320.

998. Gaston, P. S. (1993). A two-part dissertation: Part I. Grandparents as primary caregivers for their grandchildren: An attitudinal and demographic survey. Part II. Group therapy with grandparents serving as primary caregivers for their grandchildren. *Dissertation Abstracts International, 54*(05), 2750B.

999. Gaultois, A. J. (1994). A group therapy program for adult survivors of child sexual abuse: An outcome study. *Masters Abstracts International, 32*(02), 396. (University Microfilm No. AACMM-82626)
      Examined the outcome of a three-phase group therapy program for women who had been sexually abused when children. The first of the two phases, which measured outcome in terms of change in self-esteem, locus of control, and internalized shame, resulted in significant change in all areas; the second phase resulted in significant change in self-esteem for six of the eight women; in the third phase, which measured subject satisfaction through discussion, the subjects said they felt more content and in control, and less shameful.

1000. Gauthier, L., Dalziel, S., & Gauthier, S. (1987). The benefits of group occupational therapy for patients with Parkinson's disease. *American Journal of Occupational Therapy, 41*(6), 360-365.
Evaluated a group rehabilitation program using occupational therapy, designed for patients with idiopathic Parkinson's disease; 30 patients entered the treatment program and 29 were in the control group. The treatment patients perceived significant improvement in their psychological well-being, maintained their functional status after one year, and demonstrated a significant decrease of bradykinesia.

1001. Gazda, G. M. (1989). An analysis of the group counseling research literature. In *Group counseling: A developmental approach* (4th ed., pp. 247-259). Boston: Allyn & Bacon.
The purpose of Chapter 12, according to the author, "is to acquaint readers not only with the strengths and deficits of past and current research but also, because of the variables focused on, to acquaint readers with the different types of groups (clientele being served), the length and duration of group sessions, the most popular instruments used to evaluate changes, goals, and outcome criteria, and general effectiveness of group counseling."

1002. Gendron, M., Lemberg, R., Allender, J., & Bohanske, J. (1992). Effectiveness of the intensive group process-retreat model in the treatment of bulimia. Special Section: The use of group therapy in the treatment of eating disorders. *Group, 16,* 69-78.
Examined the effect of an intensive short-term group treatment and follow-up session with 24 women diagnosed with bulimia. As compared to controls, group participants significantly improved in self-esteem and in the frequency and severity of binge-purge episodes.

1003. Gershman, L., & Clouser, R. A. (1974). Treating insomnia with relaxation and desensitization in a group setting by an automated approach. *Journal of Behavior Therapy and Experimental Psychiatry, 5*(1), 31-35.

1004. Getter, H., Litt, M. D., Kadden, R. M., & Cooney, N. L. (1992). Measuring treatment process in coping skills and interactional group therapies for alcoholism. *International Journal of Group Psychotherapy, 42*(3), 419-430.

1005. Gibbard, G. S., & Hartman, J. J. (1973). The significance of utopian fantasies in small groups. *International Journal of Group Psychotherapy, 23*(2), 125-147.
Discusses the view that utopian hopes engendered by various group experiences center on the largely unconscious fantasy that the group-as-a-whole is a maternal entity. Reports on a study of two self-analytic groups participating in a course on interpersonal behavior at the University of Michigan. Findings indicate that deification, utopian hopes and messianic fantasies occur at different points in the life of the group, and serve different functions.

1006. Gildenhuys, A. A. (1990). Experiential learning as training model in group psychotherapy. *Dissertation Abstracts International, 51*(06), 3130.

1007. Gimbel, N. E. (1990). The effect of an interpersonal relationships group on psychiatric inpatients. *Masters Abstracts International, 28*(03), 368.

1008. Glass, A. P. (1995). Identifying issues important to patients on a hospital satisfaction questionnaire. *Psychiatric Services, 46,* 83-85.
Used focus groups to collect written responses to questions about satisfaction with hospital stay and ratings on scaled items.

1009. Glaubman, H., & Hartmann, E. (1978). Daytime state and night-time sleep: A sleep study after a marathon group experience. *Perceptual and Motor Skills, 46,* 711-715.
Compared the nocturnal sleep of nine subjects following a "normal" weekend and a weekend in which they participated in a psychodynamic marathon group session. Sleep latency and one measurement of D-latency were reduced after the marathon group.

1010. Glawe, V. H. (1984). A comparison of two approaches to motivating volunteerism for group counseling. *Dissertation Abstracts International, 44*(11), 3285. (University Microfilm No. AAC84-04588)

1011. Glick, I. D., Fleming, L., De Chillo, N., Meyerkopf, N., Jackson, C., Muscara, D., & Good, E. M. (1986). A controlled study of transitional day care for non-chronically-ill patients. *American Journal of Psychiatry, 143,* 1551-1556.
Transitional treatment, an intensive day program, was compared to less costly, weekly outpatient group therapy for nonchronic schizophrenics and those with major affective disorder. Although dropout rate for the weekly therapy group was significantly higher than for the transitional group, there was no significant difference in outcome.

1012. Goldberg, C. (1981). A study of change in early recollections through the use of psychodrama. *Dissertation Abstracts International, 42*(01), 354. (University Microfilm No. AAC81-10132)

1013. Golden, J. S., Price, S., Heinrich, A. G., & Lobitz, W. C. (1978). Group vs couple treatment of sexual dysfunctions. *Archives of Sexual Behavior, 7,* 593-602.

1014. Goldenberg, E., & Cowden, J. E. (1977). An evaluation of intensive group psychotherapy with male offenders in isolation units. *Corrective and Social Psychiatry and Journal of Behavior Technology, Methods and Therapy, 23,* 69-72.

1015. Goldfarb, W. (1980). Effect of group counseling on self-reported problems as influenced by group composition and time arrangement. *Dissertation Abstracts International, 40*(08), 191. (University Microfilm No. AAC80-02362)

1016. Goldstein, H. K., Cohen, A., Thames, M., & Galloway, J. P. (1974). The influence of group therapy with relative of rehabilitation clients and their families. *Small Group Behavior, 5,* 374-384.
Describes group therapy with 32 relatives of rehabilitation clients. Client's age, religion, and type of disability were related to certain characteristics of relatives and three rehabilitation center variables.

1017. Golonka, L. M. (1977). The use of group counseling with breast cancer patients receiving chemotherapy. *Dissertation Abstracts International, 37*(10), 6362A.

1018. Gonzales, D. H. (1992). A comparison of smoking patterns between counseling-assisted and unassisted heavy smokers with early chronic obstructive pulmonary disease. *Dissertation Abstracts International, 53*(02), 406A.
Retrospectively described and compared smoking patterns for 5,395 subjects in the Lung Health Study at 12 and 24 months. Assigned 3,592 subjects to a special intervention group, which received a counseling assisted smoking cessation program that included nicotine gum, and assigned 1,803 subjects to a usual care group which received no assistance to stop smoking. Found significant between and within group differences regarding smoking outcomes and smoking patterns. Although no gender differences were found for the control group, at 24 months, counseling-assisted men were more successful at remaining abstinent than counseling-assisted women. Significant demographic variables included cigarettes smoked per day, previous attempts to quit, longest period quit, and alcoholic drinks, whereas age began smoking, other smokers in household, education, and social support variables were not significant.

1019. Gonzales, H. I. (1986). Experiences in psychotherapy. *Dissertation Abstracts International, 47*(01), 317. (University Microfilm No. AAC86-06458)

1020. Gonzalez, H. S. (1980). The use and effect of training groups as pre-therapy. *Dissertation Abstracts International, 41*(01), 165. (University Microfilm No. AAC80-09968)

1021. Goodwin, J. M., Wilson, N., & Connell, V. (1992). Natural history of severe symptoms in borderline women treated in an incest group. 9th International Conference on Multiple Personality and Dissociative States (1992, Chicago, Illinois). *Dissociation Progress in the Dissociative Disorders, 5,* 221-226.

1022. Goodwin, R. A., & Mickalide, A. D. (1985). Parent-to-parent support in anorexia nervosa and bulimia. Special issue: Active roles of parents. *Children's Health Care, 14*(1), 32-37.

1023. Gordon, R. H. (1978). Efficacy of group crisis-counseling program for men who accompany women seeking abortions. *American Journal of Community Psychology, 6*(3), 239-246.
Examined the effect of a group crisis-counseling session on the anxiety level and attitudes of 46 males who accompanied women seeking legal abortions. Half the subjects participated in a two-hour counseling session while the other half remained in the waiting room, as controls. Results from the State-Trait Anxiety Inventory and other measures indicate that state anxiety decreased and attitudes toward abortion concepts generally were more positive for those in the counseling group.

1024. Gordon, V. C. (1982). Themes and cohesiveness observed in a depressed women's support group. *Issues in Mental Health Nursing, 4,* 115-125.
Middle-aged women responded to a request for women with chronic, low-grade depression; they were divided into a support group treatment and a control group. Depression decreased significantly in the treatment group.

1025. Gordon-Adams, E. J. (1987). Group counseling experiences and the self-reported behaviors and perceptions of wives of adult aphasics. *Dissertation Abstracts International, 48*(01), 108B.

1026. Gotta, H. W. (1986). Group therapist self-disclosure and its impact on the group. *Dissertation Abstracts International, 46*(07), 2073. (University Microfilm No. AAC85-19529)

1027. Gottlieb, B. H. (1982). Mutual-help groups: Members' views of their benefits and of roles for professionals. *Prevention in Human Services, 1*, 55-67.
Distinguished three self-help groups: loss-transition (LT), stress, coping and support (SCS), and groups with participants one step removed from the problem (OSR). OSR subjects reported more significant participatory gains than SCS subjects; LT subjects reported that, if placed in that position, they would be all right without the group. Of the three groups, SCS subjects most preferred indirect professional involvement.

1028. Gottschalk, L. A. (1973). An evaluation of a parents' group in a child-centered clinic. *Psychiatry, 36*(2), 157-171.

1029. Gould, E., Garrigues, C. S., & Scheikowitz, K. (1975). Interaction in hospitalized patient-led and staff-led psychotherapy groups. *American Journal of Psychotherapy, 29*, 383-390.
Compared hospitalized psychotic patients who participated in staff-led group therapy (SLG) versus patient-led group therapy with staff observing (PLG). The PLG participants talked significantly more than the SLG participants; both groups were equally able to deal with potentially disruptive psychotic behavior.

1030. Gould, E., Glick, I. D. (1976). Patient-staff judgments of treatment program helpfulness on a psychiatric ward. *British Journal of Medical Psychology, 49*, 23-33.
Patients and staff members in a psychiatric ward ranked the ward's treatment activities, from most to least helpful. Ranking agreement within the patient group was high; how staff ranked treatment was also highly related within the group. There was significant agreement between patient and staff ratings.

1031. Graf, T. M. (1975). The relative effects of a pre-release group counseling experience on the recidivist rates of a sample of unconditionally released inmates from the Mississippi State Penitentiary. *Dissertation Abstracts International, 35*(07), 4250. (University Microfilm No. AAC75-00514)

1032. Graff, R. W., Whitehead, G. I., & LeCompte, M. (1986). Group treatment with divorced women using cognitive-behavioral and supportive-insight methods. *Journal of Counseling Psychology, 33*(3), 276-281.
Assigned 12 subjects to each treatment group and 22 subjects to the control group. Pre-, post- and follow-up measures of depression, self-esteem, and neuroticism indicated that both therapies were more effective on most criteria than the control groups. At a four month follow-up, cognitive-behavioral therapy continued to be beneficial, while supportive-insight therapy was less effective.

1033. Grant, J. R. (1994). The effectiveness of cognitive-behavioral body-image therapy for women: Comparisons of individual modest-therapist contact and group therapy formats. *Dissertation Abstracts International, 54*(09), 4919. (University Microfilm No. AAC94-02342)

1034. Graybill, D., & Gabel, H. (1978). Relationship of teacher nominations for parent counseling to perceptions of children's behavior problems. *Southern Journal of Educational Research, 12,* 151-159.
Special education teachers determined that certain parents of children they taught needed parental group counseling. The teachers' nominations were related to which children, in the teachers' perception, had conduct problems; nominations were not related to the parents' perceptions of their children's behavior problems.

1035. Green, E. A., & Altmair, E. M. (1991). Attribution retraining as a structured group counseling intervention. *Journal of Counseling and Development, 69*(4), 351-355.

1036. Green, M., & Wisner, W. (1985). Evaluation of a multimodal structured group approach in treatment of depression. *Psychological Reports, 56,* 984-986.
Reports on the positive effects of a multimodal treatment program used with eight chronically depressed subjects.

1037. Greenberg, H., Seeman, J., & Cassius, J. (1978). Personality changes in marathon therapy. *Psychotherapy: Theory, Research, and Practice, 15,* 61-67.
Examined the positive personality changes of 25 participants in a 45 hour marathon therapy session.

1038. Greenberg, S. A. (1992). An investigation into the unexpressed thoughts of the members of an interpersonal growth group. *Dissertation Abstracts International, 52*(09), 4960B.

1039. Greene, L. R., & Cole, M. B. (1991). Level and form of psychopathology and the structure of group therapy. *International Journal of Group Psychotherapy, 41,* 499-521.
Examined the relationship between the subjects' psychological boundaries and group therapy's structural features. Anaclitic borderline subjects were most sensitive to structural variation and most negatively affected by impersonal and highly structured climates.

1040. Greenway, J. D., & Greenway, P. (1985). Dimensions of interaction in psychotherapeutic groups: Sensitivity to rejection and dependency. *Small Group Behavior, 16,* 245-264.
Examined dimensions of interpersonal perception among members of a therapy group focusing on personal awareness, growth, and both personal and interpersonal problems. Dependency and sensitivity to rejection were correlated with empathy, commitment, and encountering.

1041. Gregory, S. (1991). Stress management for carers. *British Journal of Occupational Therapy, 54*(11), 427-429.

Describes a pilot six-week stress management group designed for those who care for an elderly person with confusion in the home setting. The group generally consisted of four people, with the occupational therapist and physiotherapist as group leaders. Participants felt that the group had been a worthwhile experience, providing immediate support, giving guidelines for the running of similar groups, and demonstrating the positive role that could be played by consumer consultation in planning and providing services.

1042. Greif, G. L., & Drechsler, M. (1993). Common issues for parents in a methadone maintenance group. *Journal of Substance Abuse Treatment, 10,* 339-343.
Describes common themes which arose in a group of four to six parents on methadone maintenance. This group used a multimethodological approach with both structural and Bowen family therapy schools. Common themes were child-rearing problems due to: children's reactions to parental drug history; difficulty with their own parents' obstruction of reestablished parental roles; difficulty achieving daily consistency with the children; shortcomings in their own upbringing; difficulty in overcoming guilt of past neglect of their children.

1043. Griesinger, W. S. (1978). Short-term group counseling of parents of handicapped children. *Dissertation Abstracts International, 39*(02), 675A.

1044. Gross, C. B. (1985). Object representation, ego development stage and inpatient group psychotherapy. *Dissertation Abstracts International, 45*(12), 3941. (University Microfilm No. AAC85-02706)

1045. Grossman-Morris, C. F. (1987). Depression in young and old adults: The relative efficacy of cognitive versus behavioral group therapy interventions. *Dissertation Abstracts International, 47*(09), 3367. (University Microfilm No. AAC86-29069)
Compared the effectiveness of cognitive, behavioral, and socialization group therapy with younger (18- to 45-year-olds) and older (60 plus years) groups of depressed psychiatric inpatients. Some differences were found, but results were inconclusive.

1046. Gruen, B. J. (1978). Self-concept changes in women through the self-disclosing process in group counseling. *Dissertation Abstracts International, 38*(12), 7152A.

1047. Grumaer, J., & Duncan, J. A. (1982). Group workers' perceptions of their philosophical and ethical beliefs and actual ethical practices. *Journal for Specialists in Group Work, 7*(4), 231-237.

1048. Grumaer, J., & Scott, L. (1986). Group workers' perceptions of ethical and unethical behavior of group leaders. *Journal for Specialists in Group Work, 11*(3), 139-150.
There were significant differences in how 122 members of the Association for Specialists in Group Work responded to 18 ethical guidelines for group leaders. The differences were associated with variances in age, level of education, and years of experience.

1049. Guerney, B. G., Jr. (1977). *Relationship enhancement*. San Francisco: Jossey-Bass.
Reviews studies (large numbers of subjects, no-treatment controls or own-control, random assignment of subjects to groups) that evaluate the effectiveness of the Relationship Enhancement approach. The studies indicate significant improvement in communication, problem-solving, and relationships.

1050. Guilmette, T. J. (1983). A study of the effects of expectations and expectation changes of cohesion, behavior, and outcome in group counseling. *Dissertation Abstracts International, 43*(12), 4146B.
Neither high- nor low-experienced facilitators' expectations changed significantly during the course of this study of group counseling; members' expectations did increase significantly during the second half of the study. There was no significant relationship between expectations and behavioral involvement. Group cohesion was significantly correlated with members' expectations in only one of the three time periods.

1051. Guinan, J. F., Foulds, M. L., & Wright, J. C. (1973). Do the changes last? A six-month follow-up of a marathon group. *Small Group Behavior, 4*(2), 177-180.

1052. Gunter, N. C., & Bedell, J. R. (1983). The peer-managed small group versus the rehabilitation model of treatment of chronic patients. *Hospital and Community Psychiatry, 34*, 724-728.
Compared chronic patients in a small group program with patients in a rehabilitation therapy program, finding that patients in the small group program spent less time in treatment and had lower recidivism rates.

1053. Guttman, M. J. (1987). Verbal interactions of peer led group counseling. *Canadian Journal of Counseling, 21*, 49-58.
Compared verbal interaction of peer counselors who had received little training with those who had received one year of training. Found no differences between the groups except that subjects in the low training group identified themselves significantly more often with their groups than did subjects in the high training group.

1054. Hagen, R. L. (1974). Group therapy versus bibliotherapy in weight reduction. *Behavior Therapy, 5*(2), 222-234.

1055. Hajek, P., Belcher, M., & Stapleton, J. (1985). Enhancing the impact of groups: An evaluation of two group formats for smokers, *British Journal of Clinical Psychology, 24*, 289-294.
Compared two kinds of group treatment of smokers, therapist oriented (TO) and group oriented (GO); GO groups were significantly more successful than TO groups.

1056. Haley, W. E., Brown, S. L., & Levine, E. G. (1987). Experimental evaluation of the effectiveness of group intervention for dementia caregivers. *Gerontologist, 27*, 376-382.
Assigned dementia patient caregivers either to one of two kinds of support groups, or to a waiting list control group. While caregivers found the support

groups helpful, their depression, life satisfaction, social support or coping levels did not improve.

1057. Hall, Z. M. (1992). Group therapy for women survivors of childhood sexual abuse. *Group Analysis, 25,* 463-474.
Studied group therapy with women survivors of childhood sexual abuse. A female therapist did initial assessment and a male co-therapist was present for treatment, which this study contends is crucial in helping the women work through their feelings towards men. Depression fell during group therapy and ratings remained the same at a six-month follow-up.

1058. Hamblin, D. L., Beutler, L. E., Scogin, F., & Corbishley, A. (1993). Patient responsiveness to therapist values and outcome in group cognitive therapy. *Psychotherapy Research, 3,* 36-46.

1059. Hampson, R. B., & Tavormina, J. B. (1980). Relative effectiveness of behavioral and reflective training with foster mothers. *Journal of Consulting and Clinical Psychology, 48,* 294-295.
Employed foster mothers participated in one of two group parent procedures: behavioral child-rearing skills, or reflective group counseling. Results indicate that both groups improved, but in different areas. The behavioral mothers appropriately applied behavior skills, and the reflective group improved in parental attitude. Fathers reported improved child behavior and family functioning.

1060. Hansen, D. J., St. Lawrence, J. S., & Christoff, K. A. (1985). Effects of interpersonal problem-solving training with chronic aftercare patients on problem-solving component skills and effectiveness of solutions. *Journal of Consulting and Clinical Psychology, 53*(2), 167-174.

1061. Hanson, M., Cancel, J., & Rolon, A. (1994). Reducing AIDS risks among dually disordered adults. *Research on Social Work Practice, 4,* 14-27.
Studied preventive intervention designed to aid dually disordered adults change sexual behaviors that increase risk of HIV infection. Assigned subjects either to the dually disordered day treatment program, which included involvement in the AIDS awareness and prevention group, or to the waiting list. Treatment participants increased their knowledge of condom use and decreased risky sexual behavior.

1062. Hardin, J. M., Jr. (1977). The effect of group counseling on sex role expectancy of unmarried couples. *Dissertation Abstracts International, 37*(09), 4648B.

1063. Hargreaves, W. A., Showstack, J., Flohr, R., Brady, C., & Harris, S. (1974). Treatment acceptance following intake assignment to individual therapy, group therapy, or contact group. *Archives of General Psychiatry, 31,* 343-349.

1064. Harris, J. (1985). Non-professionals as effective helpers for pastoral counselors. *Journal of Pastoral Care, 39,* 165-172.
Compared four types of therapy: private, private plus group, private plus non-professional, private plus group plus non-professional. Results support the

hypothesis that professional pastoral counseling more effectively raises the subject's self-esteem when it is combined with non-professional volunteer help.

1065. Harrison, K. W. (1983). Engaging the male inpatient alcoholic in treatment through the reduction of psychological stress: An application of stress inoculation therapy. *Dissertation Abstracts International, 43*(12), 4147B.

1066. Hart, I. H. (1975). Multidisciplinary group therapy for revolving door patients. *Small Group Behavior, 6,* 204-209.

1067. Hartman, B. G. (1984). Improving interpersonal perceptual accuracy and psychological adjustment through brief perception therapy with a substance abuse population. *Dissertation Abstracts International, 45*(04), 1288. (University Microfilm No. AAC84-14957)
Randomly assigned substance abusers either to a cognitive therapy treatment group, Group Brief Perception Therapy (GBPT) (Bullmer, 1980); or to a comparison group receiving more traditional psychotherapy, Regular Group Therapy (RGT). Post-test comparisons of the two groups' three-week programs indicate that GBPT and RGT may be equally effective in improving psychological adjustment in this population.

1068. Hartman, H., & Gidron, B. (1991). Apples and oranges: The comparability of self-help groups. *Journal of Applied Social Sciences, 15,* 221-243.
Compared two types of self-help groups, immigrant groups and parents of mentally ill groups, using a control group made up of similar nonparticipants. Data, gathered in Israel, show that both groups benefit from empowerment, and that there are crucial group dissimilarities.

1069. Hartman, J. J. (1979). Small group methods of personal change. *Annual Review of Psychology, 30,* 453-476.

1070. Hartnett, R. C. (1979). Six month follow-up study on the effects of group psychotherapy with persons who have been arrested for alcohol related offenses. *Dissertation Abstracts International, 39*(11), 5557B.

1071. Hartson, D. J., & Kunce, J. T. (1973). Videotape replay and recall in group work. *Journal of Counseling Psychology, 20*(5), 437-441.

1072. Harvill, R., West, J. J., Edward, E., & Masson, R. L. (1985). Systematic group leader training: Evaluating the effectiveness of the approach. *Journal for Specialists in Group Work, 10*(1), 2-13.

1073. Hauman, R. T. (1976). The relationship of group counseling models and group facilitator personality profile to group member characteristics. *Dissertation Abstracts International, 36*(09), 5822. (University Microfilm No. AAC76-05444)

1074. Hawhlweg, K., Revenstorf, D., & Schindler, L. (1982). Treatment of marital distress: Comparing formats and modalities. *Advances in Behavior Research and Therapy, 4*(2), 57-74.
Compared behavioral marital therapy (BMT) to communication training (CT), applied in two modalities: conjoint and conjoint group. Results indicated that

both BMT modalities and conjoint CT subjects showed substantial improvement compared to controls, while subjects in conjoint group CT improved on only one of seven comparisons. In the long-term, BMT may be moderately more effective in stabilizing change than CT.

1075. Hawkins, B. L. (1982). The effect of psychological sex role on member goal orientation for small group counseling. *Dissertation Abstracts International, 42*(11), 4724. (University Microfilm No. AAC82-09877)

1076. Hawton, K. (1992). Long-term outcome studies of psychological treatments. In C. Freeman & P. Tyrer (Eds.), *Research methods in psychiatry: A beginner's guide* (2nd ed., pp. 233-246). London: Gaskell.
Reviews reasons for the importance of long-term outcome studies of at least one year following termination of treatment, discusses research designs, and how to avoid problems.

1077. Hayes, F. C. (1983). The effects of the Simontons' method including relaxation and imagery training in alleviating the psychological state of depression characteristic of cancer patients. *Dissertation Abstracts International, 43*(10), 111B.
Eight advanced carcinoma patients received Simonton training with imagery, relaxation and group counseling, while seven patients participated in the no-treatment control group. The hypothesis that treatment patients would have fewer depressive, anxiety, and defensive symptoms than controls was not supported. Discusses the factors underlying the results and the implication that effective medical management of cancer patients requires that physicians address the depression and the disease.

1078. Haynes, S. N., Woodward, S., Moran, R., & Alexander, D. (1974). Relaxation treatment of insomnia. *Behavior Therapy, 5*(4), 555-558.
Fourteen insomniac undergraduates received either relaxation training or placebo therapy. Both groups demonstrated significant improvement in their sleep patterns, but the relaxation group demonstrated significantly greater improvement than the placebo group. While relaxation can be an effective treatment method for insomnia, expectation and demand characteristics are contributing factors.

1079. Hays, D. G. (1989). The relationship of temperament and extroversion-introversion to selected group counseling outcome measures. *Dissertation Abstracts International, 49*(10), 2933A. (University Microfilm No. AAC89-00344)

1080. Hazzard, A., Rogers, J. H., & Angert, L. (1993). Factors affecting group therapy outcome for adult sexual abuse survivors. *International Journal of Group Psychotherapy, 43*, 453-468.

1081. Heather, N., Edwards, S., & Hore, B. D. (1975). Changes in construing and outcome of group therapy for alcoholism. *Journal of Studies on Alcohol, 36*(9), 1238-1253.

1082. Heckel, R. V. (1972). Predicting role flexibility in group therapy by means of a screening scale. *Journal of Clinical Psychology, 28,* 570-573.

1083. Heckel, R. V. (1975). A comparison of process data from family therapy and group therapy. *Journal of Community Psychology, 3,* 254-257.

1084. Heil, R. A., Jr. (1993). A comparative analysis of therapeutic factors in self-help groups. *Dissertation Abstracts International, 53*(08), 4373B.

1085. Heimberg, R. G., Salzman, D. G., Holt, C. S., & Blendell, K. A. (1993a). Cognitive-behavioral group treatment for social phobia: Effectiveness at five-year follow-up. *Cognitive Therapy and Research, 17,* 325-339.
Describes five-year follow-up information from 19 of the 49 subjects treated for social phobia with either cognitive behavioral group treatment (CBGT), or an alternative treatment. The CBGT subjects retained more improvement than the alternative treatment subjects. Follow-up subjects may have represented less serious impairment than the original sampling.

1086. Heimberg, R. G., Salzman, D. G. Holt, C. S., & Blendell, K. A. (1993b). "Cognitive-behavioral group treatment for social phobia: Effectiveness at five-year follow-up": Erratum. *Cognitive Therapy and Research, 17,* 597-598.
Corrected Table One by reversing superscripts e and f; amended Table is included.

1087. Heinrich, R. L., & Schag, C. C. (1985). Stress and activity management: Group treatment for cancer patients and spouses. *Journal of Consulting and Clinical Psychology, 53*(4), 439-446.

1088. Heitler, J. B. (1973). Preparation of lower-class patients for expressive group psychotherapy. *Journal of Consulting and Clinical Psychology, 41,* 251-260.
Lower-class, first-admission, psychiatric inpatients were either prepared for upcoming group therapy with a socialization interview or left naive. Compared to the naive subjects, the prepared subjects showed significant quantitative and qualitative differences in their participation in group therapy.

1089. Hellerstein, D. J., & Meehan, B. (1987). Outpatient group therapy for schizophrenic substance abusers. *American Journal of Psychiatry, 144,* 1337-1339.
Over one year, schizophrenic substance abusers who attended weekly outpatient therapy spent less days hospitalized, even if they dropped out of therapy.

1090. Helmrich, J. A. (1991). Interpersonal verbalizations and growth in group psychotherapy: An empirical study. *Dissertation Abstracts International, 52*(06), 3294B.

1091. Henning, D. D. (1984). A study of the effects of post-wedding counseling with participants of pre-marital counseling groups. *Dissertation Abstracts International, 44*(08), 2416A.
Examined the impact of a six-week post-wedding follow-up program with newly married couples who had participated in a seven-week pre-marital program.

Over six weeks, problem intensity significantly decreased in the treatment group and increased in the control condition.

1092. Henry, C. J. (1981). The effects of group counseling on divorce adjustment. *Dissertation Abstracts International, 42*(04), 1607B.

1093. Henry, M., de Rivera, J. L., Gonzalez-Martin, I. J., & Abreu, J. (1993). Improvement of respiratory function in chronic asthmatic patients with autogenic therapy. *Journal of Psychosomatic Research, 37*(3), 265-270.
      Investigated the role of stress, unpleasant emotions, and autonomic imbalance in the precipitation of asthma attacks in chronic asthma patients. Treated subjects over an eight month period with either autogenic therapy (AT) or supportive group psychotherapy, the control condition. AT subjects obtained relevant clinical improvement in respiratory function, suggesting that autogenic treatment could be an effective adjunctive treatment. The control group's bronchial function did not improve.

1094. Herder, D. D., & Redner, L. (1991). The treatment of childhood sexual trauma in chronically mentally ill adults. *Health and Social Work, 16,* 50-57.
      Used intensive group treatment, co-led by one female and one male therapist, to treat chronically mentally ill women with childhood sexual trauma. Discusses treatment goals and a case study.

1095. Hershberger, B. R. (1989). An assessment of the effectiveness of three treatment programs for battering men. *Dissertation Abstracts International, 49*(09), 4005B.

1096. Herz, M. I., Spitzer, R. L., Gibbon, M., Greenspan, K., & Reibels, S. (1974). Individual versus group aftercare treatment. *American Journal of Psychiatry, 131,* 808-812.

1097. Heuft, G., & Senf, W. (1993). Content analysis of follow-up interviews with inpatient/outpatient group psychotherapy patients. *Psychotherapy and Psychosomatics, 59,* 156-164.
      Treatment at a psychosomatic clinic in Germany consisted of group therapy on an inpatient (three months) and outpatient basis (two years). Follow-up interviews of former patients showed great difference between the start and finish of inpatient treatment. Discusses research value of former patients' evaluation of their therapy.

1098. Hickman, C. M. (1992). Effects of behavioral group leisure counseling programs on leisure independence, depression, and depression-related variables of adult women. *Dissertation Abstracts International, 53*(06), 2814B.
      Fifty-two female subjects participated in an eight week, group counseling workshop, using four leisure counseling treatment approaches: pleasant activities (PA), social skills training (SS), combined pleasant activities and social skills training (PA+SS), and relaxation (R). Found that the PA+SS group had a significantly higher mean than the R group on perceived freedom in leisure. Follow-up *t* tests revealed significant pre- and post-changes for the entire sample in perceived freedom in leisure, depression, and self-esteem.

1099. Hicks, J. S., & Wieder, D. (1973). The effects of inter-generation group counseling on clients and parents in a vocational rehabilitation agency. *Rehabilitation Literature, 34,* 358-363.
Compares two types of group therapy for parents and young adult clients in a vocational rehabilitation program. Fifty clients and 66 parents attended either inter-generational groups or separate group therapy sessions for parents and clients. Parents favored the inter-generational condition, while clients preferred the separate condition. Presents suggestions for short-term programs.

1100. Hidas, G., & Buda, B. (1973). Communication and aggression in psychoanalytic groups: The group process from the standpoint of interpersonal communication theory. *International Journal of Group Psychotherapy, 23,* 148-154.
Examined two types of psychoanalytic groups, hospitalized neurotic patients (HP) and training psychologists and psychiatrists (TP). HP's used symptoms to influence group interaction; TP groups used silence less than HP groups. The group leader's experience and knowledge was important to group control.

1101. Higgitt, A., Golombok, S., Fonagy, P., & Lader, M. (1987). Group treatment of benzodiazephine dependence. *British Journal of Addiction, 82,* 517-532.

1102. Hilkey, J. H. (1976). The effects of videotape pre-training and guided performance on selected process and outcome variables of group counseling. *Dissertation Abstracts International, 36*(07), 4261. (University Microfilm No. AAC75-29861)

1103. Hilkey, J. H., Wilhelm, C. L., & Horne, A. M. (1982). Comparative effectiveness of videotape pretraining versus no pretraining on selected process and outcome variables in group therapy. *Psychological Reports, 50(3, pt 2),* 1151-1159.
Evaluated pretraining effects on group processes by treating inmates with either pretraining plus group therapy or group therapy only. Those in pretraining began group therapy more informed on what to expect, exhibited more desirable behavior at the outset, and made greater gains in reaching individual goals.

1104. Hill, D., Weiss, D. J., Walker, D. L., & Jolley, D. (1988). Long-term evaluation of controlled smoking as a treatment outcome. *British Journal of Addiction, 83,* 203-207.
Studied smokers who, upon completing a group smoking cessation program, had achieved "controlled smoker" status, smoking one to nine cigarettes per day. One-year follow-up results indicated that attaining controlled smoking status is not a worthwhile treatment outcome.

1105. Hisli, N. (1987). Effect of patients' evaluation of group behavior on therapy outcome. Special Issue: Integration of research and practice in the field of group psychotherapy. *International Journal of Group Psychotherapy, 37,* 119-124.
Examined the effect of neurotic inpatients' self-evaluation in group therapy. Results suggest that self-evaluation may have a positive effect, mostly at the symptom level, on the outcome of therapy.

1106. Hoare, P., & Kerley, S. (1992). Helping parents and children with epilepsy cope successfully: The outcome of a group programme for patients. *Journal of Psychosomatic Research, 36,* 759-767.

1107. Hoberman, H. M., Lewinsohn, P. M., & Tilson, M. (1988). Group treatment of depression: Individual predictors of outcome. *Journal of Consulting and Clinical Psychology, 56,* 393-398.

1108. Hodges, K. K., & Brandt, D. A. (1978). Measurement of attribution of causality in counselor behavior. *Journal of Counseling Psychology, 25,* 343-348.

1109. Hoerl, R. T. (1974). Encounter groups: Their effect on rigidity. *Human Relations, 27*(5), 431-438.
      Studied changes in flexibility in 112 encounter group participants, as measured by the Flexibility and Tolerance for Ambiguity scales of the California Personality Inventory. Found significant differences between volunteer and nonvolunteer groups, but not between encounter and nonencounter groups. Concluded that treatment effects depend more upon who attends the group than on what is done.

1110. Hoffman, L. S. (1991). A comparison of consumer acceptability of three marital therapy approaches. *Dissertation Abstracts International, 52*(04), 2299B. (University Microfilm No. AAC91-18017)
      Subjects rated, on the basis of written description, three types of marital therapy for distressed couples: conjoint, group and bibliotherapy. Descriptions gave information in eight areas. Conjoint therapy received greater acceptability and preference than group or bibliotherapy. Discusses factors and reasons for consumer preferences.

1111. Hoffmann, H., Noem, A. A., & Petersen, D. (1976). Treatment effectiveness as judged by successfully and unsuccessfully treated alcoholics. *Drug and Alcohol Dependence, 1*(4), 241-246.
      Successfully and unsuccessfully treated male alcoholics evaluated six treatment methods routinely offered by a state hospital. Measured total judgment frequencies of treatment methods designated most and least helpful. The two subject groups differed significantly in which treatments they judged "least helpful", but were similar in which were "most helpful." This similarity may reflect the positive effects of previous treatment in the unsuccessful group.

1112. Hogan, P. D., & Royce, J. R. (1975-1976). Four-way sessions: The co-therapy of couples in individual and conjoint treatment. *Groups: A Journal of Group Dynamics and Psychotherapy, 7*(1), 1-11.

1113. Hogg, J. A. (1987). Comparison of cognitive and interpersonal process group therapies in the treatment of depression. *Dissertation Abstracts International, 47*(07), 3111B.

1114. Homant, R. J. (1976). Therapy effectiveness in a correctional institution. *Offender Rehabilitation, 1,* 101-113.

Making group therapy available to randomly chosen inmates from a maximum security adult institution increased therapy attendance and positively affected institutional behavior.

1115. Homant, R. J. (1986). Ten years after: A follow-up of therapy effectiveness. *Journal of Offender Counseling, Services, and Rehabilitation, 10,* 51-57.

1116. Hopf, G. I. (1994). Group art therapy with schizophrenics in a drop-in center. *Masters Abstracts International, 32*(03), 1066. (University Microfilm No. AACMM-84645)
Examined the use of open art group therapy with schizophrenics in a drop-in center; stresses the importance of this type of therapy in enhancing communication between therapist and schizophrenics.

1117. Horan, J. J., Baker, S. B., Hoffmann, A. M., & Shute, R. E. (1975). Weight loss through variations in the coverant control paradigm. *Journal of Consulting and Clinical Psychology, 43,* 68-72.

1118. Horan, T. J. (1982). The effect of group counseling on coping with occupational stress by Type A pre- and post-coronary males. *Dissertation Abstracts International, 43*(4), 1089A.
Six men participated in a structured group field study aimed at stress management for individuals with Type A behavior. The group program ran for eight two-hour sessions, with one two-hour session two months later. Individual and group feedback and mutual support were integral aspects of the program. Post-treatment and follow-up results demonstrated a decrease in overall Type A behavior pattern in each subject.   Demonstrated viability of six specific hypotheses.

1119. Hornby, G. (1992). Group parent training using reflective counselling and behavioural training procedures. *British Journal of Mental Subnormality, 38*(2), 79-86.
Evaluates the effectiveness of an eight week parent training program using a pre- and post-test research design with a treatment group and a no treatment control group, with 17 and 13 parents, respectively. The parents in the treatment group improved their knowledge of behavioral principles, but did not perceive any improvement in their children's behavior or change their own attitudes about child rearing.

1120. Hornig-Rohan, M., & Locke, S. E. (1985). *Psychological and behavioral treatments for disorders of the heart and blood vessels: An annotated bibliography.* New York: Institute for the Advancement of Health.
Bibliographic entries for the following are presented: angina pectoris, coronary artery disease, hypertension, ischemic heart disease, mixed cardiovascular disorders, myocardial infarction, and peripheral vascular disorders.

1121. Hsu, P. (1993). The improvement of the marital problems of patients suffering from depression through group counseling. *Dissertation Abstracts International, 53*(09), 3147A.
Examined the effectiveness of group therapy as an adjustment to pharmacologic therapy in treating depression and maintaining therapeutic outcomes. Forty

subjects received either combined psychopharmacologic therapy or standard pharmacologic therapy. Determined the subjects' levels of depression with the Zung Self-reported Depression Scale and determined marital adjustability with the Marital Adaptation Scale. Found that both groups improved in depression level and marital adaptation, but combined therapy was more efficacious. Makes recommendations.

1122. Huhn, R. P., Zimpfer, D. G., Waltman, D. E., & Williamson, S. (1985). A survey of programs of professional preparation for group counseling. *Journal for Specialists in Group Work, 10*(3), 124-133.
Presents survey data from 76 college and university programs for group work. Discusses program characteristics, areas of training, teaching methods, commonly used textbooks, methods of trainee assessment and program outcomes.

1123. Hulse, D. (1982). The effects of cognitive-behavioral pretraining on attraction to feedback and attraction to the group. *Dissertation Abstracts International, 42*(08), 3440A. (University Microfilm No. AAC82-00879)

1124. Hurlbert, D. F. (1993). A comparative study using orgasm consistency training in the treatment of women reporting hypoactive sexual desire. *Journal of Sex and Marital Therapy, 19,* 41-55.
Treated women reporting hypoactive sexual desire either with group intervention and orgasm consistency training (GI+OCT), or group intervention only (GI). After treatment, subjects in both groups reported sexual improvement, but at follow-up women in the GI+OCT group reported: greater sexual arousal and assertiveness (three months); and greater sexual satisfaction (six months).

1125. Hurlbert, D. F., White, L. C., Powell, R. D., & Apt, C. (1993). Orgasm consistency training in the treatment of women reporting hypoactive sexual desire: An outcome comparison of women-only groups and couples-only groups. *Journal of Behavior Therapy and Experimental Psychiatry, 24*(1) 3-13.
Evaluated and compared the effectiveness and maintenance of two group interventions using orgasm consistency training. Assigned 57 women to either a women-only group, a couples-only group, or the wait-list control group. Assessments were made on six variables, pre- and post-treatment, and at a six-month follow-up. Found treatment generally effective, but favored the couples-only group for its consistent pattern of change on all measures.

1126. Hurley, J. R. (1986). Leaders' behavior and group members' interpersonal gains. *Group, 10*(3), 161-176.

1127. Hurley, J. R., & Brooks, L. J. (1987). Group climate's principal dimension: Affiliation. *International Journal of Group Psychotherapy, 37*(3), 441-448.

1128. Hurley, J. R., & Rosenthal, M. (1978). Interpersonal rating shifts during and after AGPA's Institute groups. *International Journal of Group Psychotherapy, 28*(1), 115-121.

1129. Huston, K. (1986). A critical assessment of the efficacy of women's groups. Special Issue: Gender issues in psychotherapy. *Psychotherapy, 23,* 283-290.

1130. Hynes, K., & Wervin, J. (1977). Group psychotherapy for Spanish-speaking women. *Psychiatric Annals, 7,* 52-63.
Spanish-speaking women living in English-speaking communities participated in group therapy conducted in Spanish; in English and yoga classes; and in social activities. Most subjects overextended themselves because of concern for their children, suffered from somatic disorders citing stress as the cause, and reported feeling isolated; the group discussed child-care and came to a cooperative babysitting arrangement

1131. Ibrahim, M. A. (1974). Management after myocardial infarction: A controlled trial of the effect of group psychotherapy. *International Journal of Psychiatry in Medicine, 5*(3), 253-268.

1132. Illovsky, M. E. (1986). The therapeutic effects of two life-skill components in the treatment of psychiatric patients. *Dissertation Abstracts International, 47*(04), 1725B. (University Microfilm No. AAC86-13494)
Psychiatric inpatients participated either in life skills group training in communications and vocational skills, or in the Veterans Administration psychiatric hospital's current training, which acted as a control. The life skills participants scored higher than the control subjects; both reached the same improvement levels in psychopathology.

1133. Ingle, G. B. (1977). Attitudinal positions of clients in group psychotherapy: A function of interpersonal similarity and message type. *Dissertation Abstracts International, 37*(11), 7318. (University Microfilm No. AAC77-11245)

1134. Intagliata, J. C. (1978). Increasing the interpersonal problem-solving skills of an alcoholic population. *Journal of Consulting and Clinical Psychology, 46*(3), 489-498.

1135. Ireland, R., Paone, G., Mellstrom M., & Schornagel, T. (1976). A behaviorally oriented therapy group to facilitate inpatient hospital adjustment. *Newsletter for Research in Mental Health and Behavioral Sciences, 18,* 33-36.
Male patients, whose transfer from a locked to an open ward was a possibility, participated either in weekly meetings plus operant conditioning (OC) or in a control group of weekly meetings only. Results in the OC group were in the desired direction; three in the OC group transferred out of the locked ward, versus none in the control group.

1136. Isbell, S. E., Thorne, A., Lawler, M. H. (1992). An exploratory study of videotapes of long-term group psychotherapy of outpatients with major and chronic mental illness. *Group, 16,* 101-111.

1137. Isohanni, M., & Nieminen, P. (1992). Participation in group psychotherapy in a therapeutic community for acute patients. *Acta Psychiatrica Scandinavica, 86,* 495-501.

1138. Issacharoff, A., & Hunt, W. (1977). Observations on group process in a leaderless group of professional therapists. *Group, 1*(3), 162-171.

1139. Jacobs, M., Gatz, M., & Trick, O. L. (1974). Structured versus unstructured feedback in the training of patients to be more effective participants in group psychotherapy. *Small Group Behavior, 5,* 365-373.
Examined structured and nonstructured feedback to determine whether structured feedback helped psychiatric inpatients participate more effectively in group therapy. Found no significant differences.

1140. Jacobs, M. K., Trick, O. L., & Withersty, D. (1976). Pretraining psychiatric inpatients for participation in group psychotherapy. *Psychotherapy: Theory, Research and Practice, 13,* 361-167.
Gave newly admitted psychiatric inpatients, before therapy, specific instructions on what was desirable verbal behavior in therapy groups. The inpatients did not apply the information.

1141. Jacobson, L. (1985). Development of and in the group: An object relations perspective. *Dissertation Abstracts International, 46*(05), 1689B. (University Microfilm No. AAC85-15635)

1142. Jalowsky, H. S. (1975). The effects of group counseling membership on mildly retarded adults. *Dissertation Abstracts International, 36*(06), 3333. (University Microfilm No. AAC75-28487)

1143. Janesh, R. J. (1982). A replication study of the effects of objective evidence of expertness, nonverbal behavior and subject sex on client-perceived expertness. *Dissertation Abstracts International, 43*(03), 872B. (University Microfilm No. AAC82-19279)
Examined the effects of two types of therapist training evidence, objective (certificates, licenses) and behavioral (show of knowledge and confidence), on a client's perception of therapist-expertness. Males and females watched one of four fictional videotaped therapy sessions, with varied training evidence. Results showed no gender differences and supported the importance of objective and nonverbal behaviors in enhancing the perception of therapist-expertness.

1144. Jarrett, R. B. (1984). Mechanisms of change in cognitive-behavioral therapy in relation to depressives' dysfunctional thoughts. *Dissertation Abstracts International, 45*(01), 353B. (University Microfilm No. AAC84-08996)

1145. Jasper, F. J. (1987). Patient perception of group psychotherapy in a day hospital setting. *Dissertation Abstracts International, 47*(09), 3958B. (University Microfilm No. AAC87-01248)
Subject-participants in group therapy periodically reported their perceptions of their group and completed three Scales for progress assessment. The subjects' perceptions of the group, which were positive, stayed the same. Assessment scores indicated that subjects were moving in a therapeutic direction.

1146. Jasper, S. F. (1974). The design, implementation and evaluation of a group counseling model. *Dissertation Abstracts International, 35*(06), 3425. (University Microfilm No. AAC74-26826)

1147. Jaureguy, B. M., & Evans, R. L. (1983). Short-term group counseling of visually impaired people by telephone. *Journal of Visual Impairment and Blindness, 77,* 150-152.
Examined telephone group counseling for the visually impaired, who were divided into a counseling and a control group. After treatment scores showed significant differences between the counseling and the control groups on social involvement, but not on depression or agitation.

1148. Jeffery, R. W., & Gerber, W. M. (1982). Group and correspondence treatments for weight reduction used in the multiple risk factor intervention trial. *Behavior Therapy, 13*(1), 24-30.

1149. Jeffrey, D. B., & Christensen, E. R. (1975). Behavior therapy versus "will power" in the management of obesity. *Journal of Psychology, 90*(2), 303-311.

1150. Jensen, J. L. (1982). The relationship of leadership technique and anxiety level in group therapy with chronic schizophrenics. *Psychotherapy: Theory, Research and Practice, 19,* 237-248.
Measured anxiety of chronic schizophrenics who participated in group therapy that was either directive and structured or nondirective and nonstructured. Found no difference in anxiety between the two groups.

1151. Jensen, J. L., & McGrew, W. L. (1974). Leadership techniques in group therapy with chronic schizophrenic patients. *Nursing Research, 23,* 416-420.
Measured anxiety of two groups of male, and two groups of female schizophrenics who participated in group therapy that was either structured with directive leadership, or unstructured with nondirective leadership. Subjects in the structured group experienced more anxiety and arousal than those in the unstructured group; males had higher anxiety scores than females.

1152. Jeske, J. O. (1973). Identification and therapeutic effectiveness in group therapy. *Journal of Counseling Psychology, 20,* 528-530.
Studied whether identification with group members is related to progress in group therapy. Those who showed improvement in therapy had a significantly higher incidence of identification, and there was a positive correlation between frequency of identification and change.

1153. Jeziorski, J. C. (1994). A comparison of selection of curative factors in group therapy by borderline personality disorder and non-borderline personality disorder inpatients. *Dissertation Abstracts International, 55*(01), 47A. (University Microfilm No. AAC94-16833)
Compared borderline personality disordered (BPD) and non-BPD inpatients' determinations of which factors were helpful in their group therapy experience, finding no significant differences in the factors chosen. BPD and non-BPD subjects used group therapy in a similar way. Addresses how the groups rated their treatment and the relationship between the ratings and factors identified as helpful.

1154. Johnson, C. L. (1989). Group counseling with blind people: A critical review of the literature. *Journal of Visual Impairment and Blindness, 83,* 202-207.

Critically reviews 35 years of research on group counseling with visually impaired clients. Presents conceptual and methodological suggestions for future research.

1155. Johnson, M. (1976). An approach to feminist therapy. *Psychotherapy: Theory, Research and Practice, 13,* 72-76.

Compared feminist group therapy (FGT), consisting of female clients led by female therapists, with individual therapy of female clients by male therapists (IT). Both groups had similar problems, degrees of pretherapy distress, and degrees of post-therapy improvement, but the subjects in FGT averaged 4 months in therapy versus 10 months for those in IT. The women in FGT describe therapeutic factors that were helpful to them.

1156. Johnson, N., Russo, C., & Bundrick, C. M. (1982). Rational behavior training and changes in self-actualization. *Journal for Specialists in Group Work, 7,* 187-193.

Randomly assigned supervisors to a rational behavioral training group (RBT), which stressed use of cognitive factors in dealing with emotions, or to a control group. RBT participants became significantly more self-actualized.

1157. Johnson, T. J. (1983). Preparation of patients for short-term group psychotherapy. *Dissertation Abstracts International, 44*(01), 311B. (University Microfilm No. AAC83-09590)

Compared two groups prepared for short-term group psychotherapy to a non-prepared control group. Preparation consisted of either a role-induction film or an individual role-induction interview. Found no differences between prepared and non-prepared subjects in attendance and drop out. Prepared subjects demonstrated more favorable results in motivation, working alliance, and prognosis rating, and those prepared individually reported greater willingness to begin therapy than those prepared with a film.

1158. Jones, A. (1992). Community self-help groups for women with bulimic and compulsive eating problems. *British Review of Bulimia and Anorexia Nervosa, 6,* 63-71.

Women with compulsive eating problems (CEP) and bulimics (BU) participated in self-help group therapy, with CEP groups showing greater improvement than BU groups. Time spent in group was related to outcome. The most common reason given for leaving a group was intra-group problems; more BU women left than CEP's.

1159. Jones, B. C. (1978). The effects of a marathon experience upon on-going group psychotherapy. *Dissertation Abstracts International, 38*(08), 3887. (University Microfilm No. AAC77-32251)

1160. Jones, E. J., & McColl, M. A. (1991). Development and evaluation of an interactional life skills group for offenders. *Occupational Therapy Journal of Research, 11*(2), 80-92.

Compared two programs for adult male offenders: an interaction life skills (ILS) program, and a traditional inpatient group therapy (TT), with 12 subjects in each group. Performance was based on five outcomes. Results indicate that the ILS group took on significantly more roles than the TT group, and that the ILS subjects valued their roles more and felt more excited about participating.

1161. Jones, E. N. (1993). A performance-anxiety reduction model for group leadership training in the use of three specific group leadership techniques. *Dissertation Abstracts International, 53*(12), 4211A. (University Microfilm No. AAC93-01453)

1162. Jones, K. H. (1990). A comparison of structured role coping group interventions with and without spouse support for married, working mothers. *Dissertation Abstracts, International, 51*(02), 416A.
Assigned women who worked full-time, had a spouse employed full-time, and had at least one child under the age of 12 either to a wait-list control group or to one of two types of small counseling groups which met for four weeks for two and a half hour sessions. Counseling groups followed a highly structured manual of topics and exercises, and allowed much group discussion. The structured counseling group *with* husband participation was significantly more effective than the control group on stress, depression, role satisfaction, role effectiveness, coping skills, and equity, while the structured counseling group *without* husband participation did significantly better than the control group in improving coping skills. Discusses additional results and recommendations.

1163. Jones, M. J. (1984). The perceptions of Jungian analysts on the individuation process in group psychotherapy: A descriptive case study. *Dissertation Abstracts International, 45*(02), 672B. (University Microfilm No. AAC84-11811)

1164. Jordan, C. S., Davis, M., Kahn, P., & Sinnott, R. H. (1980). Eidetic imagery group methods of assertion training. *Journal of Mental Imagery, 4,* 41-48.

1165. Joughlin, N., Tata, P., Collins, M., & Hooper. (1991). In-patient withdrawal from long-term benzodiazepine use. *British Journal of Addiction, 86,* 449-455.

1166. Justice, B., & Justice, R. (1978). Evaluating outcome of group therapy for abusing parents. *Corrective and Social Psychiatry and Journal of Behavior Technology, Methods and Therapy, 24*(1), 45-49.

1167. Kahan, J., Kemp, B., Staples, F. R., & Brummel-Smith, K. (1985). Decreasing the burden in families caring for a relative with a dementing illness: A controlled study. *Journal of the American Geriatric Society, 33*(10), 664-670.
Examined a group support program specifically designed for relatives of patients with dementing illnesses. Twenty-two subjects participated in an eight session program using educational/support activities and a cognitive-behavioral approach, while 18 control subjects received no treatment. Treatment subjects showed significantly greater improvement on knowledge of dementia than controls, showed a reduction in depression levels, and showed a significant decrease in total family burden, while control subjects showed a significant increase.

1168. Kahl, R. D. (1978). The effects of awareness of the importance of confidentiality and lack of privileged communication statutes for group psychotherapy. *Dissertation Abstracts International, 39*(06), 2989. (University Microfilm No. AAC78-24524)

1169. Kahn, E. M., Sturke, I. T., & Schaeffer, J. (1992). Inpatient group processes parallel unit dynamics. *International Journal of Group Psychotherapy, 42,* 407-418.

1170. Kahn, E. M., Webster, P.B., & Storck, M. J. (1986). Curative factors in two types of inpatient psychotherapy groups. *International Journal of Group Psychotherapy, 36,* 579-585.

1171. Kammeier, M. L., Lucero, R. J., & Anderson, D. J. (1973). Events of crucial importance during alcoholism treatment, as reported by patients: A preliminary study. *Quarterly Journal of Studies on Alcohol, 34(4-A),* 1172-1179.

1172. Kanas, N., & Barr, M. A. (1982). Outpatient alcoholics view group therapy. *Group, 6*(1), 17-20.

1173. Kanas, N., Barr, M. A., & Dossick, S. (1985). The homogenous schizophrenic inpatient group: An evaluation using the Hill Interaction Matrix. *Small Group Behavior, 16,* 397-409.

1174. Kanas, N., DiLella, V. J., & Jones, J. (1984). Process and content in an outpatient schizophrenic group. *Group, 8,* 13-20.
        Studied the process and content of an outpatient schizophrenic group. Group discussion centered on giving advice, expressing emotion, and topics relating to interpersonal matters and reality testing.

1175. Kandel, A., Langrod, J., & Ruiz, P. (1981). Changes in future time perception of day hospital psychiatric patients in response to small group treatment approaches. *Journal of Clinical Psychology, 37,* 769-775.
        Subjects participated either in day hospital treatment plus small group treatment (DH+SG) or in day hospital treatment (DH) only. Those in the DH+SG condition showed significant improvement on Future Events and Importance, but not on Quality of Affect, Directionality, or Time Extension.

1176. Kang, S., Kleinman, P. H., Woody, G. E., & Millman, R. B. (1991). Outcomes for cocaine abusers after once-a-week psychosocial therapy. *American Journal of Psychiatry, 148,* 630-635.
        Compares 122 outpatient cocaine abusers assigned to one of three types of once-weekly therapy: psychotherapy, family therapy, or group therapy. As a whole, the subjects showed significant improvement, but this was restricted to the 23 subjects who abstained from cocaine at follow-up. There was a relationship between abstinence and absence of problems related to addiction, but no relationship between improvement and number of treatment sessions.

1177. Kaplan, H. S. (1974). Group treatment of premature ejaculation. *Archives of Sexual Behavior, 3,* 443-452.

1178. Kaplan, N. L. (1985). An investigation of the value of providing assertive social skills training to chronic pain patients. *Dissertation Abstracts International, 46*(01), 304B.

1179. Karterud, S. W. (1992). Group dreams revisited. *Group Analysis, 25,* 207-222. Examined group dreams (GDs) in an outpatient group whose members had met for four years and reported 102 dreams, 48% of which were GDs. As the group matured, the percentage of GDs rose. Examples of information reported are: One-fourth of the total dreams reported were manifest group dreams (MGDs); in 88% of the MGDs, the therapist was the dominant figure; four of the group's 26 members reported 92% of the MGDs.

1180. Kaseman, B. M. (1976). An experimental use of structured techniques in group psychotherapy. *Journal of Group Psychotherapy, Psychodrama & Sociometry, 29,* 33-39.

1181. Katz, S. E., & O'Connor, D. (1982). Conjoint cotherapist group sexual therapy. *Journal of Psychiatric Treatment and Evaluation, 4,* 173-176.

1182. Kearney, M. S. (1984). A comparative study of multiple family group therapy and individual conjoint family therapy within an outpatient community chemical dependency treatment program. *Dissertation Abstracts International, 45*(12), 3945. (University Microfilm No. AAC85-03409)
Individual, couple, and family pre- and post-treatment test results reflected no significant differences between multiple family group therapy and individual conjoint family therapy in treatment of chemical dependency.

1183. Kellerman, H., & Plutchik, R. (1978). Personality patterns of drug addicts in a therapy group: A similarity structure analysis. *Group, 2,* 14-21.
Therapists rated seven institutionalized female drug addicts, and the drug addicts rated one another, using the authors' Emotions Profile Index (EPI), a personality categorization system. Therapists' ranking reliability of overall relative maladjustment ranged from -.82 to +.98. Discusses which groups of addicts may be most accessible to treatment.

1184. Kellerman, P. F. (1987). Psychodrama participants' perception of therapeutic factors. *Small Group Behavior, 18,* 408-419.
Compared psychodrama participants' perception of which therapeutic factors were most helpful with perceptions of control group subjects, never in therapy. All subjects completed a questionnaire, founded on six categories. The psychodrama participants perceived the categories of emotional abreaction and cognitive insight as most helpful and the control group chose nonspecific healing aids.

1185. Kelly, J. A., Laughlin, C., Claiborne, M., & Patterson, J. (1979). A group procedure for teaching job interviewing skills to formerly hospitalized psychiatric patients. *Behavior Therapy, 10,* 299-310.

1186. Kelly, J. A., Murphy, D. A., Bahr, G. R., & Kalichman, S. C. (1993). Outcomes of cognitive-behavioral and support group brief therapies for depressed, HIV-infected persons. *American Journal of Psychiatry, 150*(11), 1679-1686.

1187. Kelly, M. D. (1982). The effects of pretraining on perceived attraction to group counseling. *Dissertation Abstracts International, 42*(07), 3016A. (University Microfilm No. AAC81-28020)
Examined pretraining effects on perceived attraction to group counseling using three conditions: videotaped pretraining, a control condition consisting of a presentation on the history of groups, and a second control condition of no pretraining. All subjects watched a videotape of a fictional group session and completed a questionnaire about their attraction to the group. Results showed no significant differences among the groups.

1188. Kelly, W. J. (1977). The effects of facilitative communication training and group counseling on the self-concepts of young adults. *Dissertation Abstracts International, 38*(03), 1407B.

1189. Kemp, C. G. (1970). *Foundations of group counseling.* New York: McGraw-Hill.
Provides a review of research methods and considerations and suggestions for needed research for the group counseling practitioner.

1190. Kessler, S. (1974). Treatment of overweight. *Journal of Counseling Psychology, 21,* 395-398.
Participants, motivated to form a weight reduction group, were divided randomly into one of three groups: treatment with group therapy and learning theory application; treatment with group therapy, learning theory application, plus mutual help principles; or, a control group. There was a significant difference in weight loss between the treatment and control groups, but not between the treatment groups.

1191. Kessler, S. (1978). Building skills in divorce adjustment groups. *Journal of Divorce, 2*(2), 209-216.
Compared the utility of three treatment modalities for divorce adjustment groups: structured, unstructured, and control. Criterion measures were pre-selected subscales of the Tennessee Self-Concept Scale (TSCS), the Self-Description Inventory (SDI), and the Kessler Self-Report Questionnaire (KSRC). Mean scores on the TSCS and the SFI were significantly higher for the structured group than for the unstructured and control groups. The KSRC revealed no significant differences except for the level of satisfaction with the group. Findings suggest that skill-building exercises might add an important therapeutic dimension for those adjusting to divorce.

1192. Kettlewell, P. W., Mizes, J. S., & Wasylyshyn, N. A. (1992). A cognitive behavioral group treatment of bulimia. *Behavior Therapy, 23,* 657-670.
Women with bulimia nervosa received cognitive behavioral group treatment in three groups, with varying baselines. Daily self-report bingeing and purging measures showed significant reductions.

1193. Kielhofner, G., & Brinson, M. (1989). Development and evaluation of an aftercare program for young chronic psychiatrically disabled adults. *Occupational Therapy in Mental Health, 9,* 1-25.
Chose chronic, psychiatrically disabled young adults, who were terminating inpatient hospital care, to participate in an aftercare program providing small-group sessions with structured activities and goals. There were no significant differences between the treatment and control groups, but it appeared that the program positively affected day to day life and recidivism.

1194. Kilmann, P. R. (1974). Anxiety reactions to marathon group therapy. *Journal of Clinical Psychology, 30*(3), 267-268.
Investigated the effect of marathon group therapy on state and trait anxiety. Nine university students responded to anxiety measures immediately before and after participation in a ten-hour marathon group. Results supported the hypothesis that anxiety state would decline from pre- to post-therapy while anxiety trait would remain stable; results also supported the prediction that participation in the marathon therapy would evoke heightened anxiety feelings.

1195. Kilmann, P. R. (1974). Locus of control and preference for type of group counseling. *Journal of Clinical Psychology, 30*(2), 226-227.
Subjects responded to Rotter's Internal-External Control Scale and indicated their preference for controlled versus shared leadership counseling groups. Results did not support the hypothesis that externals would prefer controlled leadership and internals, shared leadership: Externals preferred shared leadership, while internals showed no significant difference in preference.

1196. Kilmann, P. R. (1974). Marathon group therapy with female narcotic addicts. *Psychotherapy: Theory, Research and Practice, 11,* 339-342.
Assigned 84 female narcotic addicts to structured marathon therapy, unstructured marathon therapy or to the no-treatment control group. There was evidence of overall therapeutic change. The therapy groups had higher self-control and achievement scores than the control group, but there were no differences between the therapy groups.

1197. Kinder, B. N., & Kilmann, P. R. (1976). The impact of differential shifts in leader structure on the outcome of internal and external group participants. *Journal of Clinical Psychology, 32*(4), 857-863.

1198. Kindness, K., & Newton, A. (1984). Patients and social skills groups: Is social skills training enough? *Behavioral Psychotherapy, 12*(3), 212-222.

1199. Kivlighan, D. M., & Goldfine, D. C. (1991). Endorsement of therapeutic factors as a function of stage of group development and participant interpersonal attitudes. *Journal of Counseling Psychology, 38*(2), 150-158.

1200. Kivlighan, D. M., & Quigley, S. T. (1991). Dimensions used by experienced and novice group therapists to conceptualize group processes. *Journal of Counseling Psychology, 38*(4), 415-423.

1201. Kivlighan, D. M., McGovern, T. V., & Corazzini, J. G. (1984). Effects on content and timing of structuring interventions on group therapy process and outcome. *Journal of Counseling Psychology, 31*(3), 363-370.

1202. Kivlighan, D. M., Mullison, D. D., Flohr, D. G., & Proudman, S. (1992). The interpersonal structure of "good" versus "bad" group counseling sessions: A multiple-case study. *Psychotherapy, 29,* 500-508.

1203. Klein, R. H., & Carrol, R. A. (1986). Patient characteristics and attendance patterns in outpatient group psychotherapy. *International Journal of Group Psychotherapy, 36,* 115-132.
Describes patient characteristics of 719 outpatients referred for group therapy. Typically, patients were moderately to seriously disturbed, and comprised of single White working/middle class women, college students, unemployed and uneducated minority group persons. Forty-one percent never began treatment, drop-outs terminated early on, and over half of those treated were seen twelve times or less.

1204. Kleinman, P. H., Woody, G. E., Todd, T. C., & Millman, R. B. (1990). Crack and cocaine abusers in outpatient psychotherapy. *National Institute on Drug Abuse Research Monograph Series, Research Mono 140,* 24-35.

1205. Klerman, G. L., Dimascio, A., Weissman, M., Prusoff, B., & Paykel, E. (1974). Treatment of depression by drugs and psychotherapy. *American Journal of Psychiatry, 131,* 186-191.

1206. Kline, K. H. (1975). Teaching of problem-solving skills and internal locus-of-control as factors in the effectiveness of group counseling. *Dissertation Abstracts International, 36*(02), 912B.

1207. Kline, W. H. (1987). Selected predictors of outcome in the group treatment of obesity. *Dissertation Abstracts International, 47*(09), 3961B. (University Microfilm No. AAC86-29826)

1208. Kneebone, I. I., & Martin, P. R. (1992). Partner involvement in the treatment of chronic headaches. *Behaviour Change, 9*(4), 201-215.
Studied whether involving the partners of headache sufferers in a group cognitive-behavioral stress-coping intervention for chronic headaches would enhance treatment outcome. Compared partner participation treatment (PPT) to a standard treatment condition without partner participation (noPPT), and a no-treatment control condition (noT). The noPPT was effective compared to the noT; there was less evidence that PPT was effective. Addresses the possibility that partner involvement affects headache sufferers' motivation and personal responsibility for change, thereby decreasing treatment effectiveness.

1209. Koch, H. C. (1983). Changes in personal construing in three psychotherapy groups and a control group. *British Journal of Medical Psychology, 56,* 245-254.

1210. Koch, J. E. (1989). Inpatients' perceptions of therapeutic factors in group psychotherapy. *Dissertation Abstracts International, 50*(06), 2627B. (University Microfilm No. AAC89-17002)

Men and women inpatients treated with group therapy in a short-term psychiatric unit completed questionnaires and interviews to identify inpatient perceptions of therapeutic factors in group therapy. Results consistently revealed a General Therapeutic Factor and not distinct factors, contrary to reports maintaining that distinct therapeutic factors function in group therapy.

1211. Koran, L. M., & Costell, R. M. (1973). Early termination from group psychotherapy. *International Journal of Group Psychotherapy, 23,* 346-359.
Examined 11 outpatient psychotherapy groups to identify factors related to dropping out of group therapy. Participants who did not complete questionnaires that explore feelings, personality, and potential group behavior were likely to drop out. Other studies have identified factors related to drop-out, but in the present study, these were not indicative of drop-out.

1212. Kornblith, S. J., Rehm, L. P., O'Hara, M. W., & Lamparski, D. M. (1983). The contribution of self-reinforcement training and behavioral assignments to the efficacy of self-control therapy for depression. *Cognitive Therapy and Research, 7,* 499-528.

1213. Kottgen, C., Sonnichsen, I., Mollenhauer, K., & Jurth, R. (1984). Group therapy with the families of schizophrenic patients: Results of the Hamburg Camberwell-Family-Interview study: III. *International Journal of Family Psychiatry, 5,* 83-94.
Studied effects of group therapy for schizophrenic patients from high expressed emotion families, and their families. Family therapy groups were separate from patient groups and the controls received standard treatment. The therapy groups showed indications of fewer relapses than the control group, and reduced expressed emotion reactions.

1214. Kottler, J. A., & Brown, R. W. (1992). *Introduction to therapeutic counseling* (2nd ed.). Pacific Grove, CA: Brooks/Cole.
By way of surveying the relationship between research and practice in therapeutic counseling the authors, on pages 290 through 306 of Chapter 14, present a sampling of published research and basic considerations (reliability, validity, outcome effects, etc.).

1215. Krausova, L., & Hemsley, D. R. (1976). Discharge from a therapeutic community. *British Journal of Medical Psychology, 49,* 199-204.
Studied factors relating to psychiatric patients' discharge from therapeutic community type treatment. "Doctor's discharge" and "agreement between the doctor and patient" were the most important discharge determinants; subjects assessed doctors as significantly more therapeutic than group therapy, the primary treatment used, or occupational therapy. There was a significant level of agreement among staff and subjects on the subjects' condition at discharge; 78.9% of the subjects seemed improved.

1216. Kretsch, R., Goren, Y., & Wasserman, A. (1987). Change patterns of borderline patients in individual and group therapy. Special Issue: Integration of research and practice in the field of group psychotherapy. *International Journal of Group Psychotherapy, 37,* 95-112.

1217. Kriss, R. T., & Kraemer, H. C. (1986). Efficacy of group therapy for problems with post-mastectomy self-perception, body image, and sexuality. *Journal of Sex Research, 22*(4), 438-451.
Compared self-image and sexuality, positive affect, autonomy, self-sacrifice, and body touching in 62 post-mastectomy patients who received group therapy versus 51 non-mastectomy control patients. Before therapy, the post-mastectomy subjects' body image was significantly different from the control subjects', and they were lower in sexual adjustment. Results indicated that the therapy significantly improved positive affect and sexual adjustment but did not improve attitude toward the amputated breast region or increase the range of sexual activity or receptivity.

1218. Kron, L. (1984). Effects of group psychotherapy on ileitis and colitis patients and their spouses. *Dissertation Abstracts International, 44*(10), 3200B.

1219. Krone, K. P., Himle, J. A., & Nesse, R. M. (1991). A standardized behavioral group treatment program for obsessive-compulsive disorder: Preliminary outcomes. *Behavior Research and Therapy, 29,* 627-631.
Obsessive-compulsive subjects participated in an outpatient group treatment program that used a cognitive and behavioral approach. At the end of treatment, the subjects' obsession, depression and compulsion scores had significantly improved, sustained at three month follow-up. Obsession and compulsion score improvement was independent of whether the subject took antiobsessional medication.

1220. Kuhns, M. L. (1993). A comparative study between dynamic group psychotherapy and self-help support group treatment among adult children of alcoholics. *Dissertation Abstracts International, 54*(11), 5604B.

1221. Kuriansky, J. B., Sharpe, L., & O'Connor, D. (1982). The treatment of anorgasmia: Long-term effectiveness of a short-term behavioral group therapy. *Journal of Sex and Marital Therapy, 8,* 29-43.
Studied the long-term effectiveness of short-term behavioral group therapy on anorgasmia. Follow-up results of women who had been treated were mixed: Most had maintained therapeutic gains and even progressed, several had regressed, and four drop-outs reported dramatic improvements.

1222. Lack, E. R. (1986). Group psychotherapy and the cardiac rehabilitation process: A study in improving patient compliance. *Dissertation Abstracts International, 47*(05), 2170B.
Examined the impact of a short-term group psychotherapy intervention, lasting 12 weeks, on patient compliance. Data analyses of physiological and self-report measures indicate that neither psychological factors nor the presence or absence of psychological intervention significantly influenced patient compliance. Patients receiving psychological treatment attended a significantly greater percentage of the prescribed exercise sessions, and reported feeling emotionally and physically better more often than subjects receiving no psychological treatment.

1223. Lahti, S. L. (1993). An ethnographic study of the filial therapy process. *Dissertation Abstracts International, 53*(08), 2691. (University Microfilm No. AAC93-00624)

1224. Lakin, M. (1985). *The helping group: Therapeutic principles and issues.* Reading, MA: Addison-Wesley.
The author's long-standing interest in ethical issues in group treatment leads to a discussion of needed research, including: contraindications for participation in groups of various kinds, group research more relevant to clinicians' and participants' needs, investigating the relationships between specific factors in groups (group composition, leadership behavior, participant behavior), and comparisons of peer (self-help groups) with professional (treatment groups) leadership.

1225. Landau, J. M. (1993). Patient perceptions of therapeutic factors in outpatient psychotherapy groups. *Dissertation Abstracts International, 53*(08), 2692. (University Microfilm No. AACNN-69375)

1226. Lane, J. R. (1981). Group counseling effectiveness with persons arrested for driving while intoxicated. *Dissertation Abstracts International, 42*(02), 614A.

1227. LaRocca, J. M., Biersner, R. J., & Ryman, D. H. (1975). Mood effects of large group counseling among Navy recruits. *Journal of Counseling Psychology, 22,* 127-131.
Examines the utility of a group counseling program used during Navy basic training. Identified five stable mood factors in the treatment and control groups: anger, activity, depression, fatigue, and pleasure. Relative to the control group, the treatment group reported significantly less anger and more pleasure.

1228. Leak, G. K. (1980). Effects of highly structured versus nondirective group counseling approaches on personality and behavioral measures of adjustment in incarcerated felons. *Journal of Counseling Psychology, 27,* 450-523.
Compared highly structured (HS) versus traditional, nondirective group counseling with incarcerated felons. HS group counseling resulted in significantly greater empathy, in enhanced interpersonal functioning and in decreased serious infraction of rules.

1229. Lee, F. T. (1976). The effects of sex, risk-taking, and structure on prescribed group behavior, cohesion, and evaluative attitudes in a simulated early training phase of group psychotherapy. *Dissertation Abstracts International, 36*(09), 4695. (University Microfilm No. AAC76-06137)

1230. Leiblum, S. R., & Ersner-Hershfield, R. (1977). Sexual enhancement groups for dysfunctional women: An evaluation. *Journal of Sex and Marital Therapy, 3,* 139-152.

1231. Leon, M. S. (1989). Attitudes of the physically disabled towards physically disabled counselors. *Dissertation Abstracts International, 49*(07), 2862. (University Microfilm No. AAC88-12511)

1232. Levin, D., Diamond, R., & Goldstein, S. (1985). A study of alternating leadership for group psychotherapy in an aftercare clinic. *Perspectives in Psychiatric Care, 23,* 33-38.
Measured pre- and post-test improvement of schizophrenics in one of three group therapy conditions: one-leader, co-leaders, or three rotating leaders. Those in the rotating group were most improved.

1233. Levine, S. H., Bystritsky, A., Baron, D., & Jones, L. D. (1991). Group psychotherapy for HIV-seropositive patients with major depression. *Dissertation Abstracts International, 45*(3), 413-424.

1234. Lewinsohn, P. M., & Clarke, G. N. (1984). Group treatment of depressed individuals: The "Coping with Depression" course. Symposium held at the meeting of the Association for the Advancement of Behavior Therapy: Psychological treatment of unipolar depression. *Advances in Behavior Research and Therapy, 6,* 99-114.
Describes a multimodal, psycho-educational course called Coping with Depression, which has been modified for use with the elderly, high school students and outpatients who fail to respond to antidepressant treatment.

1235. Lewis, V. J., Blair, A. J., & Booth, D. A. (1992). Outcome of group therapy for body image emotionality and weight control self-efficacy. *Behavioural Psychotherapy, 20,* 155-165.
Women trying to control their weight participated in semistructured weekly group therapy, with positive results in the areas of habit, self-esteem, eating behavior, body weight reduction and attitude toward body size. Improvements were sustained and body weight decreased after the end of therapy.

1236. Liberman, R. P. (1976). Marital therapy in groups: A comparative evaluation of behavioral and interactional formats. *Acta Psychiatrica Scandinavica, 266,* 3-34.

1237. Lidren, D. M. (1994). The differential efficacy of self-help and group therapy in the treatment of panic disorder and agoraphobia: A treatment comparison study. *Dissertation Abstracts International, 54*(12), 6465. (University Microfilm No. AAC94-14791)

1238. Lieberman, M. (1975). Some limits of research on T groups. *Journal of Applied Behavioral Science, 11,* 241-249.
Compared the degree to which people seek out sensitivity training, human potential groups, psychotherapy, and women's consciousness-raising groups. The degree to which each system attracted participants varied in terms of participant distress and motivation.

1239. Lieberman, M. A., Solow, N., Bond, G. R., & Reibstein, J. (1979). The psychotherapeutic impact of women's consciousness-raising groups. *Archives of General Psychiatry, 36,* 161-168.
Examined the psychotherapeutic effects of women's consciousness-raising groups (CRGs). Changes included greater self-esteem, feelings of assertiveness, and identification with the women's movement, but few women made life-style or

behavioral changes. CRGs did not affect marriage relations or alleviate symptom distress.

1240. Lieberman, M. A., & Yalom, I. (1992). Brief group psychotherapy for the spousally bereaved: A controlled study. *International Journal of Group Psychotherapy, 42*(1), 117-132.
Compared a brief therapy group (BTG) and an untreated control group (CG), using 20 and 36 spousally bereaved subjects, respectively. Treatment consisted of eight 80-minute sessions. Over a one year period, BTG subjects showed modest improvement in role functioning and psychological states compared to CG subjects. Although there were significant changes in self-esteem and single role strain, the absence of other differences leads to the conclusion that BTG did not have a powerful effect.

1241. Lierly, J. A., Jr. (1975). Concrete versus abstract approaches in the use of group psychotherapy with hospitalized alcoholics. *Dissertation Abstracts International, 36*(06), 3053B.

1242. Lin, T. T. (1973). Counseling relationship as a function of counselor's self-confidence. *Journal of Counseling Psychology, 20,* 293-297.
Compared counselors designated as either high, moderate or low in self-confidence. The counselor's self-confidence was linearly related to the counselor's perceived empathy, warmth, intimacy, concreteness, expertness, regard, and congruence.

1243. Lipner, S. D. (1986). Aspects of recovery styles from psychosis. *Dissertation Abstracts International, 46*(11), 4020. (University Microfilm No. AAC85-29365)

1244. Little, L. F. (1981). The impact of Gestalt group psychotherapy on parents' perceptions of children identified as problematic. *Dissertation Abstracts International, 42*(02), 616A.

1245. Lobitz, W. C., & Baker, E. L. (1979). Group treatment of single males with erectile dysfunction. *Archives of Sexual Behavior, 8,* 127-138.

1246. Longo, D. J., Clum, G. A., & Yaeger, N. J. (1988). Psychosocial treatment for recurrent genital herpes. *Journal of Consulting and Clinical Psychology, 56*(1), 61-66.
Assigned 31 subjects with recurrent genital herpes to psychosocial intervention, a social support group, or a waiting list control condition. Compared to the other groups, the psychosocial intervention group reported significantly greater reductions in herpes activity and significant improvements in social support, emotional distress, and cognitive measures.

1247. Lothstein, L. M. (1978). The group psychotherapy dropout phenomenon revisited. *American Journal of Psychiatry, 135,* 1492-1495.
Describes subjects who dropped out of group therapy, even though they had been extensively screened and prepared. Proposes that the dropout phenomenon may be needed to establish group cohesiveness and may have other beneficial effects.

1248. Lothstein, L. M. (1979). Group therapy with gender-dysphoric patients. *American Journal of Psychotherapy, 33,* 67-81.

1249. Lubin, B., & Smith, P. B. (1979). Affect levels in one-day experiential groups. *Psychological Reports, 45*(1), 117-118.
Investigated affect levels (anxiety, depression and hostility) in 86 undergraduates in one day experiential groups, as a function of group composition (three levels), leader (five trainers), and elapsed time (three measurement occasions). Compared groups homogeneously on FIRO-B expressed control scores. ANCOVA yielded only one significant main effect, that of trainers on the hostility scale, and no significant interactions. Discussed the probability of insufficient time for group composition and leaders to produce significant arousal of anxiety and depression.

1250. Luka, L. P., Agras, W. S., & Schneider, J. A. (1986). Thirty month follow-up of cognitive behavioral group therapy for bulimia. *British Journal of Psychiatry, 148,* 614-615.
Examined cognitive behavioral group therapy's long-term effects on 10 bulimic subjects. Sixteen weeks after the end of therapy, the rate of induced vomiting had increased 400%, but the subjects maintained improvement on depressive symptoms.

1251. Lundgren, D. C. (1975). Interpersonal needs and member attitudes toward trainer and group. *Small Group Behavior, 6*(4), 371-388.

1252. MacKay, W., & Liddell, A. (1986). An investigation into the matching of specific agoraphobic anxiety response characteristics with specific types of treatment. *Behavior Research and Therapy, 24,* 361-364.
Examined cognitive versus relaxation group treatment with 14 agoraphobic subjects, categorized as either cognitive responders or non-cognitive responders. Subjects receiving cognitive therapy improved significantly more than those receiving relaxation therapy.

1253. MacKenzie, K. R., Dies, R. R., Coche, E., & Rutan, J. S. (1987). An analysis of AGPA Institute Groups. Special Issue: Integration of research and practice in the field of group psychotherapy. *International Journal of Group Psychotherapy, 37*(1), 55-74.
Group leader and groups traits valued by the AGPA were examined, using data from 53 two-day experiential training groups. The eight most successful groups (MSGs), characterized leaders as more charismatic, caring, skillful, and less inhibited than leaders in the least successful groups. Described MSGs as less defended and superficial, and more cohesive than less successful groups.

1254. MacKenzie, K. R., & Tschuschke, V. (1993). Relatedness, group work, and outcome in long-term inpatient psychotherapy groups. *Journal of Psychotherapy Practice and Research, 2,* 147-156.

1255. MacNair, R. R. (1993). A model of group therapy dropout and a test of client factors predicting dropout. *Dissertation Abstracts International, 53*(08), 4378. (University Microfilm No. AAC92-39758)

1256. Magden, R. F. (1975). Eight dimensions of group psychotherapy as they relate to three approaches to group therapy. *Dissertation Abstracts International, 36*(03), 1412. (University Microfilm No. AAC75-19132)

1257. Mahan, D. B. (1981). Contingency contracting as an adjunct to group counseling with substance abusers in the natural setting. *Dissertation Abstracts International, 41*(08), 3162. (University Microfilm No. AAC81-04666)
Compared three different out-patient treatments of substance abusers, consisting of traditional group counseling: plus contingency contracting with positive reinforcement, plus contingency contracting with response cost, or no contracting. Measured the subjects' depression and hostility and found no significant differences among the groups, possibly because contingency contracting requires the added control of an in-patient setting.

1258. Mahon, M. E. (1991). A comparison of therapeutic factors for ACOAs and non-ACOAs in heterogeneous psychotherapy group. *Dissertation Abstracts International, 51*(08), 4059B.

1259. Mappes, D. C. (1982). The effects of structured sociometric feedback and group counseling on personal adjustment and sociometric status. *Dissertation Abstracts International, 43*(03), 674A.

1260. Marburg, G. S. (1981). The role of brief, individual, directive and nondirective psychotherapy in facilitating self-actualization among clients who have demonstrated an internal or external locus of control. *Dissertation Abstracts International, 41*(08), 3187.

1261. Marcy, C. (1983). The effect of interpersonal skills training on the group behavior of alcoholics. *Dissertation Abstracts International, 44*(04), 1245B.

1262. Marett, K. M. (1988). A substantive and methodological review of couples group therapy outcome research. *Group, 12,* 241-246.

1263. Marino, T. M. (1984). The effects of experiential focusing on group cohesiveness and the depth of group interaction. *Dissertation Abstracts International, 44*(07), 2250. (University Microfilm No. AAC83-17268)

1264. Markewich, I. (1987). Multiple family group therapy for schizophrenic patients in a day treatment program: A comparison of patient-included and patient-excluded groups for families with different levels of expressed emotion. *Dissertation Abstracts International, 47*(07), 3117. (University Microfilm No. AAC86-14338)

1265. Markham, D. J. (1985). Behavioral rehearsals vs group systematic desensitization in assertiveness training with women. Special Issue: Gender Roles. *Academic Psychology Bulletin, 7,* 157-174.
Compared the effectiveness of behavioral rehearsal versus group systematic desensitization in assertiveness training of 45 women. Both methods improved assertiveness but did not differ from one another in amount of change.

1266. Martinez, M. (1982). A comparison of effectiveness of group assertive training and self-esteem enhancement group therapy in decreasing anxiety, depression and aggression while concurrently increasing assertiveness and self-esteem. *Dissertation Abstracts International, 42*(08), 3515A.
Assigned subjects to an assertive training (AT) group, a Self-esteem Enhancement Group Therapy (SET), or a no-treatment control. Both treatment groups combined didactic instruction with discussion, cognitive learning techniques and behavioral learning techniques. Both AT and SET were significantly effective in increasing assertiveness, but AT was a more potent treatment than SET. Both AT and SET were equally significantly effective in decreasing measures of anxiety, depression, and aggression.

1267. Mattes, J. A., Rosen, B., & Klein, D. F. (1977). Comparison of the clinical effectiveness of short- versus long-stay psychiatric hospitalization. *Journal of Nervous and Mental Disease, 165,* 387-394.

1268. Maynard, P. E. (1976). Group training for counselors: A one-year follow-up. *Counselor Education and Supervision, 15*(3), 225-228.

1269. McBride, H. S. (1976). An application of the Adlerian Group Counseling approach to nursing home staff members. *Dissertation Abstracts International, 37*(03), 1409. (University Microfilm No. AAC76-20095)

1270. McCabe, O. L., Savage, C., Kurland, A., Unger, S. (1972). Psychedelic (LSD) therapy of neurotic disorders: Short-term effects. *Journal of Psychedelic Drugs, 5,* 18-28.
Compared effects of three treatments, one low, one high LSD dosage, and conventional group therapy. Before and after treatment, subjects completed the MMPI, the Eysenck Personality Inventory and the Personal Orientation Inventory. All forms of treatment resulted in improvement, but the LSD groups, especially the high dosage group, showed greater improvement.

1271. McCallum, M., Piper, W. E., & Joyce, A. S. (1992). Dropping out from short-term group therapy. *Psychotherapy, 29,* 206-215.

1272. McCallum, M., Piper, W. E., & Morin, H. (1993). Affect and outcome in short-term therapy for loss. *International Journal of Group Psychotherapy, 43,* 303-319.
Examined the outcome of 12 psychoanalytically oriented short-term groups. Over time, positive affect, which was related to favorable income, increased.

1273. McCardel, J., & Murray, E. J. (1974). Nonspecific factors in weekend encounter groups. *Journal of Consulting and Clinical Psychology, 42*(3), 337-345.

1274. McCarrick, A. K. (1979). Analysis of interaction sequences as a method of evaluating marital group psychotherapy. *Dissertation Abstracts International, 39*(09), 5751A.

1275. McDaniel, M. F. (1991). Enhancing the psychological adjustment of visually impaired adults through cognitive group therapy. *Dissertation Abstracts International, 52*(03), 1728. (University Microfilm No. AAC91-20359)

1276. McIntosh, J. B. (1991). The effect of transpersonal and interpersonal group therapy upon the self-concept of recovering alcoholics and addicts. *Dissertation Abstracts International, 51*(07), 2269. (University Microfilm No. AAC90-22236) Randomly assigned 18 recovering alcoholics and drug addicts either to a Transpersonal Therapy (TT) group or to an Interpersonal Therapy (IT) group. Concluded that TT increased self-concept more than IT, and neither Alcoholics Anonymous (AA) nor Narcotics Anonymous (NA) involvement affected the outcome.

1277. McLachlan, J. F. (1974). Social competence and response to group therapy. *Journal of Community Psychology, 2*(3), 248-250. Studied the relationship between person perception and group therapy outcomes by developing a modified semantic differential version of R. Harrison's Person Description Instrument (PDI). Following detoxification, subjects participated in 26 hours of group therapy for 3 weeks. Initial social competence ratings of self and others predicted the subject's perception of the subject's improvement during therapy; both staff and peer ratings of the subject's initial level of social competence predicted staff ratings of therapy outcome.

1278. McLachlan, J. F. (1974). Therapy strategies, personality orientation and recovery from alcoholism. *Canadian Psychiatric Association Journal, 19*(1), 25-30. Ninety-four alcoholic inpatients received 26 hours of group therapy for three weeks. Assigned conceptual level ratings to subjects and therapists, based on responses to D. E. Hunt's paragraph completion test. Twelve to 16 months after treatment, staff members rated the patients on changes in drinking behavior. It was expected that subjects with low conceptual levels would need a more directive therapist and that those with high conceptual levels would need a more nondirective therapist. Subjects whose conceptual level matched that of their therapist had better outcomes than those who did not, with recovery rates of 70% and 50%, respectively. Aftercare matching was also related to recovery rates.

1279. McLatchie, L. R. (1982). Interpersonal problem-solving group therapy: An evaluation of a potential method of social skills training for the chronic psychiatric patient. *Dissertation Abstracts International, 42*(07), 2995. (University Microfilm No. AAC81-29186) Studied changes in interpersonal problem-solving abilities in chronic schizophrenics, randomly assigned to either a problem-solving therapy group or to a relaxation training therapy group. Dropouts acted as a control group in the Psychotic Inpatient Profile (PIP). There were no significant differences among the groups in PIP scores, or between the two therapy groups in improvement in the Means-Ends Problem-Solving Procedure (MEPS). Presents individual case studies.

1280. McNair, J. L. (1974). A comparative study of marathon placement in short-term group counseling. *Dissertation Abstracts International, 35*(05), 2692. (University Microfilm No. AAC74-23602)

1281. Meadow, D. A. (1982). The effects of a client-focused pre-group preparation interview on the formation of group cohesion and members' interactional behaviors. *Dissertation Abstracts International, 43*(04), 1294.

1282. Meier-Swickard, D. F. (1993). Comparison of group counseling for divorced single mothers. *Dissertation Abstracts International, 54*(04), 2213B.

1283. Melucci, N. J. (1992). Correlates of successful therapy reported by adult survivors of childhood sexual abuse. *Dissertation Abstracts International, 53*(05), 1403. (University Microfilm No. AAC92-27724)

1284. Merbaum, M., Avimier, R., & Goldberg. (1979). The relationship between aversion, group training and vomiting in the reduction of smoking behavior. *Addictive Behaviors, 4,* 279-285.
Examined the effects of aversion group therapy on the reduction of smoking behavior in 52 subjects. Strong aversion therapy alone reduced smoking behavior just as effectively as aversion therapy combined with self-control training.

1285. Millard, E. R. (1976). The effects of writing assignments upon rational thinking and level of self-disclosure in group counseling. *Dissertation Abstracts International, 37*(02), 813. (University Microfilm No. AAC76-17908)

1286. Miller, S. B. (1989). Treatment outcome and attrition in a comprehensive weight loss program: Group versus the combination of group with individual treatment sessions. *Dissertation Abstracts International, 50*(03), 1117. (University Microfilm No. AAC89-11407)
Randomly assigned participants in Optifast, a comprehensive weight loss program, either to group and individual therapy, or to group therapy only. Those receiving group and individual therapy received a small, nonsignificant weight loss benefit; there was no difference in attrition between the two groups. There was a significant therapist effect, with one therapist demonstrating a smaller dropout rate and more weight loss.

1287. Miller, S. E. (1980). The effects of two group approaches, psychodrama and encounter, on levels of self-actualization: A comparative study. *Dissertation Abstracts International, 41*(06), 2456A.

1288. Mitsibounas, D. N., Tsouna-Hadjis, E. D., Rotas, V. R., & Sideris, D. A. (1992). Effects of group psychosocial intervention on coronary risk factors. *Psychotherapy and Psychosomatics, 58*(2), 97-102.
Examined whether a psychosocial intervention approach aimed at resolving psychological conflicts could reduce the severity of risk factors for post-acute myocardial infarction patients. The treatment program, which lasted a year, and the control group each had 20 subjects. Compared between-group mean value of seven risk factors of coronary heart disease. Results suggest that group

psychosocial intervention with post-acute myocardial infarction patients considerably reduces some coronary-disease risk factors.

1289. Moffett, L. A., & Stoklosa, J. M. (1976). Group therapy for socially anxious and unassertive young veterans. *International Journal of Group Psychotherapy, 26,* 421-430.

1290. Montag, K. R., & Wilson, G. L. (1992). An empirical evaluation of behavioral and cognitive-behavioral group marital treatments with discordant couples. *Journal of Sex and Marital Therapy, 18*(4), 255-272.
Evaluated group behavioral (GB) and cognitive-behavioral (GCB) marital treatments across a variety of relationship dimensions and measures of individual functioning. Results demonstrated clinically significant improvement in both the GB and GCB marital treatments, as contrasted with the waiting list control group.

1291. Moran, M. (1978). Systems releasing action therapy with alcoholics: An experimental evaluation. *Journal of Clinical Psychology, 34*(3), 769-774.

1292. Morelock, C. J. (1982). Case study of crisis dynamic group psychotherapy with mixed diagnoses medically hospitalized adults. *Dissertation Abstracts International, 43*(04), 1261B.

1293. Morran, D., Keith, Stockton, R., & Bond, L. (1991). Delivery of positive and corrective feedback in counseling groups. *Journal of Counseling Psychology, 38,* 410-414.
Forty-eight personal growth group members were more willing to give positive feedback than corrective feedback to other members. Discusses explanations and implications of this finding.

1294. Morrison, J. K., Libow, J. A., Smith, F. J., & Becker, R. R. (1978). Comparative effectiveness of directive vs. nondirective group therapist style on client problem resolution. *Journal of Clinical Psychology, 34,* 186-187.
Examined the relative superiority of nondirective versus directive therapist style in problem resolution with eight neurotic subjects.

1295. Moxnes, P. (1974). Verbal communication level and anxiety in psychotherapeutic groups. *Journal of Counseling Psychology, 21,* 399-403.
Describes the finding of a curvilinear relationship between verbal behavior and experienced anxiety in a psychotherapy group. The maximum level of anxiety occurred with disclosure of private material.

1296. Moyses, C. D. (1982). The effects of three treatment approaches on locus of control of incarcerated females. *Dissertation Abstracts International, 43*(03), 675. (University Microfilm No. AAC82-17606)

1297. Muller, W. J. (1974). La Amistad: Starting an inpatient program for severely disturbed young adults. *Hospital and Community Psychiatry, 25,* 587-590.
Studied a program designed to be a model inpatient program for young adults with schizophrenia-related illness. Behavior modification was the main treatment method, supplemented with family and group therapy, and group

activities. Follow-up showed 75% of the 70 former residents improved or much improved.

1298. Murray, P. R. (1979). The effectiveness of communication training as compared to traditional group psychotherapy in an inpatient population. *Masters Abstracts International, 17*(01), 79. (University Microfilm No. AAC13-12003).

1299. Myers, E. D. (1975). Age, persistence and improvement in an open out-patient group. *British Journal of Psychiatry, 127,* 157-159.
Describes the significant correlation between age and continued attendance with 87 patients participating in group therapy. Also found significant correlations between age and symptomatic improvement, and between continued attendance and improved interpersonal relationships.

1300. Myers, J. E., Poidevant, J. M., & Dean, L. A. (1991). Groups for older persons and their caregivers: A review of the literature. *Journal for Specialists in Group Work, 16,* 197-205.

1301. Nagy, L. M., Krystal, J. H., Charney, D. S., & Merikangas, K. R. (1993). Long-term outcome of panic disorder after short-term imipramine and behavioral groups treatment: 2.9 year naturalistic follow-up study. *Journal of Clinical Psychopharmacology, 13,* 16-24.
Examined the long-term use of imipramine in 28 patients with agoraphobia with panic attacks, who had completed a course of drug and behavioral group therapy. At follow-up, half of the subjects were medication free, 8 were receiving a lower dose than at discharge, and 4 were receiving other anti-panic medications.

1302. Neal, P. J. (1983). A psychological treatment program for prevention of decubitus ulcers in spinal cord injured patients. *Dissertation Abstracts International, 44*(03), 921B.

1303. Neal, R. B. (1977). The effect of group counseling and physical fitness programs on self-esteem and cardiovascular fitness. *Dissertation Abstracts International, 38*(04), 1911A.

1304. Nero, R. S. (1985). The effect of videotape feedback on self-concept and cognitive dissonance in out-patient psychotherapy groups. *Dissertation Abstracts International, 45*(08), 2696B.
Administered the Tennessee Self-Concept Scale (TSCS) to assess self-concept and level of cognitive dissonance at pretest, post-test and at a one week follow-up. There were significant differences between the psychotherapy groups on TSCS Variability and Physical Self, but no significant differences on cognitive dissonance.

1305. Nesbit, M. (1979). The treatment of chronic pain patients via a structured group counseling approach. *Dissertation Abstracts International, 39*(09), 5331A.

1306. Neuman, N. M. (1990). Women's experiences of changes in self-esteem following participation in psychodrama: A phenomenological investigation. *Dissertation Abstracts International, 51*(04), 2116B.

1307. Newhouse, R. C., & Schwager, H. (1978). Rational behavior therapy as related to self-concept of disadvantaged adults. *Journal of Instructional Psychology, 5*(1), 35-38.

1308. Nicholas, M. W. (1990). The relationship between early group laughter and group cohesiveness in outpatient psychotherapy groups. *Dissertation Abstracts International, 51*(04), 2068. (University Microfilm No. AAC90-21069)

1309. Nichols, M. P. (1977). The delayed impact of group therapists' interventions. *Journal of Clinical Psychology, 33,* 258-262.
Examined the immediate and delayed impact of therapist interventions on 21 clients. Little immediate impact was evident, but over the sessions, the clients' level and immediacy of experience intensified.

1310. Nichols, M. P., & Taylor, T. Y. (1975). Impact of therapist interventions on early sessions of group therapy. *Journal of Clinical Psychology, 31,* 726-729.
Examined the effect of therapist style on the group therapy process. Findings suggest that individually directed, confrontive interventions lead to emotionally focused and immediacy of client responding. Furthermore, simple facilitations produce higher focusing than other types of interventions.

1311. Nicholson, P. A. (1993). Gender-related perceptions of group co-leader effectiveness. *Dissertation Abstracts International, 53*(08), 2693. (University Microfilm No. AAC92-37408)

1312. Ning, L., & Liddell, A. (1991). The effect of concordance in the treatment of clients with dental anxiety. *Behavior Research and Therapy, 29*(4), 315-322.

1313. Nir, D. (1991). A framework for eclectic group intervention. *Dissertation Abstracts International, 52*(01), 525. (University Microfilm No. AAC91-09662)

1314. Nixon, C. D., & Singer, G. H. (1993). Group cognitive-behavioral treatment for excessive parental self-blame and guilt. *American Journal on Mental Retardation, 97*(6), 665-672.
Randomly assigned 34 mothers of children with severe disabilities either to a treatment group, using behavioral and cognitive techniques to help mothers reduce their self-reported stress, or to a waiting list control condition. The mothers participated in counselor led classes, which covered topics relating to cognitive processes associated with guilt and self-blame. Results show significant reductions in measures of guilt, negative automatic thoughts, internal negative attributions, and depression. Briefly reviews theoretical and treatment literature concerning self-blame and guilt, and describes the derivative treatment.

1315. Noll, G. A., & Watkins, J. T. (1974). Differences between persons seeking encounter group experiences and others on the Personal Orientation Inventory. *Journal of Counseling Psychology, 21*(3), 206-209.

1316. Nugent, F. A. (1990). *An introduction to the profession of counseling.* Columbus, OH: Merrill.

Quotes reviewers who state that research indicates that group treatments are associated with client improvement, and that self-disclosure and feedback are basic to the effectiveness of group treatment.

1317. O'Connell, D. F. (1987). Patterns of group development and leadership style in involuntary psychotherapy groups for alcoholic abusers. *Dissertation Abstracts International, 47*(10), 3712A.

1318. O'Connell, W. E., Baker, R. R., Hanson, P. G., & Ermalinski, R. (1974). Types of "negative nonsense." *International Journal of Social Psychiatry, 20,* 122-127.
Compared psychiatric patients who were either high or low verbal participants in group therapy. High participants had higher self-esteem and lower hyper-dependency scores than did low participants.

1319. O'Dell, S., & Seiler, G. (1975). The effects of short-term personal growth groups on anxiety and self-perception. *Small Group Behavior, 6*(3), 251-271.
Examined the effects of four encounter group types: encounter, Gestalt, self-discovery, and enrichment. Examined the subject's level of anxiety, and self-evaluation of the subject's thinking, feeling and body image. Multivariate analysis of variance showed no significant differences between groups or between pre- and post-measures for any one group.

1320. O'Leary, M. A. (1985). A study of the effects of group counseling for parents who have exceptional children. *Masters Abstracts International, 23*(03), 324.

1321. O'Leary, W. C., Jr. (1975). An investigation to determine the effects of two methods of group counseling on the self-concept and work adjustment of psychiatric patients. *Dissertation Abstracts International, 36*(03), 1313A.

1322. O'Sullivan, D., Vostanis, P., & Girling, A. (1991). A description and evaluation of an intensive psychotherapy programme: Patient and staff perceptions. *International Journal of Therapeutic Communities, 12,* 233-244.
Compared patient and therapist ratings of the components of an intensive psychotherapy program. Both groups gave high ratings to small group psychotherapy, role play, and projective therapy. Therapists rated the assessment procedure, occupational therapy, and the social environment more highly than did patients.

1323. Obler, M. (1973). Systematic desensitization in sexual disorders. *Journal of Behavior Therapy and Experimental Psychiatry, 4,* 93-101.

1324. Obler, M. (1975). Multivariate approaches to psychotherapy with sexual dysfunctions. *Counseling Psychologist, 5,* 55-60.
Compared the effectiveness of two types of group treatment, Freudian versus desensitization, in treating single people with sexual dysfunctions. The desensitization group made more gains, with 80% of these subjects overcoming their dysfunctions.

1325. Oderberg, N. A. (1992). Psychotherapists countertransference in the nuclear age: Effects on therapeutic interventions. *Dissertation Abstracts International, 53*(02), 1071. (University Microfilm No. AAC92-20386)

1326. Ohlsen, M. M. (1970). *Group counseling.* New York: Holt, Rinehart & Winston.
Presents basic questions that the group counselor must ask in preparing to do research and evaluating published research.

1327. Ollerman, T. E. (1975). The effect of group counseling upon self-actualization, self-disclosure, and the development of interpersonal trust among prison inmates. *Dissertation Abstracts International, 36*(06), 3415A.

1328. Olson, J. K. (1975). The effects of instructions and positive feedback on quality and quantity of patient verbalizations in group psychotherapy. *Dissertation Abstracts International, 35*(08), 4192. (University Microfilm No. AAC75-04994)

1329. Ong, T. (1991). The effectiveness of an indigenised group counselling programme in aftercare service for drug supervisees: A one-year follow-up study. *International Journal for the Advancement of Counselling, 14,* 285-300.
Compared a group of 100 drug addicts, who had completed a group counselling program one year earlier, to a control group of 89 former addicts. Significantly more subjects from the group counseling program were free from drugs than those from the control group.

1330. Orbach, S. (1978). Social dimensions in compulsive eating in women. *Psychotherapy: Theory, Research and Practice, 15,* 180-189.

1331. Otteson, J. P. (1979). Curative caring: The use of buddy groups with chronic schizophrenics. *Journal of Consulting and Clinical Psychology, 47,* 649-651.
Compared group treatment of long-term schizophrenic males, assigning subjects to one of three groups: altruistic (buddy-oriented, with focus on buddy's discharge from the hospital), traditional (self-oriented), or no-treatment control group. Measurement of discharge and recidivism rates suggest that the altruistic group therapy was more effective.

1332. Paden, R. C., Himelstein, H. C., & Paul, G. L. (1974). Videotape versus verbal feedback in the modification of meal behavior of chronic mental patients. *Journal of Consulting and Clinical Psychology, 42,* 623.
Examined the meal behavior indexes of 28 chronic adult psychiatric patients who received videotape or verbal feedback and structured discussions. There were no significant changes in meal behavior after either treatment.

1333. Page, R. C. (1977). Marathon group counseling with imprisoned female drug abusers. *Dissertation Abstracts International, 37*(10), 6282. (University Microfilm No. AAC77-08207)

1334. Palau, J., Leitner, L., Drasgow, F., & Drasgow, J. (1974). Further improvement following therapy. *Journal of Group Psychotherapy and Psychodrama, 27,* 42-47.

After therapy, group members maintained termination levels of functioning and even continued to improve.

1335. Pallone, N. J., & Tirman, R. J. (1978). Correlates of substance abuse remission in alcoholism rehabilitation: Effective treatment or symptom abandonment? *Offender Rehabilitation, 3*(1), 7-18.

1336. Palmer, S. E., Brown, R. A., & Barrera, M. E. (1992). Group treatment program for abusive husbands: Long-term evaluation. *American Journal of Orthopsychiatry, 62* 92), 276-283.
    Evaluated the effectiveness of a 10 week group treatment program for 59 abusive husbands. Recidivism was lower for treatment subjects than controls, suggesting that short-term treatment can reduce abusive behavior in men over the long term. Nonrecidivists had higher initial depression scores, suggesting that more members of this group had begun to accept some responsibility for their behavior.

1337. Panzica, A. L. (1975). An experimental comparison of a programmed approach to activity group counseling and group-centered counseling. *Dissertation Abstracts International, 36*(04), 2032. (University Microfilm No. AAC75-22798)

1338. Parisi, J. A. (1978). An evaluation of an anticipatory socialization interview to prepare drug abusers for group psychotherapy. *Dissertation Abstracts International, 38*(08), 3900. (University Microfilm No. AAC77-32257)

1339. Parkhurst, A. E. (1989). The relationship between social anxiety, attraction to group, self-disclosure, feedback valence, and session of delivery to the acceptance of group feedback. *Dissertation Abstracts International, 49*(07), 2869. (University Microfilm No. AAC88-18961)

1340. Parloff, M. B., & Dies, R. R. (1977). Group psychotherapy outcome research, 1966-1975. *International Journal of Group Psychotherapy, 27,* 281-319.

1341. Pastushak, R. J. (1978). The effects of videotaped pretherapy training on interpersonal openness, self-disclosure, and group psychotherapy outcome measures. *Dissertation Abstracts International, 39*(02), 993B.

1342. Pattison, E. M., & Rhodes, R. J. (1974). Clinical prediction with the NOSIE-30 scale. *Journal of Clinical Psychology, 30*(2), 200-201.
    Found that scores of patients with chronic lung disease on the 30 item Nurses' Observation Scale for Inpatient Evaluation (NOSIE-30) were correlated with clinical outcome and with effective group psychotherapy participation. Results support the hypothesis that NOSIE-30 is useful with patients who are withdrawn, apathetic, and unresponsive to other clinical prognosis rating scales.

1343. Payne, W. R. (1984). The impact of metaphorical language upon self-concept and ideal self during group counseling with disabled adults: An experiment. *Dissertation Abstracts International, 44*(07), 2046A.

1344. Peake, T. H. (1979). Therapist-patient agreement and outcome in group therapy. *Journal of Clinical Psychology, 35,* 637-646.

1345. Pederson, L. L., Scrimgeour, W. G., & Lefcoe, N. M. (1975). Comparison of hypnosis plus counseling, counseling alone, and hypnosis alone in a community service smoking withdrawal program. *Journal of Consulting and Clinical Psychology, 43,* 920.
Describes the success of a combination of hypnosis plus group therapy with smoking withdrawal subjects.

1346. Penney, D. L. (1989). A comparison of psychotherapy-changers and self-changers in a naturalistic environment. *Dissertation Abstracts International, 50*(02), 756. (University Microfilm No. AAC89-01721)

1347. Peretz, M. E. (1992). The effects of psychotherapy and self-defense training on recovery of survivors of acquaintance and stranger rape. *Dissertation Abstracts International, 52*(10), 5545. (University Microfilm No. AAC92-08724)

1348. Perez, J. F. (1986). *Counseling the alcoholic group.* New York: Gardner Press.
Provides pretest and post-test evaluation data on 32 alcoholism patients treated in 10 different counseling groups, none for longer than four months. Most clients improved on personal and interpersonal dimensions.

1349. Perrin, M. M. M. (1982). Conjoint couples' group sessions for post-myocardial infarction patients and spouses. *Dissertation Abstracts International, 43*(06), 1797B.

1350. Peteroy, E. T. (1979). Effects of member and leader expectations on group outcome. *Journal of Counseling Psychology, 26*(5), 462-465.
Examined whether member and leader expectations affected self-esteem and self-actualization. Varying the level of group expectations did not significantly affect self-actualization gain but did affect self-esteem change. There were significant differences between the experimental and control groups on the dependent variables. Discusses results and recommends future research on group leaders' expectations.

1351. Pevsner, R. K. (1981). Parent training and group therapy versus individual family therapy in the treatment of child behavior problems. *Dissertation Abstracts International, 41*(09), 3538B.

1352. Pincus, A. L. (1993). Extending interpersonal problems to include the 'big five' personality dimensions. *Dissertation Abstracts International, 54*(06), 3379. (University Microfilm No. AACNN-79702)

1353. Pinney, E. L., Wells, S. H., & Fisher, B. (1978). Group therapy training in psychiatric residency programs: A national survey. *American Journal of Psychiatry, 135*(12), 1505-1508.
Questioned directors of the 256 approved American psychiatric residency programs about the availability, content, and orientations of group therapy training. Results include: Seventy-eight percent of the responding programs offered group therapy training, and programs offered a full range of theoretical orientations.

1354. Piper, W. E., Debbane, E. G., & Garant, J. (1977). An outcome study of group therapy. *Archives of General Psychiatry, 34,* 1027-1032.

1355. Piper, W. E., Debbane, E. G., & Garant, J. (1977). Group psychotherapy outcome research: Problems and prospects of a first-year project. *International Journal of Group Psychotherapy, 27,* 321-341.
      Describes a program designed to provide group therapy for outpatients, to train group therapists, and to study the outcome of group therapy.

1356. Piper, W. E., Doan, B. D., Edwards, E. M., & Jones, B. D. (1979). Co-therapy behavior, group therapy process and treatment outcome. *Journal of Consulting and Clinical Psychology, 47,* 1081-1089.

1357. Piper, W. E., McCallum, M., & Azim, H. F. A. (1992). *Adaptation to loss through short-term group psychotherapy.* New York: Guilford Press.
      Studied 154 patients (109 began 1 of 16 therapy groups), in treatment and control groups. Treatment was conducted by experienced therapists whose treatment technique was validated by tape-recorded sessions. The concept of "psychological mindedness" and psychodynamic treatment were central to the project. Treated patients improved significantly over control subjects.

1358. Piper, W. E., & Perrault, E. L. (1989). Pretherapy preparation for group members. *International Journal of Group Psychotherapy, 39,* 17-34.
      A review of 20 studies during the period from 1962 to 1987 reveals numerous shortcomings in methodology and design, rendering conclusions about the positive benefits of pretherapy preparation premature.

1359. Piran, N., Langdon, L., Kaplan, A. S., & Garfinkel, P. E. (1990). Program evaluation. In N. Piran & A. S. Kaplan (Eds.), *A day hospital group treatment program for anorexia nervosa and bulimia nervosa* (pp. 139-150). New York: Brunner/Mazel.
      Explored the efficacy of therapeutic elements in the Day Hospital Program in improving 44 patients' eating behavior and attitudes. Those with anorexia experienced significant weight gain while those with bulimia experienced a significant drop in bingeing and vomiting episodes.

1360. Platt, J. J., Husband, S. D., Hermalin, J., & Cater, J. (1993). A cognitive problem-solving employment readiness intervention for methadone clients. *Journal of Cognitive Psychotherapy, 7,* 21-33.

1361. Pokorny, A. D., Miller, B. A., Kanas, T., & Valles, J. (1973). Effectiveness of extended aftercare in the treatment of alcoholism. *Quarterly Journal of Studies on Alcohol, 34*(2), 435-443.

1362. Polinskey, T. G. (1992). The effects of a group counseling grief recovery program for clients experiencing bereavement. *Dissertation Abstracts International, 52*(11), 3830. (University Microfilm No. AAC92-04733)

1363. Pool-Trafton, S. K. (1992). The relationship of cognitive complexity level and time for processing on acceptance of feedback. *Dissertation Abstracts International, 52*(10), 3532. (University Microfilm No. AAC92-08961)

1364. Powers, R. J. (1978). Enhancement of former drug abusers' career development through structured group counseling. *Journal of Counseling Psychology, 25,* 585-587.
   Used career development treatment, a slightly modified version of Daane's Vocational Exploration Group (VEG), on 120 former drug abusers. Those treated had greater career plan clarity, maturity of career attitude, and competence than those in the control group. Both groups found meaning in career development activities.

1365. Price, R. H., & Curlee-Salisbury, J. (1975). Patient-treatment interactions among alcoholics. *Journal of Studies on Alcohol, 36*(5), 659-669.

1366. Prince, R. M., Ackerman, R. E., & Barksdale, B. S. (1973). Collaborative provision of aftercare services. *American Journal of Psychiatry, 130*(8), 930-932.
   Data from 1,182 chronic psychotic patients demonstrate that group aftercare methods make more efficient use of personnel and are significantly more effective than traditional individual-aftercare.

1367. Proedrou, R. D. (1975). The adjunctive use of videotape feedback in group psychotherapy. *Dissertation Abstracts International, 35*(10), 6519. (University Microfilm No. AAC75-07665)

1368. Quintano, J. H. (1974). Effects of content centered group counseling on memory recall in alcoholic brain damaged subjects, *Dissertation Abstracts International, 35*(04), 1988A.

1369. Rahe, R. H., Ward, H. W., & Hayes, V. (1979). Brief group therapy in myocardial infarction rehabilitation: Three to four year follow-up of a controlled trial. *Psychosomatic Medicine, 51*(3), 229-242.

1370. Ramseyer, M. S. (1984). Curative factors in psychodrama with substance abusers. *Dissertation Abstracts International, 44*(09), 2905. (University Microfilm No. AAC83-09708)

1371. Rangitsch, S. M. (1990). Elaboration and evaluation of a personal-transpersonal group counseling model. *Dissertation Abstracts International, 51*(06), 3144. (University Microfilm No. AAC90-33077)

1372. Rappaport, E. (1979). General versus situation-specific trait anxiety in prediction of state anxiety during group therapy. *Psychological Reports, 44*(3, Pt 1), 715-718.

1373. Ratto, R. (1992). Situational and trait affiliativeness as related to inpatient group psychotherapy outcome. *Dissertation Abstracts International, 53*(02), 1073. (University Microfilm No. AAC92-16347)

1374. Reed, R. A. (1987). Premenstrual syndrome: The comparative efficacy of three group therapy interventions. *Dissertation Abstracts International, 47*(10), 4312. (University Microfilm No. AAC87-03602)

1375. Reed, R. P. (1975). Group psychotherapy effects on internal-external locus-of-control. *Dissertation Abstracts International, 36*(06), 3065. (University Microfilm No. AAC75-28673)

1376. Reid, V. L. (1979). The influence of group counseling on the recently divorced. *Dissertation Abstracts International, 39*(08), 4737A.

1377. Reinfeld, W. V. (1976). The effects of a group psychotherapy intervention on clients with an external locus-of-control. *Dissertation Abstracts International, 36*(08), 5056. (University Microfilm No. AAC76-02257)

1378. Reiss, D., & Costell, R. (1977). The multiple family group as a small society: Family regulation of interaction with nonmembers. *American Journal of Psychiatry, 134,* 21-24.
Describes the inter-generational dynamics of 18 families participating in group counseling. Changes in either the parents' or the adolescents' group participation levels were rapidly matched by the other generation.

1379. Rempel, K., Hazelwood, E., & McElheran, N. (1993). Brief therapy group for mothers of troubled children. *Journal of Systematic Therapies, 12*(1), 32-48.

1380. Renjilian, D. A. (1990). Individual versus group therapy for obesity: Matching clients with treatments. *Dissertation Abstracts International, 51*(05), 2633. (University Microfilm No. AAC90-25006)

1381. Resick, P. A., Schnicke, M. K. (1992). Cognitive processing therapy for sexual assault victims. *Journal of Consulting and Clinical Psychology, 60,* 748-756.
Evaluated cognitive processing therapy (CPT) in treating rape victims' post-traumatic stress disorder (PTSD) symptoms. CPT group members showed significant improvement in pre- to post-treatment measures of PTSD and depression, maintained for six months, but comparison group members showed no change.

1382. Resnick, R. J., Lira, F., & Wallace, J. H. (1977). On the effectiveness of group counseling: A look at the group leader in the correctional setting. *Criminal Justice and Behavior, 4,* 77-85.
Compared three types of leaders in group counseling in a correctional setting: psychologists, social workers and correctional counselors. Those in psychologist-led groups showed greater motivation and better adjustment in work settings. The results were attributed to the inmates' perception of the leader's influence on their parole recommendations. Influence is seen as a threat to the inmate's freedom, rendering group counseling by an influential person, e.g., a correctional counselor, less effective than by a psychologist.

1383. Richards, R. L. (1992). An examination of interpersonal process in successful and unsuccessful group psychotherapy participants. *Dissertation Abstracts International, 52*(12), 6669. (University Microfilm No. AAC92-10205)

Contrasted the interpersonal behavior of group therapy members who improved (Is) with that of members who deteriorated (Ds). Ds used hostile compliance and hostile autonomy more frequently than Is. Furthermore, Ds used interpersonal processes that allowed them to avoid confronting their problems, whereas Is used interpersonal styles that enabled them to confront their problems.

1384. Richter, D. (1975). Investigation of the short-term and long-term effects of an audio-taped group counseling treatment on a volunteer sample of cigarette smokers. *Dissertation Abstracts International, 35*(09), 5829. (University Microfilm No. AAC75-05656)

1385. Rimm, D. C., Hill, George, A., Brown, N. N., & Stuart, J. E. (1974). Group-assertive training in treatment of expression of inappropriate anger. *Psychological Reports, 34*(3, Pt. 1), 791-798.
Assigned subjects with a history of inappropriate expressions of anger either to an assertiveness training group (ATA) or to a placebo group (PG). The seven subjects in the ATA showed significantly greater improvement in objective measures of assertion and comfort than did the six subjects in the PG.

1386. Roback, H., Purdon, S. E., Ochoa, E., & Block, F. (1993). Effects of professional affiliation on group therapists' confidentiality and behaviors. *Bulletin of the American Academy of Psychiatry and the Law, 21*(2), 147-153.

1387. Roback, H. B., & Strassberg, D. S. (1975). Relationship between perceived therapist-offered conditions and therapeutic movement in group psychotherapy. *Small Group Behavior, 6,* 345-352.
Examined the relationship between therapeutic outcome and the patient's perception of therapist empathy, positive regard, and other therapist-offered conditions in a population of 12 hospitalized chronic schizophrenics. Differences in therapeutic outcome were not explained by perceived therapeutic conditions.

1388. Robak, R. (1991). Loss and bereavement groups in the treatment of recovering addicts. *Death Studies, 15,* 293-301.
Loss and bereavement groups helped recovering addicts identify purpose and meaning for their recovery.

1389. Roberts, A. K. P. (1994). The effects of imagery, group therapy or laughter/humor on quality of life in cancer patients. *Dissertation Abstracts International, 54*(10), 5401B.
Examined differential treatment effects of three group psychotherapeutic interventions, mental imagery, group therapy, laughter/humor, and a control condition. Treatment involved two hour biweekly sessions over a one month period with cancer patients. Hypothesized that all methods would produce statistically significant decreases in total mood disturbance, depression, anxiety, and subjective pain levels, with more superior improvements for the laughter/humor group. Results partially confirmed these forecasts; all groups showed statistically significant decreases in anxiety.

1390. Roberts, L. J. (1990). Giving and receiving help: Group behavioral predictors of outcomes for members of a mutual help organization. *Dissertation Abstracts International, 50*(10), 4783. (University Microfilm No. AAC89-24932)

1391. Robinson, A. L. (1983). Effects of a biofeedback monitored, guided imagery-based group counseling approach on post-divorce adjustment. *Dissertation Abstracts International, 43*(12), 3815A.

1392. Robinson, R. M. (1980). The relationship of dimensions of interpersonal trust with group-cohesiveness, group status, and immediate outcome in short-term group counseling. *Dissertation Abstracts International, 40*(10), 5016B.

1393. Robison, F. F., & Hardt, D. A. (1992). Effects of cognitive and behavioral structure and discussion of corrective feedback outcomes on counseling group development. *Journal of Counseling Psychology, 39*, 473-481.
      Compared a cognitive-behavioral (CBT) with a behavioral treatment (BT) in group therapy for their effects on high and low risk takers' attitudes and corrective feedback production. CBT in combination with a discussion activity enhanced low risk takers' attraction to their groups and to feedback.

1394. Rochester, S. R., Vachon, M. L., & Lyall, W. A. (1974). Immediacy in language: A channel to care of the dying patient. *Journal of Community Psychology 2*, 75-76.
      Describes group therapy discussion sessions with 20 nurses aimed at allowing the nurses to explore their own fears of dying and attitudes toward dying patients. After therapy, nurses decreased their non-immediacy tendency in discussing and dealing with dying patients.

1395. Roe, J. E., & Edwards, K. J. (1978). Relationship of two process measurement systems for group therapy. *Journal of Consulting and Clinical Psychology, 46*, 1545-1546.
      Describes the analysis of 42 group therapy sessions using 4 Hill Interaction Matrix variables. Identified three underlying factors of group process: initiating skills, responding skills and discussion skills. Suggests that the Hill Matrix fails to tap a qualitative dimension of group process.

1396. Roessler, R., Cook, D., & Lillard, D. (1977). Effects of systematic group counseling on work adjustment clients. *Journal of Counseling Psychology, 24*, 313-317.

1397. Roessler, R. T. (1978). An evaluation of personal achievement skills training with the visually handicapped. *Rehabilitation Counseling Bulletin, 21*(4), 300-305.
      Thirty-four visually challenged clients participated in either a structured personal-adjustment training program (PAT) relying on verbal, braille, and motor modes of presentation, or in a control condition. From pre- to post-treatment, PAT subjects increased significantly in self-esteem and tended to make greater progress in goal attainment than did control subjects. An equivalent proportion of PAT and control subjects developed a more optimistic view of life. Neither group changed on the locus of control scale.

1398. Roffman, R. A., Klepsch, R., Wertz, J. S., & Simpson, E. E. (1993). Predictors of attrition from an outpatient marijuana-dependence counseling program. *Addictive Behaviors, 18,* 553-566.
Studied participant attrition in a marijuana-dependence counseling program, using two types of outpatient group counseling. The 23 early dropouts were younger, less financially stable and had more psychological distress than treatment completers. The 43 late dropouts were similar to the 146 treatment completers in these categories, and similar to the 23 early dropouts in their lower rates of abstinence.

1399. Rogers, E. S. (1981). The effects of structured experiential training on the psycho-social adjustment, vocational activity and goal attainment of severely disabled individuals. *Dissertation Abstracts International, 42*(06), 2510. (University Microfilm No. AAC81-26611)

1400. Rohde, R. I. (1989). The effect of structured feedback on goal attainment, attraction to group, and satisfaction with the group in small group counseling. *Dissertation Abstracts International, 49*(09), 2542. (University Microfilm No. AAC88-24182)

1401. Rohde, R. I., & Stockton, R. (1994). Group structure: A review. *Journal of Group Psychotherapy, Psychodrama & Sociometry, 46,* 151-158.
Presents a conceptual and research review of group structure in group counseling. Emphasizes the need to explore structure in group counseling as a multidimensional construct.

1402. Rohrbaugh, M., & Bartels, B. D. (1975). Participants' perceptions of curative factors in therapy and growth groups. *Small Group Behavior, 6,* 430-456.
Evaluated Yalom's Q-sort in terms of its construct validity, finding perceptions of curative factors to be complex and not easily dimensionalized.

1403. Roosa, B. A. (1986). Alcoholism treatment and medical utilization. *Dissertation Abstracts International, 46*(08), 2822B.
Examines the relationship of modality and amount of outpatient alcoholism treatment to subsequent medical service use (MSU) in a health maintenance organization (HMO). The hypothesis that MSU would decrease after beginning alcoholism treatment was generally not supported. Compares present study to previous studies and discusses the differences in patient characteristics and data analysis procedures which might account for the different findings; suggests future research.

1404. Rootes, L. E. (1993). A comparison of staff and patient perspectives of substance abuse treatment and its effectiveness. *Dissertation Abstracts International, 53*(09), 4967. (University Microfilm No. AAC93-03571)

1405. Roschenwimmer, S. C. (1991). Bulimia nervosa and affective disorder: Toward identification of theoretically and clinically relevant subgroups of bulimia nervosa. *Dissertation Abstracts International, 51*(97), 3581. (University Microfilm No. AAC90-27360)

1406. Rose, S. D. (1989). *Working with adults in groups: Integrating cognitive-behavioral and small group strategies.* San Francisco: Jossey-Bass.
Presents a comprehensive discussion of the use of assessment instruments in cognitive-behavioral group therapy by the practitioner and the researcher. The author demonstrates how the clients' problems and resources can best be assessed in groups.

1407. Rose, S. D., Siemon, J. B., & O'Bryant, K. (1979). Use of the group in therapy by members of the AABT. *Behavior Therapist, 2*(4), 21-23.

1408. Rosen, B., Katzoff, A., Carillo, C., & Klein, D. F. (1976). Clinical effectiveness of "short" versus "long" psychiatric hospitalization: I. Inpatient results. *Archives of General Psychiatry, 33,* 1316-1322.

1409. Rosenberg, H., & Bonoma, T. V. (1974). A social influence rating method for group interaction and some pilot results on group therapy process. *Personality and Social Psychology Bulletin, 1,* 259-262.
Evaluated five inpatient and outpatient groups using the Social Influence Rating System (SIRS). Found that therapy was composed of influence-related rather than overt-influence gestures.

1410. Rosenthal, L. (1979). An investigation of the relationship between therapists' orientations and their preferences for interventions in group psychotherapy. *Dissertation Abstracts International, 39*(08), 3757. (University Microfilm No. AAC78-24106)

1411. Rosenzweig, S. P., & Folman, R. (1974). Patient and therapist variables affecting premature termination of group psychotherapy. *Psychotherapy: Theory, Research and Practice, 11,* 76-79.
Examines variables affecting premature termination of group therapy with 26 male Veterans Administration patients. Although psychological tests failed to predict terminators, therapists' attitudes and predictions as well as education successfully distinguished between terminators and continuers.

1412. Ross, W. F., McReynolds, W. T., & Berzins, J. I. (1974). Effectiveness of marathon group psychotherapy with hospitalized female narcotics addicts. *Psychological Reports, 34,* 611-616.
Female narcotic addicts participated in either a 17-hour marathon experience or in 2-hour group psychotherapy sessions for two weeks. Both treatments decreased post-test scores on the MMPI on the "neurotic triad"; the marathon treatment effected change in specific attitudes toward criminal and drug subcultures.

1413. Rowan, J. (1983). *The reality game: A guide to humanistic counselling and therapy.* Boston: Routledge & Kegan Paul.
Critiques much group therapy research because of the vagueness of the concept of outcome, the inexperienced therapists used in many studies, the brevity of the therapy group in many of the studies, and the fact that many of the studies treated a narrow range of patients, for example, students with test anxiety. The author believes that the patient's choice behavior is the most significant human

quality, which is omitted in most of these investigations, and presents a new paradigm for doing humanistically valid research.

1414. Rozaire-Brown, B. C. (1987). Confidentiality as a group norm and its concomitant effect on self-disclosures by participants in personal growth groups. *Dissertation Abstracts International, 47*(07), 2462. (University Microfilm No. AAC86-19221)

1415. Rule, W. R., & McKenzie, D. H. (1977). Early recollections as a variable in group composition and in facilitative group behavior. *Small Group Behavior, 8,* 75-82.
Compared a group of 48 counselors divided according to Adler's concepts of more- and less-secure. Early recollection rating and early recollection security did not correlate with increased empathy and sincerity.

1416. Sachs, D. L. (1975). The impact of group counseling on self-esteem and other personality characteristics. *Dissertation Abstracts International, 35*(11), 7068A.

1417. Sadowski, A. F. (1990). Facilitating self-disclosure in group counseling through videotape pretraining. *Dissertation Abstracts International, 50*(11), 3486A.

1418. Safran, D. A. (1987). The efficacy of group psychotherapy in prison. *Dissertation Abstracts International, 47*(08), 3543. (University Microfilm No. AAC86-26536)

1419. Sage, J. A. W. (1984). Men's group therapy: A feminist and Jungian model. *Dissertation Abstracts International, 45*(03), 1029. (University Microfilm No. AAC84-12906)

1420. Sakai, C. E. (1993). Outcome differences in the treatment of major depression with Axis II disorders. *Dissertation Abstracts International, 54*(04), 2221. (University Microfilm No. AAC93-24588)

1421. Saltzberg, L. H. (1981). A comparison of RET group therapy, RET group therapy with bibliotherapy, and bibliotherapy only treatments. *Dissertation Abstracts International, 41*(07), 3018A.

1422. Salvendy, J. T., & Joffe, R. (1991). Antidepressants in group psychotherapy. *International Journal of Group Psychotherapy, 41,* 465-480.
Describes the impact of antidepressant drug therapy with patients in long-term group therapy experiencing a therapeutic impasse. Subjects reported improvement in mood, increased ability to think, plan and make decisions.

1423. Sanders, J. F., Orling, R. A., Brown, R., & Davis, B. (1993). Rational behavior training effectiveness for White and Nonwhite incarcerated felons. *Psychological Reports, 73,* 1056-1058.

1424. Sanders, M. J. (1986). Prediction of perceived effectiveness of therapeutic factors in group therapy with psychiatric inpatients using MMPI scores. *Dissertation Abstracts International, 46*(12), 4414. (University Microfilm No. AAC85-27062)

1425. Santarsiero, L. J. (1990). The effects of cognitive pretraining on cohesion and self-disclosure in small interpersonal learning groups: An analog study. *Dissertation Abstracts International, 50*(07), 3175B.

1426. Saporito, T. J. (1977). The effects of group size and leader style on level of empathic understanding and self-concept of members of an experiential course in group counseling. *Dissertation Abstracts International, 38*(03), 1234A.

1427. Saunders, D. G., & Hanusa, D. (1986). Cognitive-behavioral treatment of men who batter: The short-term effects of group therapy. *Journal of Family Violence, 1*(4), 357-372.
Ninety-two men who had abused women participated in a study of structured cognitive-behavioral group treatment for men who abuse women, consisting of 12 skill sessions and 8 process group sessions. Recorded subjects' pre- and post-therapy scores regarding attitudes toward women, anger, jealousy, and depression. The assessments were correlated with reports of violence by the partners. Presents changes in the subjects.

1428. Savage, C., & McCabe, O. L. (1973). Residential psychedelic (LSD) therapy for the narcotic addict: A controlled study. *Archives of General Psychiatry, 28,* 808-814.
Compared the rehabilitative effectiveness of LSD therapy during a six-week residential halfway house setting versus an outpatient clinic program with daily urine monitoring and weekly group psychotherapy. Throughout the first year after treatment, the LSD therapy group had greater abstinence than the control group.

1429. Sawyer, P. K. (1989). Group psychotherapy preparation with inpatients. *Dissertation Abstracts International, 50*(03), 1121. (University Microfilm No. AAC89-12749)

1430. Sayger, T. V., Szykula, S. A., & Sudweeks, C. (1992). Treatment side effects: Maternal positive and negative attributes of child-focused family therapy. *Child and Family Behavior Therapy, 14*(1) 1-9.

1431. Schacht-Lavine, L. J. (1982). The effectiveness of psychodrama in developing empathy: A training method using role reversal, doubling, and mirroring. *Dissertation Abstracts International, 43*(03), 676. (University Microfilm No. AAC82-19493)

1432. Schaffer, J. B., & Dreyer, S. F. (1982). Staff and inpatient perceptions of change mechanisms in group psychotherapy. *American Journal of Psychiatry, 139*(1), 127-128.
Results indicated a low correlation between what staff and patient perceive to be the two most important change mechanisms in group therapy.

1433. Schechter, W. M. (1992). Participants' learning styles, personality types and learning in a T-group. *Dissertation Abstracts International, 53*(02), 1110. (University Microfilm No. AAC92-18713)

1434. Schedler, D. E. (1980). The impact of the Ohlsen triad model of couples group counseling in treatment-training workshops for clergy and spouses. *Dissertation Abstracts International, 41*(06), 2459A.

1435. Scheidlinger, S. (1994). An overview of nine decades of group psychotherapy. *Hospital and Community Psychiatry, 45,* 217-225.

1436. Schindler, L., Hahlweg, K., & Revenstorf, D. (1983). Short- and long-term effectiveness of two communication modalities with distressed couples. *American Journal of Family Therapy, 11*(3), 54-64.
Compared 16 couples in a conjoint modality (CG), 19 in a conjoint group modality (CGM), and 17 in a waiting list control group. CM couples showed improvement in 5 of 7 outcome variables when compared to the control group, while the CGM couples improved on 2 of the 7 variables. At one year follow-up, both modalities' initial gains had substantially reduced.

1437. Schinke, S. P., & Rose, S. D. (1976). Interpersonal skill training in groups. *Journal of Counseling Psychology, 23*(5), 442-448.

1438. Schinke, S. P., Schilling, R. F., Kirkham, M. A., & Gilchrist, L. D. (1986). Stress management skills for parents. *Journal of Child and Adolescent Psychotherapy, 3*(4), 293-298.
Examined group stress management skills intervention with 13 mothers and 10 fathers of developmentally disabled children. Post-test and six month follow-up results showed that, compared to the no-intervention control group, the intervention parents had better attitudes toward their children and had improved ability to manage anger and cope with stress. Also, the observed interactions between intervention parents and their children were more positive.

1439. Schmidt, M. I. (1987). Forgiveness as the focus theme in group counseling. *Dissertation Abstracts International, 47*(11), 3985. (University Microfilm No. AAC87-05162)

1440. Schneider, J. A., & Agras, W. S. (1985). A cognitive behavioral group treatment of bulimia. *British Journal of Psychiatry, 146,* 66-69.
Examines the effectiveness of a cognitive-behavioral group therapy for bulimia with 13 women aged 17 to 51 years. Found significant changes in depression levels, attitudes, and assertiveness, and vomiting decreased dramatically.

1441. Schneider, K. S. (1975). Helpfulness of treatment and alcoholic characteristics. *Perceptual and Motor Skills, 41*(3), 690.
Alcoholic inpatients rated group therapy, the program in general, and being away from drinking as the most helpful treatment methods. In general, ratings of helpfulness were unrelated to such variables as age, number of previous hospitalizations, level of education, and score on Rotter's Internal-External Control Scale.

1442. Schneidman, B., & McGuire, L. (1976). Group therapy for non-orgasmic women: Two age levels. *Archives of Sexual Behavior, 5,* 239-247.

1443. Scholing, A., & Emmelkamp, P. M. (1993). Exposure with and without cognitive therapy for generalized social phobia: Effects of individual and group treatment. *Behaviour Research and Therapy, 31,* 667-681.

1444. Schramski, T. G., Feldman, C. A., Harvey, D. R., & Holiman, M. (1984). A comparative evaluation of group treatments in an adult correctional facility. *Journal of Group Psychotherapy, Psychodrama & Sociometry, 36,* 133-147.
      Male inmates in a medium-security prison received group treatments of either psychodrama, anger therapy, values clarification, or decision making; there was a no treatment control group. Each treatment had a positive effect on behavior. Psychodrama significantly helped bring about improved attitudes and significantly decreased distressing symptoms.

1445. Schrenk, L. (1986). Psychotherapists' attitudes toward alcoholics and their treatment: Toward development of a treatment model. *Dissertation Abstracts International, 47*(01), 389B.
      Evaluated psychotherapists' attitudes toward alcoholics and alcoholism treatment, the impact of alcoholism training on therapists' attitudes, and the effect of using familiar psychological terms to explain the Twelve Steps of Alcoholics Anonymous (AA) on therapists' attitudes toward AA.

1446. Schroeder, D. J., Bowen, W. T., & Twemlow, S. W. (1982). Factors related to patient attrition from alcoholism treatment programs. *International Journal of Addictions, 17*(3), 463-472.

1447. Schuh, M. G. (1981). The relationship of patient and therapist variables to group therapy recommendations. *Dissertation Abstracts International, 42*(03), 1190B.

1448. Schum, R. L. (1983). Group counseling in prison: Effects on locus of control attitudes and on adjustment behaviors. *Dissertation Abstracts International, 44*(06), 1977. (University Microfilm No. AAC83-23920)
      Compared Rotter Scale Locus of Control (LOC) scores and prison adjustment behavior (PAB) measures of young male prisoners in a federal prison who received either directive or nondirective group counseling; there was a no-treatment control condition. LOC score changes showed no difference among the groups, and there were no relationships between LOC attitudes and PAB measures.

1449. Schweigler, J. L. (1981). The effects of structured group therapy and assertion training on a female alcoholic population. *Dissertation Abstracts International, 41*(11), 4612A.

1450. Scott, M. J., & Stradling, S. G. (1987). Evaluation of a group programme for parents of problem children. *Behavioural Psychotherapy, 15*(3), 224-239.
      Examined the results of a behaviourally based parental assistance program for low income and state-dependent single parents. Pre- and post-testing indicated that the program significantly reduced parental depression, inward and outward irritability, the perceived number and intensity of child behavior problems, and the level of perceived child conduct problems, impulsivity, and anxiety. The subjects' child management skills significantly improved. The reduction in child behavior problems was maintained at three and six month follow-up, and

improvement in parental depression and irritability was maintained at three-month follow-up.

1451. Scurfield, R. M., Corker, T. M., Gongla, P. A., & Hough, R. L. (1984). Three post-Vietnam "rap/therapy" groups: An analysis. *Group, 8,* 3-21.
Vietnam combat veterans participated in three rap/therapy groups, each with a different type of facilitator and approach: a male psychiatrist with experience working with Vietnam veterans, a male psychiatrist with less experience in this area, or a male and female social worker. The groups were similar in how they functioned, what issues they discussed most, the major theme of the rap/therapy, and the time frames addressed.

1452. Sechrest, L., & Bootzin, R. (1975). Preliminary evaluation of psychologists in encounter groups. *Professional Psychology, 6*(1), 69-79.
Examined 257 psychologists and 315 undergraduates with regard to the prevalence and nature of encounter groups (EGs). Results indicate that "encounterists" (Es) tended to be younger and had obtained their highest degrees more recently than the "non-encounterist" control group members; Es also tended to have an Ed.D. rather than a Ph.D. Generally, Es held favorable attitudes toward EGs, but a substantial minority reported experiencing or witnessing adverse reactions.

1453. Seelye, E. E. (1979). Relationship of socioeconomic status, psychiatric diagnosis and sex to outcome of alcoholism treatment. *Journal of Studies on Alcohol, 40*(1), 57-62.
Examined data on age, gender, socioeconomic status (SES), psychiatric diagnosis, and therapeutic outcome on the first 100 admissions to the Alcoholism Treatment Unit of the New York Hospital, Cornell Medical Center. Fifty-four subjects were upper SES; the secondary diagnosis was psychoneurosis in 30 subjects and personality disorder in 49 subjects. The program consisted of individual psychotherapy, group therapy, Alcoholics Anonymous (AA) meetings, and drug therapy, if needed. Subject follow-up ranged from 2.5 months to 5 years.

1454. Seigel, S. M., Rootes, M. D., & Traub, A. (1977). Symptom change and prognosis in clinic psychotherapy. *Archives of General Psychiatry, 34,* 321-329.

1455. Seldman, M. L., & McBrearty, J. F. (1975). Characteristics of marathon volunteers. *Psychological Reports, 36*(2), 555-560.
Surveyed the extent of undergraduate interest in marathon groups and the personality characteristics of marathon volunteers (MVs). Compared levels of dependency and sense of well-being in MVs versus nonvolunteers from the same university. Findings suggest that MVs have a lower sense of well-being and greater needs for independence. Integrates results with previous findings and relates results to the controversy concerning marathon participants' level of adjustment.

1456. Self, M. C. (1990). Comparison of the effectiveness of two interventions for the treatment of agoraphobia. *Dissertation Abstracts International, 50*(10), 3158. (University Microfilm No. AAC90-05358)

1457. Sellschopp, R. A. (1977). Behavioral characteristics in inpatient group psychotherapy with psychosomatic patients. *Psychotherapy and Psychosomatics, 28,* 316-322.
Compares the group participation characteristics of 45 patients characterized as either psychoneurotic or psychosomatic. Psychosomatic patients showed greater emotional content and greater frequency of interaction, while psychoneurotic patients showed greater inner engagement and contributed more to group satisfaction.

1458. Serok, S., & Bar, R. (1984). Looking at Gestalt group impact: An experiment. *Small Group Behavior, 15,* 270-277.
Examined the effectiveness of Gestalt group therapy in increasing self-concept with thirty-three 25- to 35-year-olds. Compared to the control condition, self-concept and decisiveness significantly improved in the Gestalt group.

1459. Serok, S., Rabin, C., & Spitz, Y. (1984). Intensive Gestalt group therapy with schizophrenics. *International Journal of Group Psychotherapy, 34,* 431-450.
Schizophrenics assigned to Gestalt group therapy, when compared to the control group, showed some improvement in self- and other-perception and significant improvement in the presentation of body image.

1460. Serok, S., & Zemet, R. M. (1983). An experiment of Gestalt group therapy with hospitalized schizophrenics. *Psychotherapy: Theory, Research and Practice, 20,* 417-424.
Examined level of reality differentiation and perception in schizophrenics in a Gestalt group therapy (GG) compared to a control group (CG). Rorschach results showed a significant increase in one measurement of reality perception in the GG versus the CG.

1461. Setaro, J. L. (1986). Aerobic exercise and group counseling in the treatment of anxiety and depression. *Dissertation Abstracts International, 47*(06), 2633B.
Placed 180 subjects experiencing mild to moderate depression and anxiety in one of six groups: cognitive group counseling (CG); aerobic exercise (AE); non-aerobic activity (nonA); cognitive group counseling and aerobic exercise (CG+AE); cognitive group counseling and a non-aerobic activity (CG+nonA); and, no treatment. CG was more effective than either AE or nonA in treating both depression and anxiety. The combination of CG and an activity, either aerobic or non-aerobic, more effectively treated depression than did CG, but this was not the case with anxiety.

1462. Sexton, H. (1993). Exploring a psychotherapeutic change sequence: Relating process to inter-sessional and post-treatment outcome. *Journal of Consulting and Clinical Psychology, 61,* 128-136.

1463. Shaffer, C. S., Shapiro, J., Sank, L. I., & Coghlan, D. J. (1981). Positive changes in depression, anxiety, and assertion following individual and group cognitive behavior therapy intervention. *Cognitive Therapy and Research, 5*(2), 149-157.

1464. Shakir, S. A., Volkmar, F. R., Bacon, S., & Pfefferbaum, A. (1979). Group psychotherapy as an adjunct to lithium maintenance. *American Journal of Psychiatry, 136,* 455-456.
Subjects with bipolar affective illness who received lithium maintenance and long-term group psychotherapy reported positive experiences with group therapy.

1465. Shapiro, D. A., Caplan, H. L., Rohde, P. D., & Watson, J. P. (1975). Personal questionnaire changes and their correlates in a psychotherapeutic group. *British Journal of Medical Psychology, 48,* 207-215.
Examined changes in group members over the course of group psychotherapy, finding no general pattern of improvement. There was suggestion of an inverse relationship between changes during therapy and those occurring after termination of therapy.

1466. Shapiro, J., Sank, S. I., Shaffer, C. S., & Conovan, D. C. (1982). Cost effectiveness of individual vs group cognitive behavior therapy for problems of depression and anxiety in an HMO population. *Journal of Clinical Psychology, 38,* 674-677.
Compared the use of interpersonal group therapy, individual cognitive behavior therapy, and a cognitive behavior group therapy with 44 outpatients with anxiety and or depression. All groups significantly improved and no differential effects were found.

1467. Shapiro, J. L. (1978). *Methods of group psychotherapy and encounter: A tradition of innovation.* Itasca, IL: F. E. Peacock.
Reviews research on group psychotherapy produced in the previous 25 years and uses the studies to make points regarding the importance of methodology and study design.

1468. Shapiro, N. (1992). The self-help group as an intervention in postpartum depression. *Dissertation Abstracts International, 53*(02), 1077B.
Reviews the history and literature of the self-help movement and discusses its role in the delivery of human services. Presents a historical overview of the evolution of group psychotherapy; discusses ways in which professionals and self-help groups can be mutually beneficial, and how training of facilitators might offer a paradigm for a new alliance between professionals and the self-help movement.

1469. Shaskan, D. A., & Moran, W. L. (1985). Influence of group psychotherapy: A thirty-eight year follow-up. *American Journal of Psychoanalysis, 45,* 93-94.
Describes a 38 year follow-up with 9 subjects and therapists from a counseling group. Found low and high measures of avoiding, along with high measures of being engaged.

1470. Shatin, L., & Kymissis, P. (1975). A study of transactional group image therapy. *American Journal of Art Therapy, 15,* 13-18.
Describes group sessions, phases of group development, individual changes, and test results of seven participants aged 22 to 50 years in transactional group image therapy at a mental hygiene clinic.

1471. Shaul, S. L. (1981). Loneliness: A comparison of two group counseling strategies with adults. *Dissertation Abstracts International, 42*(04), 1560A.
Divided 66 adults into one of three conditions, each with two groups: the first condition was patterned after cognitive-behavioral treatment, the second was supportive, nondirective treatment patterned after Rogers; the third was a delayed-treatment control. Groups met once weekly for eight weeks. Found strong support for the effectiveness of group counseling treatment in the management of loneliness and depression in adults. Detected no significant differences between the post-test means of the two treatment conditions. The study confirmed the utility of considering loneliness as a construct related to, but separate from depression and low self-esteem.

1472. Shawver, L., & Lubach, J. (1977). Value attribution in group psychotherapy. *Journal of Consulting and Clinical Psychology, 45,* 228-236.
Examines participants' verbalizations in group therapy sessions for value attribution—target person, those they blamed, and those not involved.

1473. Shealy, R. C. (1979). The effectiveness of various treatment techniques on different degrees and durations of sleep-onset insomnia. *Behavior Research and Therapy, 17,* 541-546.
Compared the use of five group therapy techniques with 40 female insomniacs: relaxation without muscle tension, stimulus control plus relaxation without muscle tension, placebo, self-monitoring, and waiting list. The two relaxation groups showed significantly greater improvement in sleep-onset latency.

1474. Sheets, C. H. (1989). Co-dependency and the healing process. *Dissertation Abstracts International, 49*(10), 4560. (University Microfilm No. AAC88-27201)

1475. Shen, W. W., Sanchez, A. M., & Huang, T. (1984). Verbal participation in group therapy: A comparative study on New Mexico ethnic groups. *Hispanic Journal of Behavioral Sciences, 6*(3), 277-284.
Alcoholic inpatient subjects in group therapy consisted of 102 White, 126 Mexican American, and 37 Native American individuals. White subjects exhibited significantly higher verbal participation than did the other subjects. Discusses factors related to this and implications for therapy with ethnic groups.

1476. Shepherd, R. H. (1992). Group psychotherapy for wife abusers: Client variables that affect treatment outcome. *Dissertation Abstracts International, 52*(10), 3533A.

1477. Sherry, P., & Hurley, J. R. (1976). Curative factors in psychotherapeutic and growth groups. *Journal of Clinical Psychology, 32*(4), 835-837.

1478. Shewchuk, L. A. (1977). Preliminary observations on an intervention program for heavy smokers. *International Journal of the Addictions, 12,* 323-336.

1479. Shihadeh, E. S., & Nedd, A. N. (1974). The perceptions of penitentiary inmates and staff. *Journal of Social Psychology, 92,* 217-224.

1480. Shipley, R. H. (1977). Effect of a pre-group collective project on the cohesiveness of inpatient therapy groups. *Psychological Reports, 41,* 79-85.

1481. Shipton, B., & Spain, A. (1980). The influence of client fees on evaluations by clients of counseling outcome. *Psychology: A Quarterly Journal of Human Behavior, 17,* 1-4.
Compared client evaluations of counseling outcome for clients asked to pay versus those paying nothing. Found no differences between the two groups.

1482. Shirreff, N. R. (1989). Group psychotherapy with mentally retarded persons using a mediation model. *Dissertation Abstracts International, 50*(01), 353. (University Microfilm No. AAC89-08198)

1483. Siegel, G. S. (1987). Effects of multiple family support group therapy on measures of adaptability, cohesion, family strengths, and coping strategies for families with a psychiatrically hospitalized child. *Dissertation Abstracts International, 48*(03), 612A.

1484. Siemens, H. (1993). A Gestalt approach in the care of persons with HIV. *Gestalt Journal, 16*(1), 91-104.
Evaluated Gestalt methodology as support for gay males who were HIV seropositive. Used two treatment and one control group to examine psychosocial influences on the subjects' biomedical status; the first treatment group was modeled on stress-management (SM) and the second on experiential-Gestalt methodology (EG). One goal of group therapy was for subjects to see the foreground as being the HIV-positiveness and the background as being the whole life. Data on the impact of therapy on the immune system indicate slightly better results for EG subjects than for other subjects. Both therapy approaches were comparable within most parameters, such as mood change, sense of well-being, and depression. However, the EG subjects showed a slightly smaller decrease in T-cell numbers than did the SM subjects.

1485. Sigrell, B. (1992). The long-term effects of group psychotherapy: A thirteen year follow-up study. Special Section: Research and the group psychotherapist. *Group Analysis, 25,* 333-352.

1486. Silbergeld, S. (1975). Changes in serum dopamine-b-hydroxylase activity during group psychotherapy. *Psychosomatic Medicine, 37,* 352-367.
Describes increases in the level of dopamine-b-hydroxylase in five married couples participating in group psychotherapy.

1487. Silon, B. (1987). A group therapy treatment model for panic disorder and agoraphobia with an Adlerian emphasis. *Dissertation Abstracts International, 47*(11), 4665. (University Microfilm No. AAC87-02974)

1488. Silver, G. M. (1978). Systematic presentation of pre-therapy information in group psychotherapy: Its relationship to attitude and behavioral change. *Dissertation Abstracts International, 38*(09), 4481. (University Microfilm No. AAC77-32501)

1489. Silver, R. J., & Conyne, R. K. (1977). Effects of direct experience and vicarious experience on group therapeutic attraction. *Small Group Behavior, 8*(1), 83-92.

Evaluated the relative effectiveness of direct (DE) versus vicarious experience (VE) in therapy sessions in bringing about positive feelings for the group experience. DE was associated with significantly more positive feelings for the group experience than was VE.

1490. Sinclair-Brown, W. (1981). A TA/redecision psychotherapy program for mothers who physically abuse and/or seriously neglect their children. *Dissertation Abstracts International, 42*(02), 788B.

1491. Sinfneos, P. E. (1975). Criteria for psychotherapeutic outcome. *Psychotherapy and Psychosomatics, 26*(1), 49-58.
Used twelve outcome criteria to evaluate various psychotherapies at a clinic. Examination of 53 patients treated by 14 therapists in short- and long-term therapies revealed impressive changes in motivation for change, self-esteem, and interpersonal relations in the short-term psychotherapy group.

1492. Singleton, S. P., Neale, A. V., Hess, J. W., & Dupuis, M. H. (1987). Behavioral contracting in an urban health promotion projects. Special Issue: Research on preventive behavior: An overview. *Evaluation and the Health Professions, 10,* 408-437.
Examined behavioral contracting in individual and group counseling with 223 adults at high risk for cardiovascular problems.

1493. Sisson, C. J., Sisson, P. J., & Gazda, G. M. (1977). Extended group counseling with psychiatry residents: HIM and Bonney Scale compared. *Small Group Behavior, 8,* 351-360.
Compared descriptions of group processes obtained from the Hill Interaction Matrix (HIM) and the Bonney Scale in a counseling group of 10 psychiatric residents.

1494. Sisson, P. J., Sisson, C. J., & Gadza, G. M. (1973). Extended group counseling with psychiatry residents: An interaction process analysis. *Small Group Behavior, 4,* 466-475.
Describes the interaction process of a counseling group consisting of 10 psychiatric residents.

1495. Sklare, G., Petrosko, J., & Howell, S. (1993). The effect of pre-group training on members' level of anxiety. *Journal for Specialists in Group Work, 18*(3), 109-114.

1496. Skoloda, T. E., Alterman, A. I., & Gottheil, E. (1974). Drinking pattern on a fixed interval drinking decisions program. *Newsletter for Research in Mental Health and Behavioral Sciences, 16*(2), 31-32.
Describes the application of the Fixed Interval Drinking Decisions (FIDD) program to 98 male alcoholics. The three stages are: predrinking, in which alcohol is not available; drinking decisions, in which subjects must decide whether or how much to drink; and post-drinking, with alcohol again unavailable. Individual and group psychotherapy was initiated during the first phase. Forty-three subjects remained abstinent, 37 drank moderately, and 18 drank regularly. Analyzes and discusses drinking patterns.

1497. Slavin, R. L. (1993). The significance of here-and-now disclosure in promoting cohesion in group psychotherapy. *Group, 17,* 143-150.
Examined here-and-now disclosure with there-and-then disclosure for comparative effects on group cohesion with 88 patients in group psychotherapy. Here-and-now disclosure was a greater predictor of cohesion.

1498. Slocum, Y. S. (1987). A survey of expectations about group therapy among clinical and nonclinical populations. Special issue: Integration of research and practice in the field of group psychotherapy. *International Journal of Group Psychotherapy, 37*(1), 39-54.

1499. Smillie, A. L. (1991). The effects of group interventions on attitudes and stress in parents of learning-disabled and educable mentally impaired adolescents. *Dissertation Abstracts International, 52*(03), 808A.
Evaluated the effects of a support group, counseling group, and educational group on the attitudes and stress levels of parents of learning-disabled and educable mentally impaired adolescents. Results indicated significant change in parents' attitudes but no significant decrease in parents' stress levels. There were no significant findings regarding birth order, type of disability, and income level of family. Discusses the need for future research.

1500. Smith, C. W. (1977). Releasing pressure caps: Using TA with women whose husbands have had strokes. *Transactional Analysis Journal, 7*(1), 55-57.
TA program with wives of stroke victims emphasized concepts such as existence of choices, personal needs for support and recognition, awareness of significant changes in the marriage relationship, and identifying and entering into an anger/grieving process. TA program results included relief of pressures from guilt, anger, grief, and a shift from acceptance of a primarily caretaking role to the construction of a personally meaningful life. These changes were accompanied by a marked alleviation of previously reported physical and emotional stress.

1501. Smith, J. W., Frawley, P. J., & Polissar, L. (1991). Six- and twelve-month abstinence rates in inpatient alcoholics treated with aversion therapy compared with matched inpatients from a treatment registry. *Alcoholism Clinical and Experimental Research, 15*(5), 862-870.
Subjects who were treated for alcoholism in an inpatient multimodal program that included aversion therapy (AT), were matched, post hoc, on 17 baseline variables with a control condition from a national treatment registry. The control received inpatient treatment emphasizing individual and group counseling but not AT. Subjects treated with AT had significantly higher alcohol abstinence rates at 6 and 12 months.

1502. Smith, R. R., Jenkins, W. O., Petko, C. M., & Warner, R. W. (1979). An experimental application and evaluation of Rational Behavior Therapy in a work release setting. *Journal of Counseling Psychology, 26,* 519-525.

1503. Soeken, D. R. (1979). Feedback in short-term married couples group psychotherapy. *Dissertation Abstracts International, 40*(05), 2899A.

188 Research on Group Treatment Methods

1504. Soeken, D. R., Manderscheid, R. W., Flatter, C. H., & Silbergeld, S. (1981). A controlled study of quantitative feedback in married couples brief group psychotherapy. *Psychotherapy: Theory, Research and Practice, 18*(2), 204-216. Used a two-group, two-stage design to assess the impact of delayed written feedback on the process and outcome of brief group psychotherapy for married couples. Results indicated that therapy plus feedback led to the assessment of greater behavioral change than therapy alone; feedback variables showed more significant changes in the expected directions than did the nonfeedback variables; compared to therapy alone, therapy plus feedback more effectively increased the degree of congruence between self- and peer-rating, and between self- and therapist-ratings.

1505. Sokoloff, D. W. (1990). Effects of personality disorder on outcome in short-term group therapy for bulimia nervosa. *Dissertation Abstracts International, 51*(04), 2075. (University Microfilm No. AAC90-23683)

1506. Soldz, S., Budman, S., & Demby, A. (1992). The relationship between main actor behaviors and treatment outcome in group psychotherapy. *Psychotherapy Research, 2,* 52-62.

1507. Soldz, S., Budman, S., Demby, A., & Feldstein, M. (1990). Patient activity and outcome in group psychotherapy: New findings. *International Journal of Group Psychotherapy, 40,* 53-62.
Examined the relationship between patient pre-therapy symptom status and patient verbal activity during time-limited group psychotherapy with 90 non-psychotic patients aged 21 to 25. Found that subjects who were more troubled before therapy began were more likely to become main actors during therapy.

1508. Soldz, S., Budman, S., Demby, A., & Merry, J. (1993). Representation of personality disorders in circumplex and five-factor space: Explorations with a clinical sample. *Psychological Assessment, 5,* 41-52.

1509. Solomon, G. S., & Ray, J. B. (1984). Irrational beliefs of shoplifters. *Journal of Clinical Psychology, 40,* 1075-1077.
Examines a psychoeducational group counseling program designed to reduce recidivism with 94 adult shoplifters. At one year follow-up, there was only one repeat offense.

1510. Solomon, S. D. (1982). Individual versus group therapy: Current status in the treatment of alcoholism. *Advances in Alcohol and Substance Abuse, 2,* 69-86.

1511. Somers, J. E. (1991). The effects of a program of instructional counseling for optimism. *Dissertation Abstracts International, 52*(06), 2030. (University Microfilm No. AAC91-29573)

1512. Spence, S. H. (1985). Group versus individual treatment of primary and secondary female orgasmic dysfunction. *Behavior Research and Therapy, 23,* 539-548.
Examined the effectiveness of individual versus group behavioral therapy with 50 orgasmically dysfunctional women, aged 22 to 51 years. Both treatment

conditions improved more than the control group, and participants in individual therapy improved slightly more than those in group therapy.

1513. Spencer, K. R. (1989). Group treatment: Adult females incestuously abused as children. *Masters Abstracts International, 27*(03), 348. (University Microfilm No. AAC13-36199)
Used group therapy to increase assertiveness in adult females, who experienced incest as children, with mixed results.

1514. Spencer, P. G., Gillespie, C. R., & Ekisa, E. G. (1983). A controlled comparison of the effects of social skills training and remedial drama on the conversational skills of chronic schizophrenic inpatients. *British Journal of Psychiatry, 143,* 165-172.

1515. Spiegel, D., & Bloom, J. R. (1983). Group therapy and hypnosis reduce metastatic breast carcinoma pain. *Psychosomatic Medicine, 45*(4), 333-339.

1516. Spiegel, D., & Glafkides, M. C. (1983). Effect of group confrontation with death and dying. *International Journal of Group Psychotherapy, 33*(4), 433-447.

1517. Spinal, P. (1984). Group resistance and leader intervention: An interactional analysis. *Small Group Behavior, 15,* 417-424.
Examines group leader interventions used to break down group resistance within a group of six women at a battered women's shelter.

1518. Spira, J. L. (1992). Educational therapy: Existential, educational, and counseling approaches to behavioral medicine intervention. *Dissertation Abstracts International, 53*(05), 1410. (University Microfilm No. AAC92-28864)

1519. Spiro, R. D. (1992). A comparison of three techniques utilized in conjoint group psychotherapy to improve the sexual and interactive attitudes of heterosexual dyads. *Dissertation Abstracts International, 53*(01), 574. (University Microfilm No. AAC92-07298)

1520. Spitz, H. I., Kass, F., & Charles, E. (1980). Common mistakes made in group psychotherapy by beginning therapists. *American Journal of Psychiatry, 137*(12), 1619-1621.
Surveyed 42 senior group therapy supervisors about beginning therapists' most and least common errors. Most common mistakes were related to the handling of patients who reject help, who monopolize the group, or complain; to the discussion of transference issues; and to the desire to be liked by the group. Least common mistakes were related to violating confidentiality; to consciously disliking the group; and to handling length of sessions and group member hospitalizations.

1521. Spitzer, A., Webster-Stratton, C., & Hollinsworth, T. (1991). Coping with conduct-problem children: Parents gaining knowledge and control. *Journal of Clinical Child Psychology, 20*(4), 413-427.

1522. Srivastava, K. I. (1985). Socio-psychological factors of stammering and the problem of rehabilitation of statements. *Indian Psychological Review, 29,* 24-34.

Examined the effect of group therapy on the stammering of 80 subjects, 10 years or older. Subjects showed improved adjustment in family, schools, offices and other public places. Found stammering to be related to physical and sociopsychological factors.

1523. Stallone, T. M. (1993). The effects of psychodrama on inmates within a structured residential behavior modification program. *Journal of Group Psychotherapy, Psychodrama & Sociometry, 46,* 24-31.
Inmates with adjustment problems participated in psychodrama group therapy within a structured residential behavior modification program, with positive results.

1524. Stalonas, P. M., & Kirschenbaum, D. S. (1985). Behavioral treatments for obesity: Eating habits revisited. *Behavior Therapy, 16,* 1-14.
Examined three perspectives from which 32 obese patients, aged 14 to 53, were monitored: self-report, therapist rating, and spouse rating. All three perspectives showed equally strong and positive associations with weight loss.

1525. Stanton, H. E. (1975). Change in self-insight during an intensive group experience. *Small Group Behavior, 6*(4), 487-493.
Measured the effect of an intensive weekend group experience on subjects' self-insight, as defined by Gross's Self-Insight Scale (SIS). The scale's reliability and validity data showed a reliability coefficient of 0.92 and a 0.57 point-biserial correlation. Experimental subjects demonstrated significant differences on the pre- and post-tests, whereas control subjects' measures remained unchanged. Concluded that the SIS has considerable validity and reliability as a measure of insight.

1526. Stanton, H. E. (1976). Hypnosis and encounter group volunteers: A validation study of the sensation-seeking scale. *Journal of Consulting and Clinical Psychology, 44*(4), 692.

1527. Staunton, G. J. (1981). An account of a research project designed to investigate the effects of preparing patients for group psychotherapy. *British Journal of Projective Psychology and Personality Study, 26,* 17-19.
Describes findings that suggest the importance of supportive rather than instructive preparation for patients about to enter group therapy.

1528. Stehouwer, R. S., Bultsma, C. A., & Blackford, I. T. (1985). Developmental differences in depression: Cognitive-perceptual distortion in adolescent versus adult female depressives. *Adolescence, 20,* 291-299.
Examined the success of group psychotherapy in reducing the cognitive-perceptual distortion of 50 depressed 13 to 54 year old female psychiatric inpatients; compared cognitive-perceptual distortion in the adolescent and adult subjects.

1529. Stein, E., & Brown, J. D. (1991). Group therapy in a forensic setting. *Canadian Journal of Psychiatry, 36,* 718-722.
Examined the capacity of 30 violent criminals from 25 to 62 years old, who had been found not guilty by reason of insanity, to develop group dynamics in

therapy. Found that the subjects possessed personality characteristics that precluded the development of therapeutic group dynamics.

1530. Steinfeld, G. J., & Mabli, J. (1974). Perceived curative factors in group therapy by residents of a therapeutic community. *Criminal Justice and Behavior, 1,* 278-288.

1531. Steinmetz, J. L., Lewinsohn, P. M., & Antonuccio, D. O. (1983). Prediction of individual outcome in a group intervention for depression. *Journal of Consulting and Clinical Psychology, 51,* 331-337.
Describes group therapy with 75 subjects suffering from depressive disorder. All subjects improved, but those who improved the most had greater perceptions of mastery and greater reading ability, were younger, conceived of their families as supportive, and were not receiving additional treatment.

1532. Stephens, R. S., & Roffman, R. A. (1993). Adult marijuana dependence. In J. S. Baer, G. A. Marlatt, & R. J. McMahon (Eds.), *Addictive behaviors across the life span: Prevention, treatment, and policy issues* (pp. 202-218). Newbury Park, CA: Sage.
Reviews research on personality characteristics of marijuana users and the effectiveness of treatment programs; presents research in support of the authors' proposed group treatment model.

1533. Stephenson, N. L., Boudewyns, P. A., & Lessing, R. A. (1977). Long-term effects of peer group confrontation therapy used with polydrug abusers. *Journal of Drug Issues, 7,* 135-149.

1534. Stern, M. J., Plionis, E., & Kaslow, L. (1984). Group process expectations and outcome with post-myocardial infarction patients. *General Hospital Psychiatry, 6*(2), 101-108.

1535. Steuer, J. L., & Clarke, E. O. (1982). Family support groups within a research project on dementia. *Clinical Gerontologist, 1*(1), 87-95.
Examined three support groups for caregivers of patients with senile dementia as part of a larger study of Alzheimer's disease. Two of the groups were closed and time limited, and one was structured and open ended. The most supportive and cohesive group was unstructured and time limited.

1536. Stevens, E. V., & Salisbury, J. D. (1984). Group therapy for bulimic adults. *American Journal of Orthopsychiatry, 54,* 156-161.
Describes the use of group therapy, which combined behavioral methods and psychodynamic understanding, in treating women with bulimia. Five of the eight subjects dramatically reduced bingeing and purging episodes.

1537. Stewart, J. E. (1986). Rehabilitation of the violence-prone criminal: An evaluation of a group therapy approach. *Dissertation Abstracts International, 46*(08), 2826. (University Microfilm No. AAC85-22993)

1538. Stier, R. J. (1978). The effect of verbal reinforcement on self-referent statements in an experimental study of group counseling. *Dissertation Abstracts International, 38*(07), 4060. (University Microfilm No. AAC77-27980)

1539. Stiles, W. B., Tupler, L. A., & Carpenter, J. C. (1982). Participants' perceptions of self-analytic group sessions. *Small Group Behavior, 13,* 237-254. Examined changes within a group therapy cohort across sessions, describing subjects' reactions on three dimensions: evaluation, potency, and activity.

1540. Stockton, R., Rhode, R. I., Haughey, J. (1992). The effects of structured group exercises on cohesion, engagement, avoidance, and conflict. *Small Group Research, 23*(2), 155-168.
At the beginning of each of six weekly group sessions, subjects participated in a structured group exercise, and at the end of each session, subjects completed the Attraction Scale and the Group Climate Questionnaire. A repeated measures ANOVA indicated significant interaction between time and structure for cohesion, engagement, and avoidance. The main effect of structure was significant only for the conflict variable.

1541. Stockton, R., Robison, F. F., & Morran, D. K. (1983). A comparison of the HIM-B with the Hill Interaction Matrix model of group interaction styles: A factor analysis study. *Journal of Group Psychotherapy, Psychodrama & Sociometry, 36,* 449-467.

1542. Stokes, J. P., & Tait, R. C. (1979). The Group Incidents Questionnaire: A measure of skill in group facilitation. *Journal of Counseling Psychology, 26,* 250-254.

1543. Stone, W. N., Rodenhauser, P., & Markert, R. J. (1991). Combining group psychotherapy and pharmacotherapy: A survey. *International Journal of Group Psychotherapy, 41*(4), 449-464.
Results indicated that overall, clinicians favored including medicated patients in their outpatient psychotherapy groups.

1544. Stone, W. N., & Rutan, J. S. (1984). Duration of treatment in group psychotherapy. *International Journal of Group Psychotherapy, 34,* 93-109.
Examined the dropout rates of 147 adult patients attending group therapy. Individual therapy concurrent with, or prior to, group therapy contributed to subjects staying in group therapy.

1545. Stoudenmire, J. (1973). Group counseling in hospital trainees coming from "culturally deprived" backgrounds. *Journal of Community Psychology, 1,* 295-296.

1546. Strassberg, D. S., Roback, H. B., Anchor, K. N., & Abramowitz, S. I. (1975). Self-disclosure in group therapy with schizophrenics. *Archives of General Psychiatry, 32,* 1259-1261.
Schizophrenics in group therapy who self-disclosed more made less progress in therapy than those who divulged less.

1547. Streitman, S. R. (1981). Other and self-perceptions of the social behavior of depressed patients in psychotherapy. *Dissertation Abstracts International, 42*(03), 1195. (University Microfilm No. AAC81-19870)

1548. Strupp, H. H., & Bloxom, A. L. (1973). Preparing lower-class patients for group psychotherapy: Development and evaluation of a role-induction film. *Journal of Consulting and Clinical Psychology, 41*, 373-384.

1549. Subich, L. M., & Coursol, D. H. (1985). Counseling expectations of clients and non-clients for group and individual treatment modes. *Journal of Counseling Psychology, 32*, 245-251.
Examined those already in group or individual counseling, those seeking group or individual counseling, and those not seeking counseling for differences in counseling expectations.

1550. Subramanian, K. (1986). Group training for the management of chronic pain in interpersonal situations. Special issue: Research in social group work. *Social Work with Groups, 9*(3), 55-69.
Used 21 chronic pain patients to examine a group pain management treatment program that emphasized modeling and behavioral rehearsal. Results indicated that this treatment effectively reduced dysfunctions and could help increase coping skills.

1551. Suga, L. J. (1987). Control of chronic low-back pain: Treatment differentials. *Dissertation Abstracts International, 47*(10), 4316B.
Divided 29 subjects into three groups, receiving five sessions of: hypnotherapy with psychoeducation, cognitive behavioral therapy with psychoeducation, or psychoeducation only. No significant reduction in reported pain occurred as a function of treatment, psychoeducation or time. Level of hypnotic susceptibility neither enhanced nor interfered with any treatment effect.

1552. Sultan, F. E. (1984). The female offender's adjustment to prison life: A comparison of psychodidactic and traditional supportive approaches to treatment. Special Issue: Gender issues, sex offenses, and criminal justice: Current trends. *Journal of Offender Counseling, Services and Rehabilitation, 9*, 49-56.
Randomly assigned new female inmates in a correctional facility to a support group, a psychodidactic-intervention support group, or a control group. When compared to the control group, the two treatment groups reported a significant decrease in psychosomatic symptoms; when compared to one another, the treatment groups showed no significant differences.

1553. Sumlin, D. L. (1979). An affective-cognitive group counseling procedure for use with parents of handicapped children: A comparative study of its effectiveness for changing attitudes and training parents in a method of child guidance. *Dissertation Abstracts International, 39*(07), 4186A.

1554. Sutton, C. (1992). Training parents to manage difficult children: A comparison of methods. *Behavioural Psychotherapy, 20*(2), 115-139.
Parents of preschool children participated in one of four parent training conditions: group, home visit, telephone, or waiting list control. Assessments conducted pre- and post-intervention and at 12 to 18 month follow-up indicated clinical improvement for all three active intervention conditions, compared to the control condition. However, there were no significant differences among the three active intervention conditions at post-intervention and follow-up.

1555. Swetz, A., Jr. (1983). The differential effects of the length of intervals between sessions on the process and outcome of time limited group psychotherapy with incarcerated males. *Dissertation Abstracts International, 44*(06), 222. (University Microfilm No. AAC83-23593)

1556. Tableman, B., Marciniak, D., Johnson, D., & Rodgers, R. (1982). Stress management training for women on public assistance. *American Journal of Community Psychology, 10*(3), 357-367.

1557. Tallant, S., Rose, S. D., & Tolman, R. M. (1989). New evidence for the effectiveness of stress management training in groups: Special Issue: Empirical research in behavioral social work. *Behavior Modification, 13*(4), 431-466.
Examined the effectiveness of stress management treatment in a structured small group setting, which included teaching the cognitive-behavioral skills of relaxation, cognitive restructuring, and assertiveness. Treatment subjects evidenced significant pre- to post-test reductions for all dependent measures of stress, compared to the wait-list control subjects.

1558. Tallant, S. H. (1986). Meta-analysis: Statistical considerations and applications in small group treatment research. *Social Work with Groups, 9,* 43-53.
Reviews and discusses the advantages of using meta-analytic procedures in small group treatment research, and suggests minimal criteria for the inclusion of studies in a meta-analysis.

1559. Tavormina, J. B. (1975). Relative effectiveness of behavioral and reflective group counseling with parents of mentally retarded children. *Journal of Consulting and Clinical Psychology, 43*(1), 22-31. Evaluated the relative effectiveness of behavioral versus reflective group counseling for mothers of children with mental retardation. Both types of counseling had a beneficial effect relative to the untreated controls, but the behavioral method resulted in a significantly greater magnitude of improvement. The consistency of these results across measures strongly suggests the superiority of the behavioral technique for counseling parents of children with mental retardation.

1560. Taylor, C. B., Farquhar, J. W., Nelson, E., & Agras, S. (1977). Relaxation therapy and high blood pressure. *Archives of General Psychiatry, 34*(3), 339-342.
Divided 31 subjects receiving medical treatment for essential hypertension into three groups: relaxation therapy (RT), nonspecific therapy (NonST), and medical treatment only (MT). At post-treatment, the RT group showed a significant reduction in blood pressure compared with the NonST and MT, even when those subjects whose medication was increased were excluded from the data analysis. At the six month follow-up, the RT group showed a slight decrement in treatment effects while both NonST and MT groups showed continued improvement.

1561. Taylor, G. S. (1983). The effect of nonverbal doubling on the emotional response of the double. *Journal of Group Psychotherapy, Psychodrama & Sociometry, 36*(2), 61-68.

1562. Taylor, W. F., & Hoedt, K. C. (1974). Classroom-related behavior problems: Counsel parents, teachers, or children? *Journal of Counseling Psychology, 21,* 3-8.
Compared the effectiveness of group counseling with parents and teachers and group counseling with students alone in reducing classroom behavior problems of 372 children. Analysis showed that the indirect approach with the adults was more effective than the direct approach with the children.

1563. Telch, C. F. (1985). A comparison of coping skills instruction and support group counseling in alleviating psychological distress among cancer patients. *Dissertation Abstracts International, 46*(04), 1349B.
Compared the relative efficacy of a comprehensive coping skills training approach (CST) versus supportive group therapy (SGT) in alleviating cancer patients' psychological distress among cancer patients. CST included relaxation and stress management, communication training, cognitive restructuring and problem-solving, feelings management, and pleasant activities. Behavioral strategies included homework assignments, self-monitoring, goal setting, self-reinforcement, participant modeling and behavioral rehearsal. Results indicated a marked and consistent superiority of CST intervention over SGT and the no treatment condition. Additionally, CST subjects significantly improved compared to their own pre-test levels.

1564. Telch, M. J., Hannon, R., & Telch, C. F. (1984). A comparison of cessation strategies for the outpatient alcoholic. *Addictive Behaviors, 9*(1), 103-109.
Examined the effectiveness of three treatments in disrupting alcoholics' drinking responses: group-administered covert sensitization (CVS), supportive group therapy (SGT), and a nonspecific control treatment. Although SGT was significantly more effective than the other conditions in reducing the subjects' reported daily drinking, there were no significant differences found in the measures of blood alcohol concentrations or in the subjects' ratings of frequency of urges to drink. Over time, all three groups' urge rating reports significantly improved.

1565. Telch, M. J., Lucas, J. A., Schmidt, N. B., Hanna, H. H. (1993). Group cognitive-behavioral treatment of panic disorder. *Behavior Research and Therapy, 31,* 279-287.
Examined the effectiveness of cognitive-behavioral group therapy with 34 panic disorder patients. At post-treatment, 85% of treated subjects were panic free, compared to 30% of controls.

1566. Templer, D. I., Ruff, C. F., & Simpson, K. (1974). Alleviation of high death anxiety with symptomatic treatment of depression. *Psychological Reports, 35,* 216.
Thirty-one hospitalized depressed patients received drug, group and occupational therapy, designed solely to reduce depression; this treatment decreased patients' levels of depression and death anxiety.

1567. Tepperman, J. H. (1985). The effectiveness of short-term group therapy upon the pathological gambler and wife. *Journal of Gambling Behavior, 1,* 119-130.
Examined the effectiveness of conjoint group therapy with 20 pathological gamblers and their wives. Found no significant differences in defensiveness,

marital compatibility and communication between those participating in therapy and the controls.

1568. Teri, L., & Lewinsohn, P. M. (1986). Individual and group treatment of unipolar depression: Comparison of treatment outcome and identification of predictors of successful treatment outcome. *Behavior Therapy, 17,* 215-228.
Compared group and individual therapy in treating 66 subjects with unipolar depression. Subjects in both conditions improved with no differences between the two groups.

1569. Terkelson, C. (1976). Making contact: A parent-child communication skill program. *Elementary School Guidance and Counseling, 11*(2), 89-99.
Six elementary school students and 6 parents attended 12 counseling sessions aimed at developing skills in listening, conflict resolution, and value identification. Parents and children were counseled separately during the first six sessions and together in the remaining six sessions. Comparison of pre- and post-treatment responses showed some positive gains in parent-child communication. The children reported a greater change in their parents' behavior toward them than the parents reported about themselves.

1570. Textor, M. R. (Ed.). (1989). *The divorce and divorce therapy handbook.* Northvale, NJ: Jason Aronson.
Presents limited in-program data on adolescent members of the therapy program (consumer satisfaction, common themes, and factors related to self-reported adjustment difficulties).

1571. Thakar, B. (1975). An evaluation of the effectiveness of rehabilitated schizophrenics as co-leaders in a selected group counseling situation. *Dissertation Abstracts International, 35*(08), 4200. (University Microfilm No. AAC74-25024)

1572. Thomas, J. L. (1991). Examining self-acceptance of learning disability in young adults through counseling and vocational outcomes. *Dissertation Abstracts International, 52*(06), 3279B.

1573. Threadcraft, H. L. (1993). Mixed gender co-leadership in group counseling with adult women survivors of child sexual abuse. *Dissertation Abstracts International, 54*(01), 95. (University Microfilm No. AAC93-13075)
Compared self-concept and depression scores of adult women who were sexually abused as children and who participated in group therapy with either women co-facilitators or male-female co-facilitators. Results suggest improved self-concept and depression scores in the male-female co-facilitation group.

1574. Tiedemann, G. L., & Johnston, C. (1992). Evaluation of a parent training program to promote sharing between young siblings. *Behavior Therapy, 23,* 299-318.
Evaluates the effectiveness of individual and group formats of a parenting program in promoting sharing between young siblings. Parents were given information and taught behavioral techniques. The observations and reports of sharing behavior evinced the program's positive effects, sustained over a six week follow-up period.

1575. Todres, R. (1982). Professional attitudes, awareness and use of the self-help groups. *Prevention in Human Services, 1*(3), 91-98.
Surveyed 308 professional mental and physical health practitioners in Toronto about self-help programs. Practitioners indicated that they were somewhat familiar with the groups in their community, held favorable attitudes toward them, and were prepared to refer their clients to groups that may be helpful to them.

1576. Tolman, R. M., & Bhosley, G. (1989). A comparison of two types of pregroup preparation for men who batter. Special Issue: Advances in group work research. *Journal of Social Service Research, 31*(2), 33-43.

1577. Tolman, R. M., & Rose, S. D. (1989). Teaching clients to cope with stress: The effectiveness of structured group stress management training. Special Issue: Advances in group work research. *Journal of Social Service Research, 13*(2), 45-66.

1578. Tomsovic, M. (1976). Group therapy and changes in self-concept of alcoholics. *Journal of Studies on Alcohol, 37*(1), 53-57.
Administered the Tennessee Self-Concept Scale to 162 male alcoholic veterans in a rehabilitation program before and after they had participated in 1 of 2 types of group therapy, an open-ended elective group (OG) or a closed encounter group (CG). The CG subjects had significantly greater improvements in self-concept than the OG subjects, who only improved on the Physical Self scale. For both groups, the relatively highest and lowest gains were on the Physical Self and Social Self scales, respectively.

1579. Toomey, T. C., & Sanders, S. (1983). Group hypnotherapy as an active control strategy in chronic pain. *American Journal of Clinical Hypnosis, 26*(1), 20-25.
Examined a group-based hypnotic approach designed to generate coping strategies with five chronic pain subjects. Pre- and post-testing measures indicated a decrease in reported subjective estimates of pain. Discusses defective cognitive-attitudinal coping skills as characteristic of chronic pain states.

1580. Toro, P. A., Rappaport, J., & Seodman, E. (1987). Social climate comparison of mutual help and psychotherapy groups. *Journal of Consulting and Clinical Psychology, 55,* 430-431.

1581. Toseland, R. W., & Hacker, L. (1985). Social workers' use of self-help groups as a resource for clients. *Social Work, 30*(3), 232-237.
Results of a survey to 247 professional social workers indicate that respondents were generally familiar with and participated in self-help groups (SHGs). A significant number of respondents thought that SHGs generally discourage members from seeking professional help and did support social worker involvement with SHGs.

1582. Toseland, R. W., Kabat, D., & Kemp, K. (1983). Evaluations of a smoking cessation group treatment program. *Social Work Research and Abstracts, 19,* 12-19.

Used a quasi-experimental design to evaluate group treatment for 39 long-term heavy smokers; 47% stopped smoking and 38% reduced their smoking.

1583. Towers, D. A. (1986). Cognitive focusing as an attentional self-regulation strategy in the treatment of substance abuse. *Dissertation Abstracts International, 47*(05), 2146B.

1584. Townsend, J. E. (1981). The effects of ego deficits on parenting an MBD child, examined in parental group therapy. *Dissertation Abstracts International, 42*(05), 2300A.

1585. Townsend, R. E., House, J. F., & Addario, D. (1975). A comparison of biofeedback, mediated relaxation and group therapy in the treatment of chronic anxiety. *American Journal of Psychiatry, 132*(6), 598-601.
Compared the effectiveness of two types of treatment for chronic anxiety: biofeedback-mediated electromyographic (EMG) relaxation versus group psychotherapy. Results indicated significant decreases in the feedback group's EMG levels, mood disturbance, trait anxiety, and state anxiety; no such decreases occurred in the psychotherapy group. Suggests that EMG feedback can be an important adjunct therapy for chronic anxiety.

1586. Tracey, D. A., Briddell, D. W., & Wilson, G. T. (1974). Generalization of verbal conditioning to verbal and nonverbal behavior: Group therapy with chronic psychiatric patients. *Journal of Applied Behavior Analysis, 7,* 391-402.
Hospitalized psychotic females received token rewards, contingent on two types of positive verbal statements, those about available optional activities, and those about people. Positive activities statements generalized to actual activity participation; positive people statements did not generalize.

1587. Tracy, D. (1986). Group hypnotherapy: A treatment for depression. *Dissertation Abstracts International, 47*(04), 1748. (University Microfilm No. AAC86-14922)

1588. Trammell, W. B. (1986). The effect of observing psychotherapy groups on learning multiple-attending skills. *Dissertation Abstracts International, 47*(04), 1749. (University Microfilm No. AAC86-14580)

1589. Treadwell, T. W., Leach E., & Stein, S. (1993). The Social Networks Inventory: A diagnostic instrument measuring interpersonal relationships. *Small Group Research, 24*(2), 155-178.

1590. Trifone, J. M. (1994). Education and empowerment: The development of a ten-week group therapy model for the treatment of battered women. *Dissertation Abstracts International, 55*(02), 608B.

1591. Tschuschke, V. (1986). Relationships between psychological and psychophysiological variables in the group therapeutic setting. *International Journal of Group Psychotherapy, 36,* 305-312.

1592. Turner, J. A. (1982). Comparison of group progressive-relaxation training and cognitive-behavioral group therapy for chronic low back pain. *Journal of Consulting and Clinical Psychology, 50*(5), 757-765.

1593. Ukeritis, M. D. (1978). A study of value convergence in a group psychotherapy setting. *Dissertation Abstracts International, 38*(09), 4488. (University Microfilm No. AAC78-01842)

1594. Unger, R. A. (1993). Influences affecting therapist attitudes and approaches to managing conflict in psychotherapy groups. *Dissertation Abstracts International, 54*(03), 100. (University Microfilm No. AAC93-20487)

1595. Upper, D., Livingston, L., Conners, G. J., & Olans, J. (1982). Evaluating a social and coping skills training groups for psychiatric day hospital patients. *International Journal of Partial Hospitalization, 1*(3), 203-211.

1596. Vachon, M. L. (1980). A controlled study of self-help intervention for widows. *American Journal of Psychiatry, 137,* 134-138.
Examines an intervention program that provided emotional support and practical assistance to 68 widows. Program subjects followed the same general course of bereavement as controls, but their progress was accelerated.

1597. Valle, S. K., & Marinelli, R. P. (1975). Training in human relations skills as a preferred mode of treatment for married couples. *Journal of Marriage and Family Counseling, 1*(4), 359-365.
Ten couples experiencing marital difficulties participated in either a traditional therapy group (TTG), which emphasized cathartic release and problem solving, or a training group (TG) consisting of a systemic didactic and experiential approach, which emphasized the ability to discriminate and communicate helpfully. Results indicate significant improvement in interpersonal skills and overall functioning in the TG as compared to the TTG.

1598. Van Boemel, G. B., & Rozee, P. D. (1992). Treatment for psychosomatic blindness among Cambodian refugee women. Special Issue: Refugee women and their mental health: Shattered societies, shattered lives: II. *Women and Therapy, 13,* 239-266.

1599. Van Dyck, B. J. (1980). An analysis of selection criteria for short-term group counseling clients. *Personnel and Guidance Journal, 59,* 226-230.
Describes five short-term counseling groups in which quality of communication, goal specificity, goal identification, and willingness to discuss problems openly were significantly related to counseling outcomes.

1600. VanderVoort, D. J., & Fuhriman, A. (1991). The efficacy of group therapy for depression: A review of the literature. *Small Group Research, 22,* 320-338.

1601. Vandewater, S. R. (1982). The social organization of group therapy sessions: An analysis of client-therapist interaction in a community mental health center. *Dissertation Abstracts International, 42*(08), 3780.

1602. Vandewater, S. R. (1983). Discourse processes and the social organization of group therapy sessions. *Sociology of Health and Illness, 5,* 275-296.
Describes the social organization, hierarchical and sequential organization of activities of 48 group therapy sessions involving 17- to 30-year-olds.

1603. Vannicelli, M. (1989). *Group psychotherapy with adult children of alcoholics: Treatment techniques and countertransference considerations.* New York: Guilford Press.
Comments on the paucity of research studies regarding group treatment of this category of patient, adult children of alcoholics, and on the inadequacy of the few studies in the literature.

1604. Vera, M. I. (1993). Group therapy with divorced persons: Empirically evaluating social work practice. *Research on Social Work Practice, 3*(1), 3-20.

1605. Verinis, J. S. (1980). Alcoholic inpatients' evaluation of different group experiences. *Psychological Reports, 46*(3, Pt 2) 1155-1158.
Evaluated open-ended discussion versus structured-behavioristic group experiences for the presence or absence of certain curative factors and for the usefulness of each type of group. Both groups were evaluated positively and results indicated that each group had something specific to offer.

1606. Vicary, J. R., & Good, R. (1983). The effects of a self-esteem counseling group on male prisoners' self-concept. *Journal of Offender Counseling, Services and Rehabilitation, 7,* 107-117.
Studied the effects on young male inmates of a self-esteem workshop that stressed family related self-concept. Found a significant increase in family related self-esteem, but not in other types of self-concept.

1607. Videka, S. L. (1982). Effects of participation in a self-help group for bereaved parents: Compassionate Friends. *Prevention in Human Services, 1,* 69-77.
Examined personal growth and depression levels in bereaved parents who were involved, in differing degrees, with Compassionate Friends groups. Those who were most involved with this self-help group were more likely to sustain a sense of positive personal growth than those who were involved to a lesser degree; there were no differences in the area of depression.

1608. Vidmar, L. A. L. (1985). A multidimensional psychotherapy for women incest victims. *Dissertation Abstracts International, 46*(01), 317. (University Microfilm No. AAC85-07081)

1609. Viljoen, G. (1993). The experience of interaction by the inpatient during short-term group psychotherapy. *Masters Abstracts International, 32*(01), 348.

1610. Vogel, J. P. (1981). A qualitative approach to the process of insight in psychodrama psychotherapy. *Dissertation Abstracts International, 41*(12), 4695. (University Microfilm No. AAC81-10163)

1611. Voigt, H., & Weininger, R. (1992). Intervention style and client progress in time-limited group psychotherapy for adults sexually abused as children. *Psychotherapy, 29,* 580-585.
Examined activating and (AIs) stabilizing interventions (SIs) in group therapy with women who had been sexually abused as children. During initial sessions, SIs were more effective than AIs but by the fourth session, SIs were less effective than AIs. AIs were more effective with the third to sixth sessions of therapy.

1612. von Rad, M. (1979). Comments on theory and therapy of psychosomatic patients with a follow-up study. *Psychotherapy and Psychosomatics, 32,* 118-127.

1613. Vostanis, P., & O'Sullivan, D. (1992). Evaluation of therapeutic factors in group psychotherapy by therapists in training. Special Section: Research and the group psychotherapist. *Group Analysis, 25,* 325-332.
Compared the perceptions of outpatients, therapists in training, and therapists with extensive experience, in evaluating therapeutic factors in group psychotherapy. The perceptions of therapists in training were closer to those of the outpatients than to the perceptions of the experienced therapists.

1614. Wagoner, J. L., & Piazza, N. J. (1993). Group therapy for adult substance abusers on probation. *Journal of Offender Rehabilitation, 19*(3-4), 41-56.

1615. Wahl, D. J. (1986). Group counseling and mediation: Similarities in conflict resolution processes and conflict intervention methods. *Dissertation Abstracts International, 46*(12), 3607A.
Examined group counseling and mediation, two conflict resolution processes using a trained neutral party. Presented specific characteristics to identify the group stages involved in the conflict resolution process, and to establish similarities between group counseling and mediation. Methods examined included statements used for bridging, confronting, gatekeeping, identifying, informing, interpreting, questioning, summarizing, and supporting.

1616. Waldo, M. (1986). Group counseling for military personnel who battered their wives. *Journal for Specialists in Group Work, 11*(3), 132-128.
Twenty-three military personnel who had abused their spouses were treated with small support groups that used communication, conflict resolution, and other skills to manage anger. Evaluated the therapy's effectiveness with pre- and post-test measures.

1617. Walker, B. A. (1977). Group counseling to effect changes in personality variables for therapist trainees. *Educational Research Quarterly, 2*(3), 70-79.
Investigated how self-report test measures of dogmatism, flexibility and nonauthoritarianism related to leader and peer ratings of these same variables.

1618. Walker, C. (1977). Effect of group psychotherapy on bereavement with spouses of dying cancer patients. *Dissertation Abstracts International, 38*(10), 5049B.

1619. Walker, R. B., & Latham, W. L. (1977). Relationship of a group counseling course, hours in counselor education, and sex to empathic understanding of counselor trainees. *Counselor Education and Supervision, 16,* 269-174.

1620. Walker, W. B., & Franzini, L. R. (1985). Low-risk aversive group treatments, physiological feedback, and booster sessions for smoking cessation. *Behavior Therapy, 16,* 263-274.
Compared the use of taste-satiation and focused-smoking techniques in a smoking cessation program. Taste-satiation was more effective than focused-smoking techniques in reducing or eliminating smoking.

1621. Wallace, S. A. (1993). Health risk appraisal counseling: Effect on employee health behaviors, beliefs, and locus-of-control. *Dissertation Abstracts International, 54*(04), 1247. (University Microfilm No. AAC93-14308)

1622. Walls, N. R. (1985). Assessment of rape survivors' adaptation to assault and a comparison of two types of group therapy for rape survivors. *Dissertation Abstracts International, 46*(05), 1703. (University Microfilm No. AAC85-08023)

1623. Walsh, J. A., & Phelan, T. W. (1974). People in crisis: An experimental group. *Community Mental Health Journal, 10,* 3-8.

1624. Walsh, P. J. (1994). Empathy and therapist theoretical orientation. *Dissertation Abstracts International, 55*(03), 1196. (University Microfilm No. AAC94-21231)

1625. Waring, E. M., Stalker, C. A., Carver, C. M., & Gitta, M. Z. (1991). Waiting list controlled trial of cognitive marital therapy in severe marital discord. *Journal of Marital and Family Therapy, 17*(3), 243-256.

1626. Washington, T. M. M. (1993). Comparison of the effectiveness of individual versus group counseling on reducing low density lipoprotein cholesterol levels. *Masters Abstracts International, 31*(01), 285.

1627. Watkins, J. T., Noll, G. A., & Breed, G. R. (1975). Changes toward self-actualization. *Small Group Behavior, 6*(3), 272-281.
Examined the impact of length and number of sessions in producing positive results in sensitivity group sessions. Results indicated that neither the marathon nor massed group encounter was superior in producing positive results.

1628. Watson, J. P., & Lacey, J. H. (1974). Therapeutic groups for psychiatric in-patients. *British Journal of Medical Psychology, 47,* 307-312.
Twelve psychiatric inpatients reported more anxiety before and after group sessions than before and after control periods. Inpatients also reported more anxiety after, rather than before, group sessions.

1629. Watterson, J. M. (1994). A model for the treatment of sex offenders in a community mental health setting. *Dissertation Abstracts International, 54*(11), 5995. (University Microfilm No. AAC94-13245)
Examined a community-based group therapy program for treatment of sex offenders, using the MMPI-2 and the Tennessee Self-Concept Scale (Form C) for measurement, and a waiting list control group for comparison. Those who had completed more therapy sessions manifested more significant decreases in psychopathological variables and more significant increases in self-concept, and gave more honest responses.

1630. Webster, D., & Schwartzberg, S. L. (1992). Patients' perception of curative factors in occupational therapy groups. *Occupational Therapy in Mental Health, 12,* 3-24.
Thirty-five short-term inpatients rated the most valued aspects of occupational group therapy. Cohesion was the most valued factor; instillation of hope and altruism were rated highly.

1631. Weide, U. (1986). The effect of classical psychodrama on anxiety and depression: Psychodrama with incarcerated public offenders. *Dissertation Abstracts International, 46*(09), 2818. (University Microfilm No. AAC85-25609) Evaluated psychodrama's effectiveness in decreasing anxiety and depression in incarcerated inmates.   Volunteers participated in one of three conditions: classical psychodrama treatment, an attention placebo consisting of substance abuse education, or no treatment. Anxiety and depression levels decreased in all subjects in the three groups.

1632. Weiner, M. F. (1984). Outcome of psychoanalytically oriented group psychotherapy. *Group, 8,* 3-12.
Discusses 100 outpatients' responses to group therapy.   Most subjects also required individual therapy or medication in conjuncture with group therapy.

1633. Weiner, M. F. (1992). Group therapy reduces medical and psychiatric hospitalization. *International Journal of Group Psychotherapy, 42,* 267-275.

1634. Weininger, R. B. (1991). Intervention style and client progress in time-limited group psychotherapy for adults sexually abused as children. *Dissertation Abstracts International, 52*(02), 1087. (University Microfilm No. AAC91-20018) The effectiveness of active and stabilizing interventions in group therapy with women vary with the needs and phases of group development.   Work with groups of women who were sexually abused as children showed that at the beginning and end of the series of sessions, when there was greater need for structure and support, stabilizing interventions were more effective, while toward the middle of the series, the more challenging, activating interventions were more productively used by the group.

1635. Weinstock, M. (1974). Toward a treatment of alienation: A comparison of group counseling approaches. *Dissertation Abstracts International, 35*(05), 2785.

1636. Weiss, C. R. (1988). Cognitive-behavioral group therapy for the treatment of premenstrual distress. *Dissertation Abstracts International, 49*(06), 2389. (University Microfilm No. AAC88-12402)

1637. Welch, R. R. (1990). Altering expectations about group counseling and its effect on the development of attraction to group in growth groups. *Dissertation Abstracts International, 50*(07), 1951. (University Microfilm No. AAC89-25331)

1638. Wemhoff, R. T. (1978). The effects of two different counseling orientations and procedures on self-actualization of group counseling participants. *Dissertation Abstracts International, 39*(06), 3386A.

1639. Wenzel, L. B. (1989). Coping with illness-related stress during recovery from early-stage gynecologic cancer. *Dissertation Abstracts International, 50*(04), 1659B.

1640. Wertlieb, D., Budman, S., Demby, A., & Randall, M. (1982). The stress of marital separation: Intervention in a health maintenance organization. *Psychosomatic Medicine, 44*(5), 437-448.

1641. Wertz, R. T. (1981). Veterans Administration cooperative study on aphasia: A comparison of individual and group treatment. *Journal of Speech and Hearing Research, 24*(4), 580-594.

1642. West, E. D. (1982). Randomized comparative trial of a ward discussion group. *British Journal of Psychiatry, 141,* 76-80.
Describes the ineffectiveness of a discussion group used with 74 psychiatric patients.

1643. Wetzel, M. C., Kinney, J. M., Beavers, M. E., Harvey, R. I., & Urbancik, G. W. (1976). Action Laboratory: Behavioral group therapy in a traditional context. *International Journal of Group Psychotherapy, 26,* 59-70.

1644. Wheeler, I., O'Malley, K., Waldo, M., & Murphey, J. (1992). Participants' perception of therapeutic factors in groups for incest survivors. *Journal for Specialists in Group Work, 17,* 89-95.

1645. Whipple, A. G. (1991). A comparison of the self-concept and career maturity of recovering alcoholics before and after participation in the employment program for recovering alcoholics (EPRA). *Dissertation Abstracts International, 52*(03), 858A.

1646. Whitaker, D. S. (1985). *Using groups to help people.* London: Routledge & Kegan Paul.
Discourages use of outcome evaluation as redundant to prove the effectiveness of group treatment, but worthwhile to determine who benefits most and why. When conducted for the approved purposes, the author maintains that outcome evaluation should focus on (a) identifying outcome variables, (b) assessing whether change has taken place, and (c) demonstrating that outcome is related to the group experience. Process-outcome research can be used primarily for exploratory purposes.

1647. White, J., Keenan, M., & Brooks, N. (1992). Stress control: A controlled comparative investigation of large group therapy for generalized anxiety disorder. *Behavioural Psychotherapy, 20*(2), 97-113.

1648. White, W. C., & Boskind-White, M. (1981). An experimental-behavioral approach to the treatment of bulimarexia. *Psychotherapy: Theory, Research and Practice, 18,* 501-507.
Describes a multidimensional group therapy program used with 14 bulimarexic women. Subjects' scores on the Body Cathexis Scale improved significantly, and 10 subjects eliminated or reduced binge behaviors.

1649. Whitney, D., & Rose, S. D. (1989). The effect of process and structured content on outcome in stress management groups. Special Issue: Advances in group work research. *Journal of Social Service Research, 13*(2), 89-104.
Examined stress reduction under 4 conditions: group process (GP), high structure (HS), combined process and structure (GP&HS), and waiting-list control (WLC). GP, HS, and GP&HS fared significantly better than the WLC on one dependent measure, the hassles scale (Lazarus, 1981). While not

statistically significant, the conditions that enhanced group process, viz., GP and GP&HS, were generally superior to those that did not.

1650. Wieder, D., & Hicks, J. (1973). A study of motivational techniques in the long-term sheltered workshop. *Training School Bulletin, 70,* 43-50.
Compared small group counseling versus immediate reinforcement of client productivity in a rehabilitation workshop with 66 clients. Neither treatment increased client productivity, but group therapy participants increased social interaction significantly.

1651. Wierzbicki, M., & Bartlett, T. S. (1987). The efficacy of group and individual cognitive therapy for mild depression. *Cognitive Therapy and Research, 11*(3), 337-342.
Two therapy groups used A. T. Beck and colleagues' (1979) cognitive therapy for depression in either group therapy (GT), individual therapy (IT), with nine subjects in each treatment condition, or a control condition (CC). Results from MANOVA demonstrated a significant treatment by time interaction. IT subjects improved more than subjects in the other groups. GT subjects showed greater improvement than the CC subjects, with no significant differences between these two groups.

1652. Wijesinghe, O. B., & Wood, R. R. (1976). A repertory grid study of interpersonal perception within a married couples' psychotherapy group. *British Journal of Medical Psychology, 49,* 287-293.

1653. Wilfley, D. E., Agras, W. S., Telch, C. F., & Rossiter, E. M. (1993). Group cognitive-behavioral therapy and group interpersonal psychotherapy for the non-purging bulimic individual: A controlled comparison. *Journal of Consulting and Clinical Psychology, 61,* 296-305.
Examined the roles of eating behavior and interpersonal factors in an effort to understand and treat the non-purging bulimic person. Compared group cognitive-behavioral and group interpersonal psychotherapy with 56 women diagnosed as bulimic. Both groups showed significant improvement in binge eating.

1654. Willage, D. E. T. (1981). The effects of informing patients of the limits of confidentiality on group psychotherapy. *Dissertation Abstracts International, 41*(09), 3595. (University Microfilm No. AAC81-06554)

1655. Willett, E. A. (1973). Group therapy in a methadone treatment program: An evaluation of changes in interpersonal behavior. *International Journal of the Addictions, 8,* 33-39.

1656. Williams, R. C. (1981). A clinical study of the effects of prior structuring on cohesiveness in counseling groups. *Dissertation Abstracts International, 42*(06), 2555. (University Microfilm No. AAC81-27176)

1657. Williams, S. M. (1980). A comparison of the effectiveness of psychotherapy and behavior therapy for incarcerated sex offenders. *Dissertation Abstracts International, 41*(02), 704.

Studied Rational Behavior Therapy's effect on subjects in a work release setting, as measured by three life-career management skills: interpersonal relations, money management, and leisure time activities. One group was treated with, and another was treated without significant others; there was a no-treatment control group. All treated subjects showed significant improvement in all skill areas, while no-treatment subjects demonstrated insignificant change. Greater improvement was indicated for those in treatment with significant others versus those in treatment alone.

1658. Wilson, B., & Moffat, N. (1992). The development of group memory therapy. In B. Wilson & N. Moffat (Eds.), *Clinical management of memory problems* (2nd ed., pp. 243-273). San Diego: Singular Publishing Group.
The Rivermead memory group (RMG), consisting of 12 men and 8 women patients, completed the Prose Recall Test, the Digit Span Test, Paired Associate Learning, The Rivermead Behavioral Memory Test, The Kapur and Pearson Rating Scale, and a version of Harris' questionnaire on the use of memory aids. The RMG showed no specific benefits compared to a matched control condition.

1659. Wilson, C. J., Muzekari, L. H., Schneps, S. A., & Wilson, D. M. (1974). Time-limited group counseling for chronic home hemodialysis patients. *Journal of Counseling Psychology, 21*(5), 376-379.
Compared the effects of six group counseling (GC) sessions versus a comparable no-treatment control (NTC) on 18 chronic home hemodialysis subjects. Scores on Rotter's Internal-External Control Scale and selected California Personality Inventory Scales revealed no significant between group differences. The GC subjects showed pre- to post-testing changes on two of the measures. A one year follow-up of 11 of the subjects suggested that hemodialysis patients use the defense mechanism of denial to adapt to their condition.

1660. Wilson, G. L., & Wilson, L. J. (1991). Treatment acceptability of alternative sex therapies: A comparative analysis. *Journal of Sex and Marital Therapy, 17,* 35-44.

1661. Wilson, G. T. (1989). Behavior therapy. In R. J. Corsini & D. Wedding (Eds.), *Current psychotherapies* (4th ed., pp. 241-270). Itasca, IL: F. E. Peacock.
Presents research strategies used by behavior therapists to evaluate their group work.

1662. Winick, C., & Weiner, M. F. (1986). Professional activities and training of AGPA members: A view over 2 decades. *International Journal of Group Psychotherapy, 36*(3), 471-476.
Current survey responses of AGPA members concerning their backgrounds and professional activities, when compared with 1961 and 1971 results, showed that during the last 20 years, a broader base of acceptance of group psychotherapy had occurred in the U.S.

1663. Winter, D. A., & Trippett, C. J. (1977). Serial change in group psychotherapy. *British Journal of Medical Psychology, 50,* 341-348.

1664. Winters, N. L. (1984). The effects of sociometric grouping on socializing behavior of psychiatric outpatients. *Dissertation Abstracts International, 44*(07), 2286. (University Microfilm No. AAC83-25923)

1665. Wirshing, W. C., Marder, S. R., Eckman, T. A., & Liberman, R. P. (1992). Acquisition and retention of skills training methods in chronic schizophrenic outpatients. *Psychopharmacology Bulletin, 28,* 241-245.

1666. Wise, T. N., Cooper, J. N., & Ahmed, S. (1982). The efficacy of group therapy for patients with irritable bowel syndrome. *Psychosomatics, 23*(5), 465-469.
For six weeks, 20 adults with irritable bowel syndrome participated in group therapy that incorporated behavioral and didactic techniques. Found a significant reduction in dysphoric emotions, despite the persistence of somatic complaints. Discusses results in the context of subject locus of control and field dependence-independence.

1667. Withersty, D., & Jolley, M. (1974). Effectiveness of family presence in therapy: A preliminary study. *Family Therapy, 1*(3), 257-262.
Examined whether the involvement of family members in psychiatric treatment is a significant factor in recidivism and re-employment rate. Studied family presence or absence at five different points during treatment. An analysis of the records of 80 inpatients revealed no difference between those patients who had family members present during hospitalization and those who did not. Implications for the value of this therapeutic technique are noted.

1668. Wogan, M. (1977). Influencing interaction and outcomes in group psychotherapy. *Small Group Behavior, 8,* 25-46.
Discusses the success of greater leader activity in increasing group oriented discussion with 52 group therapy members.

1669. Wold, P., & Steger, J. (1976). Social class and group therapy in a working class population. *Community Mental Health Journal, 12,* 335-341.
Examines the characteristics of 279 twenty- to forty-year-olds who applied to a clinic for therapy. Social class did not affect the assignment of applicants to therapy, and 45% of those referred to group therapy stayed in therapy for at least two years.

1670. Woldenberg, L. (1976). Psychophysical changes in feeling therapy. *Psychological Reports, 39,* 1059-1062.

1671. Wolf, E. M., & Crowther, J. H. (1992). An evaluation of behavioral and cognitive-behavioral group interventions for the treatment of bulimia nervosa in women. *International Journal of Eating Disorders, 11,* 3-15.

1672. Wolf, P. R., & DeBlassie, R. R. (1982-1983). A comparison of holistic and behavioral group approaches in facilitating weight loss, personality change, and self-concept change in adult women. *Journal of Obesity and Weight Regulation, 2,* 195-202.
Compared the effectiveness of behavioral and holistic group therapy with 96 overweight adult women. Both therapy groups lost significantly more weight

and changed significantly more on a physical self-concept scale than did the control group.

1673. Wollersheim, J. P. (1977). Follow-up of behavioral group therapy for obesity. *Behavior Therapy, 8,* 996-998.

1674. Wollersheim, J. P., & Wilson, G. L. (1991). Group treatment of unipolar depression: A comparison of coping, supportive, bibliotherapy, and delayed treatment groups. *Professional Psychology: Research and Practice, 22,* 496-502. Examined group treatment of depression by comparing coping, supportive, bibliotherapy, and delayed treatment groups; randomly assigned subjects to different conditions. All conditions showed significant therapeutic gains, sustained at follow-up.

1675. Wolpert, J. (1990). Differential response to chemical dependency treatment among alcoholics with or without additional psychiatric disorders. *Dissertation Abstracts International, 51*(05), 2665B.

1676. Wong, E. L. (1976). Role of recent life changes upon participants in group psychotherapy. *Dissertation Abstracts International, 37*(04), 1934. (University Microfilm No. AAC76-22407)

1677. Wood, R. Y. (1984). Partners of post-mastectomy women: Needs assessment and client participation in the development of specifications for an educational curriculum. *Dissertation Abstracts International, 45*(03), 819B.

1678. Woods, M. M. (1980). Relevance, activity, and inter-member familiarity as parameters of group structure: Effects on early group development. *Dissertation Abstracts International, 41*(02), 705.

1679. Wooley, S. C., Blackwell, B., & Winget, C. (1978). A learning theory model of chronic illness behavior: Theory, treatment, and research. *Psychosomatic Medicine, 40,* 379-401.
Used a learning model of chronic illness behavior in treating subjects referred to inpatient psychosomatic care. This model emphasizes social reinforcement and avoidance of activities integral to psychosomatic symptomatology. Preliminary results showed improvement in some areas, and at one year follow-up, improvement or failure corresponded to whether the subject had returned to an intact family or to the medical care system, respectively.

1680. Wooley, S. C., & Lewis, K. G. (1987). Multifamily therapy within an intensive treatment program for bulimia. *Family Therapy Collections, 20,* 12-24.
Describes an intensive treatment program for bulimia in which six to eight women lived in a hotel apartment for 3.5 weeks and were responsible for their own food preparation. They also participated in daily food and psychotherapy groups, daily body image therapy, individual sessions, educational seminars and family therapy. Results indicate that the program was successful.

1681. Worthen, V. K., & Malony, H. N. (1973-1974). Potential strengths: A comparative study of positive and negative oriented marathon group experiences for couples. *Interpersonal Development, 4,* 243-253.

1682. Wright, F., Hoffman, X. H., & Gore, E. M. (1988). Perspectives on scapegoating in primary groups. *Group, 12,* 33-44.

1683. Wright, P. J. (1989). Grief recovery: A comparison of group therapies for widows. *Dissertation Abstracts International, 50*(01), 357. (University Microfilm No. AAC88-27685)

1684. Wright, T. L., & Duncan, D. (1986). Attraction to group, group cohesiveness, and individual outcome: A study of training groups. *Small Group Behavior, 17,* 487-492.
Examines four training groups consisting of 8 men and 19 women; group outcome was related to attraction to the group.

1685. Wynne, A. R. (1978). Movable group therapy for institutionalized patients. *Hospital and Community Psychiatry, 29,* 516-519.
As part of a normalization program, chronic psychotic inpatients received group therapy in parks and restaurants in the community. After one year, 50% of the 40 subjects had been discharged; after three years, 75% had been discharged. Discusses rate of discharge, emotional growth, and symptom improvement.

1686. Yalom, I. D. (1974). Group therapy and alcoholism. *Annals of the New York Academy of Sciences, 233,* 85-103.

1687. Yalom, I. D. (1977). The impact of a weekend group experience on individual therapy. *Archives of General Psychiatry, 34,* 399-415.
Compared the use of affect-arousing groups and Gestalt therapy groups in a weekend group experience with thirty-three 20- to 63-year-olds. At six week follow-up, both groups showed greater improvement in individual therapy than did the controls. However, at 12 weeks, there were no demonstrable differences.

1688. Yalom, I. D. (1978). Alcoholics in interactional group therapy: An outcome study. *Archives of General Psychiatry, 35*(4), 419-425.

1689. Yalom, I. D. (1985). *The theory and practice of group psychotherapy* (3rd ed.). New York: Basic Books.
Although the author prefers idiographic measures (individually tailored measures) over nomothetic measures, and while increased student research sophistication helps students better evaluate the therapy they use and the research of others, he believes it important that students be aware of the usual outcome study that employs nomothethic methods.

1690. Yassen, J., & Glass, L. (1984). Sexual assault survivors groups: A feminist practice perspective. *Social Work, 29,* 252-257.
Assessed the benefits of group therapy co-lead by women for women who had been raped, finding post-group benefits in the areas of self-esteem, assertiveness and personal relationships.

1691. Yates, A. J., & Sambrailo, F. (1984). Bulimia nervosa: A descriptive and therapeutic study. *Behavior Research and Therapy, 22,* 503-517.

Examined the use of cognitive behavioral group therapy with 24 women diagnosed with bulimia nervosa. Although anxiety and depression scores decreased, causality was questionable.

1692. Yoak, M., Chesney, B. K., & Schwartz, N. H. (1985). Active roles in self-help groups for parents of children with cancer. Special issue: Active roles of parents. *Children's Health Care, 14*(1), 38-45.

1693. Youmans, R. D. (1974). Differences in behavior related to participation and nonparticipation in jail group counseling. *Dissertation Abstracts International, 35*(01), 113. (University Microfilm No. AAC74-14320)

1694. Zarit, S. H., Anthony, C. R., & Boutselis, M. (1987). Interventions with caregivers of dementia patients: Comparison of two approaches. *Psychology and Aging, 2*, 225-232.
Examined the relative utility of family counseling and support groups in relieving stress for caregivers of patients with dementia. Both treatments succeeded in significantly reducing stress, which was maintained at the one year follow-up.

1695. Zastowny, T. R., Janosik, E., Trimborn, S., & Milanese, E. (1982). Cognitive orientation: Identified curative factors, and depression and predictors for treatment outcomes in group therapy programs for alcoholism. *Psychological Reports, 50*(2), 477-478.

1696. Zeiss, R. A., Christensen, A., Levine, A. G. (1978). Treatment for premature ejaculation through male-only groups. *Journal of Sex and Marital Therapy, 4*, 139-143.

1697. Zettle, R. D., Haflich, J. L., Reynolds, R. A. (1992). Responsivity of cognitive therapy as a function of treatment format and client personality dimensions. *Journal of Clinical Psychology, 48*, 787-797.
Found individual and group cognitive therapy equally effective in reducing depression in 27 subjects. Sociotropic subjects in group therapy and autonomous subjects in individual therapy showed the greatest improvement, which is consistent with Beck's (1983) model.

1698. Zibbell, R. A. (1992). A short-term, small-group education and counseling program for separated and divorced parents in conflict. *Journal of Divorce and Remarriage, 18*(1-2), 189-203.
Experimented with a small-group educational and skills training approach to divorce education and conflict resolution. Three groups of couples, referred because of child-centered conflict, underwent a four week group education experience. The groups attitudes toward parental cooperation improved significantly; self-reported behavior also improved, but not at a significant level.

1699. Zidar, S. R. (1992). Some effects of group counseling on the self-concept of women who experienced childhood sexual abuse. *Masters Abstracts International, 30*(02), 198. (University Microfilm No. AAC13-46729)

1700. Zimpfer, D. G. (1988). Marriage enrichment programs: A review. *Journal for Specialists in Group Work, 13*, 44-53.

Presents a critical review of 14 studies of group marital enrichment programs, focusing on the use of control groups, follow-up evaluation, types of outcome measures used, personality factors, etc.

1701. Zimpfer, D. G. (1991). Pretraining for group work: A review. *Journal for Specialists in Group Work, 16,* 264-269.

1702. Zimpfer, D. G., Waltman, D. E., Williamson, S. K., & Huhn, R. P. (1985). Professional training standards in group counseling—idealistic or realistic. *Journal for Specialists in Group Work, 10*(3), 134-143.
Surveyed 76 college or university group counseling programs, accumulating data related to level of training, number of courses offered at each level, prior preparation or affiliation of students, average enrollment, population served, content areas, purpose, teaching methods, philosophical bases, and assessment techniques.

1703. Zohn, J., & Carmody, T. (1978). Training opportunities in group treatment methods in APA-approved clinical psychology programs. *Professional Psychology, 9*(1), 50-62.
Results indicate that program emphasis and student interest in training in group treatment methods have increased significantly over the past five years, but that staff and funds for training have not increased at the same rate.

1704. Zuboy, J. W. (1979). An investigation of the effects of focusing ability upon outcome in group psychotherapy. *Dissertation Abstracts International, 39*(11), 6555. (University Microfilm No. AAC79-10322).

1705. Zucker, A. H., & Waksman, S. (1972-1973). Results of group therapy with young drug addicts. *International Journal of Social Psychiatry, 18,* 267-279.
Group therapy of 11 young heroin addicts begun during hospitalization and continued after discharge was beneficial, supporting the idea that transition from hospital to community requires active intervention.

5

The Elderly

1706. Abler, R. M. (1989). Cognitive/Behavioral and Relational/Interpersonal group counseling: Effects of an eight-week approach on affective status among independent-living elderly adults. *Dissertation Abstracts International, 51*(02), 969. (University Microfilm No. AAC90-12431)
Compared the use of cognitive/behavioral and relational/interpersonal group counseling with a group of 37 elderly adults. Initially, the relational/interpersonal group had significantly greater reductions in depression, but these reductions were not maintained at six month follow-up. Neither approach reduced hopelessness.

1707. Abraham, I. L., Neundorfer, M. M., & Currie, L. J. (1992). Effects of group interventions on cognition and depression in nursing home residents. *Nursing Research, 41,* 196-202.

1708. Abraham, I. L., Neundorfer, M. M., & Terris, E. A. (1993). Effects of focused visual imagery on cognition and depression among nursing home residents. *Journal of Mental Imagery, 17,* 61-76.

1709. Abraham, I. L., & Reel, S. J. (1992). Cognitive nursing interventions with long-term care residents: Effects on neurocognitive dimensions. *Archives of Psychiatric Nursing, 6,* 356-365.

1710. Anderson, L. (1985). Intervention against loneliness in a group of elderly women: An impact evaluation. *Social Science and Medicine, 20,* 355-364.
Describes participation of 108 women, who admitted feeling lonely, in an intervention group based on availability of a confidant, social comparison, and personal control. Subjects reported less feelings of loneliness and meaninglessness, more social contacts, higher self-esteem and ability to trust, and lower blood pressure.

1711. Andersson, G., Melin, L., Scott, B., & Lindberg, P. (1995). An evaluation of a behavioural treatment approach to hearing impairment. *Behavioral Research and Therapy, 33,* 283-292.

Twenty-four hearing impaired elderly persons participated in either behavioral group treatment, consisting of video self-modelling, exposure, applied relaxation, and various coping skills, or an untreated control group. Pre- and post-treatment assessments used a structured video interview that measured coping behavior, visual analogue scales and a questionnaire; also conducted a follow-up telephone interview. Judged the treatment program as beneficial.

1712. Atkinson, R. M., Tolson, R. L., & Turner, J. A. (1993). Factors affecting outpatient treatment compliance of older male problem drinkers. *Journal of Studies on Alcohol, 54,* 102-106.
Two hundred and five male problem drinkers, from 55 to 79 years old, attended a weekly outpatient therapy group. Those with later onset of alcohol problems, spousal participation, and drinking and driving offenses were more likely to abstain from drinking and to attend therapy.

1713. Austad, C. S. (1992). The Wisdom Group: A psychotherapeutic model for elderly persons. *Psychological Reports, 70,* 356-358.
Describes group therapy with five male psychiatric inpatients, older than 68 years, designed to foster reminiscing and communication, and to raise self-esteem. The group was effective in that subjects participated and appeared to appreciate the experience.

1714. Baine, S., Saxby, P., & Ehlert, K. (1987). Reality orientation and reminiscence therapy: A controlled cross-over study of elderly confused people. *British Journal of Psychiatry, 151,* 220-231.
In a controlled cross-over design, 15 elderly residents of a large home were involved in reminiscence therapy and reality orientation. Reality orientation followed by reminiscence therapy produced significantly more cognitive and behavioral improvement than either the reverse pattern or the control group.

1715. Baker, B. E. (1990). A study of the effect of a six-week counseling group on well-being and depression scores and rating of self-perceived health of elderly African American participants. *Dissertation Abstracts International, 51*(06), 2125. (University Microfilm No. AAC90-27441)

1716. Baker, R. M. (1994). The effects of a reminiscing group therapy intervention on institutionalized older adults. *Dissertation Abstracts International, 54*(12), 6452. (University Microfilm No. AAC94-10125)

1717. Barnes, G. S. (1989). Cognitive-behavior therapy and desired-control with depressed elderly adults. *Dissertation Abstracts International, 51*(04), 2051. (University Microfilm No. AAC90-23844)
Compared 21 depressed elders participating in either a problem solving training group or a control group which encouraged problem solving but did not teach new skills. Both groups appeared to benefit equally from therapy.

1718. Becker, P. W., & Conn, W. H. (1978). Beer and social therapy treatment with geriatric psychiatric patient groups. *Addictive Diseases: An International Journal, 3,* 429-436.

1719. Berland, D. I., & Poggi, R. (1979). Expressive group psychotherapy with the aging. *International Journal of Group Psychotherapy, 29,* 87-108.
Describes a group therapy process with 72- to 99-year-old residents of a retirement home.

1720. Beutler, L. E., Scogin, F., Kirkish, P., & Schretlen, D. (1987). Group cognitive therapy in the treatment of depression in older adults. *Journal of Consulting and Clinical Psychology, 55,* 550-556.

1721. Birkett, D. P., & Boltuch, B. (1973). Remotivation therapy. *Journal of the American Geriatrics Society, 21,* 368-371.
Compared the use of remotivation therapy with conventional group therapy in a group of 39 ambulant geriatric inpatients. No statistically significant advantage was found for remotivation therapy.

1722. Boehnlein, J. K., & Sparr, L. F. (1993). Group therapy with WWII ex-POWs: Long-term post-traumatic adjustment in a geriatric population. *American Journal of Psychotherapy, 47,* 273-282.

1723. Bogovich, K. (1984). Development, implementation, and evaluation of an activities of daily living training program for psychiatric elderly inpatients. *Dissertation Abstracts International, 45*(11), 3429.
Psychogeriatric inpatients participating in Activities of Daily Living Training group therapy were compared to those participating in control and placebo groups. Found a significant difference on four of five instruments designed to measure cognition, behavior, locus of control, life satisfaction, and personal and social competence.

1724. Boone, F. M. (1987). Teaching the older adult: An adaptive process using psychodrama. *Dissertation Abstracts International, 47*(08), 2846. (University Microfilm No. AAC86-20105)

1725. Brand, E., & Clingempeel, W. G. (1992). Group behavioral therapy with depressed geriatric inpatients: An assessment of incremental efficacy. *Behavior Therapy, 23,* 475-482.
Compared the use of standard hospital treatment with behavioral group therapy with a group of depressed geriatric inpatients. Although both groups improved, at post-test, the behavioral group therapy participants exhibited normal depression scores.

1726. Cetingok, M., & Hirayama, H. (1983). Evaluating the effects of group work with the elderly: An experiment using a single-subject design. *Small Group Behavior, 14,* 327-335.
Found no success with this group approach, which was designed to improve the mental health status and the level of knowledge of illness and health care for 15 elderly patients.

1727. Christopher, F. (1987). The effects of group psychotherapy on mental status, social adaptation, and depression in elderly persons in long-term care with age-onset organic brain syndrome. *Dissertation Abstracts International, 47*(12), 4289. (University Microfilm No. AAC87-06305)

1728. Cooper, F. W. (1983). The effects of two group approaches on self-esteem among the elderly. *Journal of Reality Therapy, 3,* 32.

1729. Crutchfield, H. C. (1994). The effects of a movement therapy program on the self-efficacy and the morale of institutionalized elderly. *Dissertation Abstracts International, 54*(10), 5092. (University Microfilm No. AAC94-07729)
A formal group movement therapy program did not significantly affect the self-efficacy and morale of its 100 institutionalized elderly participants.

1730. deVries, B., & Petty, B. J. (1992). Peer-counseling training: Analysis of personal growth for older adults. *Educational Gerontology, 18,* 381-393.
Twenty-one 56 to 78 year old participants in a peer counseling training program showed significant improvement in life satisfaction after 12 months.

1731. Dhooper, S. S., Green, S. M., Huff, M. B., & Austin-Murphy, J. (1993). Efficacy of a group approach to reducing depression in nursing home elderly residents. *Journal of Gerontological Social Work, 20,* 87-100.
Reports on an eclectic group approach to reducing depression with 16 elderly depressed nursing home residents, from 64 to 94 years of age. On post-test, mean scores on the Self-Rating Depression Scale significantly decreased.

1732. Ernst, P. (1977). Treatment of the aged mentally ill: Further unmasking of the effects of a diagnosis of chronic brain syndrome. *Journal of the American Geriatrics Society, 25,* 466-469.

1733. Ernst, P. (1978). Sensory stimulation of elderly patients: Preliminary report on the treatment of patients with chronic brain syndrome in an old-age home. *Israel Annals of Psychiatry and Related Disciplines, 16,* 315-326.
Examined the utility of group psychotherapy and sensory stimulation in reducing social and emotional isolation in six elderly patients diagnosed with chronic brain syndrome. Symptoms that served as the basis for the original diagnosis were eliminated. Discusses the relationship of isolation and the development of psychiatric symptoms in the elderly.

1734. Evans, R. L., & Jaureguy, B. M. (1981). Group therapy by phone: A cognitive behavioral program for visually impaired elderly. *Social Work in Health Care, 7,* 79-90.
Twelve blind, isolated elderly individuals participated in group tele-conference discussions; those subjects who were at risk for affective disorder were quickly identified and provided with information and socialization. Results indicated significant changes in behavior and task-centered goal attainment.

1735. Evans, R. L., Smith, K. M., Werkhoven, W. S., Fox, H. R., & Pritzl, D. O. (1986). Cognitive telephone group therapy with physically disabled elderly persons. *Gerontologist, 26,* 8-11.

1736. Evans, R. L., Werkhoven, W., & Fox, H. R. (1982). Treatment of social isolation and loneliness in a sample of visually impaired elderly persons. *Psychological Reports, 51,* 103-108.

1737. Fielden, M. A. (1990). Reminiscence as a therapeutic intervention with sheltered housing residents: A comparative study. *British Journal of Social Work, 20,* 21-44.
According to pre- and post-nine week data (General Health Questionnaire, the Philadelphia Geriatric Center Morale Scale, sociometric ratings, and behavioral ratings), group therapy intervention improved psychological well-being, life satisfaction, and socialization patterns.

1738. Frey, D. E., Kelbley, T. J., Durham, L., & James, J. S. (1992). Enhancing the self-esteem of selected male nursing home residents. *Gerontologist, 32,* 552-557.

1739. Gallagher, D. E. (1979). Comparative effectiveness of group psychotherapies for reduction of depression in elderly outpatients. *Dissertation Abstracts International, 39*(11), 5550.

1740. Goldwasser, A. N., Auerback, S. M., & Harkins, S. W. (1987). Cognitive, affective, and behavioral effects of reminiscence group therapy on demented elderly. *International Journal of Aging and Human Development, 25,* 209-222.
Compared reminiscence group therapy with supportive group therapy and a no-treatment control group for 27 elderly nursing home residents with dementia, using the Mini-Mental State Examination, the Beck Depression Inventory, and an index of daily living activities. Reminiscence therapy was superior to supportive therapy and to the control group, but no group was superior to the others on cognitive or behavioral functioning.

1741. Grossman-Morris, C. F. (1987). Depression in young and old adults: The relative efficacy of cognitive versus behavioral group therapy interventions. *Dissertation Abstracts International, 47*(09), 3367. (University Microfilm No. AAC86-29069)
Compared the effectiveness of cognitive, behavioral, and socialization group therapy with younger (18- to 45-year-olds) and older (60 plus years) groups of depressed psychiatric inpatients. Some differences were found, but results were inconclusive.

1742. Hendrix, F. G. (1982). The effect of structured group counseling on the anxiety level of primary caretakers of geriatric patients. *Dissertation Abstracts International, 42*(10), 4300A.

1743. Hern, B. G., & Weis, D. M. (1991). A group counseling experience with the very old. Special Issue: Group work with the aging and their caregivers. *Journal for Specialists in Group Work, 16,* 143-151.
Used remotivation group therapy and structured reminiscence with six female nursing home residents, aged 85 to 99 years, who avoided social interactions. Residents experienced reduced feelings of alienation and isolation, and became more talkative.

1744. Jasin, G. R. (1986). The effect of cognitive-behavioral therapy, therapist competency, and group process on depression among the elderly. *Dissertation Abstracts International, 47*(09), 3957. (University Microfilm No. AAC96-23829)

1745. Jessum, K. L. (1978). The effects of group counseling on geriatric patients institutionalized in long-term care facilities. *Dissertation Abstracts International, 39*(02), 677.

1746. Johnson, W. Y., & Wilborn, B. (1991). Group counseling as an intervention in anger expression and depression in older adults. *Journal for Specialists in Group Work, 16,* 133-142.
Found no improvement in either awareness or expression of anger in 17 women, aged 65 to 95 years, who participated in group counseling sessions focusing on anger awareness.

1747. Kahan, J., Kemp, B., Staples, F. R., & Brummel-Smith, K. (1985). Decreasing the burden in families caring for a relative with a dementing illness: A controlled study. *Journal of the American Geriatric Society, 33*(10), 664-670.
Examined a group support program specifically designed for relatives of patients with dementing illnesses. Twenty-two subjects participated in an eight session program using educational/support activities and a cognitive-behavioral approach, while 18 control subjects received no treatment. Treatment subjects showed significantly greater improvement on knowledge of dementia than controls, showed a reduction in depression levels, and showed a significant decrease in total family burden, while control subjects showed a significant increase.

1748. Katz, M. M. (1976). Behavioral change in the chronicity pattern of dementia in the institutional geriatric resident. *Journal of the American Geriatrics Society, 24,* 522-528.
Used a combination of modified reality orientation, remotivation, activity and milieu group therapies with 108 residents of an extended care facility who had organic brain syndrome or senile dementia, with a mean age of 84 years. Sixty-four percent of the residents improved or remained the same and eighteen percent deteriorated.

1749. Kemp, B. J., Corgiat, M., & Gill, C. (1991-1992). Effects of brief cognitive-behavioral group psychotherapy on older persons with and without disabling illness. *Behavior, Health and Aging, 2,* 21-28.

1750. Kiley, R. H. (1977). A study of group psychotherapy using resocialization counseling with socially withdrawn institutionalized geriatric patients. *Dissertation Abstracts International, 37*(09), 5703. (University Microfilm No. AAC77-05953)

1751. Kuharek, J. M. (1991). Behavioral group therapy on depressed inpatient elderly: A comparative study. *Dissertation Abstracts International, 52*(01), 265. (University Microfilm No. AAC91-15886)

1752. Ladish, C. (1993). Group treatment for depressed elderly: A comparison of cognitive-behavioral and supportive approaches. *Dissertation Abstracts International, 54*(12), 6464. (University Microfilm No. AAC94-14786)
Twenty-two moderately to severely depressed elderly outpatients participated in a cognitive-behavioral treatment group or a support group. At completion of treatment, both groups showed marked improvement.

1753. Leung, S. N., & Orrell, M. W. (1993). A brief cognitive behavioral therapy group for the elderly: Who benefits? *International Journal of Geriatric Psychiatry, 8,* 593-598.

1754. Lieberman, M. A., & Bliwise, N. G. (1985). Comparisons among peer and professionally directed groups for the elderly: Implications for the development of self-help groups. *International Journal of Group Psychotherapy, 35,* 155-175. In a study of 108 elderly subjects, those in professionally led groups improved more than subjects in either the peer led or control group conditions.

1755. Lund, D. A., Dimond, M. F., & Juretich, M. (1985). Bereavement support groups for the elderly: Characteristics of potential participants. *Death Studies, 9,* 309-321.

1756. McCrone, S. H. (1991). Resocialization group treatment with the confused institutionalized elderly. *Western Journal of Nursing Research, 13,* 30-45.

1757. McLeod, J., & Ryan, A. (1993). Therapeutic factors experienced by members of an out-patient therapy group for older women. *British Journal of Guidance and Counselling, 21,* 64-72.
Examined the group experiences of eight women, mean age 55 years, to identify therapeutic factors. The women identified existential awareness as the most important mechanism, but they varied on which group processes were most therapeutic.

1758. Miller, P. M., Hersen, M., Eisler, R. M., & Hemphill, D. P. (1973). Electrical aversion therapy with alcoholics: An analogue study. *Behavior Research and Therapy, 11*(4), 491-497.
Assigned 30 male chronic alcoholic inpatients matched on age, education, and length of problem drinking to one of three treatment conditions: electrical aversion conditioning (high shock paired with alcohol sips); control conditioning (very low shock paired with alcohol sips); and, confrontational group psychotherapy. Found no statistically significant differences among the groups in either reduced alcohol consumption or attitudes toward alcohol. Data trends support the idea that effects of electrical aversion may be more related to factors such as therapeutic instructions, expectancy, specificity of the procedure, or experimental demand characteristics than to conditioning factors.

1759. Morton, I., & Bleathman, C. (1991). The effectiveness of validation therapy in dementia: A pilot study. *International Journal of Geriatric Psychiatry, 6,* 327-330.
Describes the usefulness of group validation therapy for five 69- to 78-year-old subjects with short-term memory loss. After therapy, subjects were able to maintain discussions for longer periods than prior to therapy.

1760. Moss, E. P. (1976). A study of the relationship between group counseling, social activities, and aspects of life adjustment of older, sheltered workshop clients. *Dissertation Abstracts International, 37*(02), 979. (University Microfilm No. AAC76-19038)

1761. Myers, J. E., Poidevant, J. M., & Dean, L. A. (1991). Groups for older persons and their caregivers: A review of the literature. *Journal for Specialists in Group Work, 16,* 197-205.

1762. Nashef, A. A. (1981). The effects of group therapy on the affective states, social distance, interpersonal locus of control, life satisfaction, and ward behavior among the institutionalized aged. *Dissertation Abstracts International, 42*(01), 384.

1763. Newton, N. A., & Lazarus, L. W. (1992). Behavioral and psychotherapeutic interventions. In J. E. Birren, R. B. Sloane, G. D. Cohen, N. R. Hooyman, B. D. Lebowitz, M. Wykie, & D. E. Deutchman (Eds.), *Handbook of mental health and aging* (2nd ed.). San Diego: Academic Press.
Summarizes research in such substantive areas as reality orientation, expressive group therapy, socialization groups, reminiscence or life review therapy, and group therapy.

1764. Orten, J. D., Allen, M., & Cook, J. (1989). Reminiscence groups with confused nursing center residents: An experimental study. *Social Work in Health Care, 14,* 73-86.
Tested effectiveness of reminiscence groups in improving social behavior with the elderly. Three groups of residents, aged 58 to 101 years, met for 16 sessions, with inconclusive results.

1765. Parsons, W. A. (1984). Reminiscence group therapy with older persons: A field experiment. *Dissertation Abstracts International, 45*(04), 1040. (University Microfilm No. AAC84-15147)

1766. Pearce, S. S. (1979). The effect of structured group counseling on levels of depression among retired women in institutional and non-institutional settings. *Dissertation Abstracts International, 39*(07), 4064. (University Microfilm No. AAC79-00278)

1767. Plotkin, D. A., & Wells, K. B. (1993). Partial hospitalization (day treatment) for psychiatrically ill elderly patients. *American Journal of Psychiatry, 150,* 266-271.
Examined the effects of group therapy in a day treatment facility for 100 patients aged 56 to 87 years. Within about three months, 57% of the subjects had improved. Improvement was highest for subjects diagnosed with mood disorders, those possessing better initial functioning and social support, and those able to avoid stressful events.

1768. Powell, R. R. (1974). Psychological effects of exercise therapy upon institutionalized geriatric mental patients. *Journal of Gerontology, 29,* 157-161.
Evaluated the effectiveness of exercise versus social therapy on cognitive and behavioral characteristics of 30 elderly mental patients. Compared to the social therapy and the control conditions, the exercise therapy group improved significantly on two of three cognitive tests. There were no significant differences in behavioral characteristics.

1769. Pugel, L. J. (1994). Interpretation and adaptation of five treatment modalities (including hypnotic techniques and psychotherapy approaches) in the treatment of long-term care residents. *Dissertation Abstracts International, 54*(11), 5601. (University Microfilm No. AAC94-10241)

1770. Richman, J. (1979). A couples therapy group on a geriatric service. *Journal of Geriatric Psychiatry, 12,* 203-213.

1771. Rowland, K. F., & Haynes, S. N. (1978). A sexual enhancement program for elderly couples. *Journal of Sex and Marital Therapy, 4,* 91-113.
After participating in a group sexual enhancement program, 10 married couples aged 51 to 71 years, reported significant increases in sexual satisfaction, frequency of certain sexual activities, and positive attitudes about life and marital satisfaction.

1772. Schor, M. M. (1988). Therapeutic effects of group counseling with visually-impaired elderly adults. *Dissertation Abstracts International, 49*(01), 41. (University Microfilm No. AAC88-04339)

1773. Sedutto, M. H. (1991). Geriatric case management targeting the informal caregiver. *Dissertation Abstracts International, 52*(03), 1381. (University Microfilm No. AAC91-24777)
Examined the utility of providing support services, including individual and group counseling, to caregivers of elderly persons who were at high risk for nursing home placement. Results were inconclusive due to methodological weaknesses.

1774. Sheikh, A. J., Mason, D., & Taylor, A. (1993). An experience of an expressive group with the elderly. *British Journal of Psychotherapy, 10,* 77-82.
This impressionistic study favorably evaluated expressive group therapy, as applied during 15 sessions with seven elderly day hospital patients, aged 61 to 80 years.

1775. Singer, V. I., Tracz, S. M., & Dworkin, S. H. (1991). Reminiscence group therapy: A treatment modality for older adults. Special Issue: Group work with the aging and their caregivers. *Journal for Specialists in Group Work, 16,* 167-171.

1776. Steffes, E. J. (1991). Improving quality of life for residents in nursing homes. *Dissertation Abstracts International, 51*(10), 5077. (University Microfilm No. AAC90-35068)
Investigated the use of three techniques designed to improve the mood of nursing home residents. Subjects who received child visitations reported positive feelings, those who received group counseling reported mixed feelings, and those who received peer visitation reported negative feelings. However, two additional measures did not yield the same results. Discusses the validity of using the Life Satisfaction Index with nursing homes residents.

1777. Steuer, J. L. (1984). Cognitive-behavioral and psychodynamic group psychotherapy in treatment of geriatric depression. *Journal of Consulting and Clinical Psychology, 52,* 180-189.

1778. Stones, M. J., Ivany, G., & Kozma, A. (1994). Anticipating attendance in reminiscence therapy with measures of mood and happiness. *Social Indicators Research, 32,* 251-262.
Measures of mood and psychological well-being successfully predicted attendance in a group of 19 independent living volunteer residents, with a mean age of 74.

1779. Turbow, S. R. (1975). Geriatric group day care and its effect on independent living: A thirty-six month assessment. *Gerontologist, 15,* 508-510.

1780. Tutaj, G. A. (1975). The effectiveness of group counseling in alleviating depression among the aged. *Dissertation Abstracts International, 36*(05), 2653. (University Microfilm No. AAC75-23417)

1781. Usdan, T. D. F. (1981). Effects of a counseling skill training program for older adults on selected variables. *Dissertation Abstracts International, 41*(10), 4296. (University Microfilm No. AAC81-07248)

1782. Vickers, R. (1976). The therapeutic milieu and the older depressed patient. *Journal of Gerontology, 31,* 314-317.

1783. Viney, L. L., Benjamin, Y. N., & Preston, C. A. (1989). An evaluation of personal construct therapy for the elderly. *British Journal of Medical Psychology, 62,* 35-41.
Evaluates the effectiveness of short-term personal construct therapy with 30 elderly subjects with a mean age of 74 years by comparing results with two control groups: 46 well-functioning elderly persons and 30 elderly persons matched with therapy patients for age, gender, and type of chronic illness. At immediate post-therapy, the therapy group showed less anxiety and depression than did the well-functioning control group; at 12 week follow-up, the therapy group showed less anxiety, depression, and indirectly expressed anger than the matched group.

1784. Waller, M., & Griffin, M. (1984). Group therapy for depressed elders. *Geriatric Nursing, 5,* 309-311.

1785. Weiner, M. B., & Weinstock, C. S. (1979-1980). Group progress of community elderly as measured by tape recordings, group tempo, and group evaluation. *International Journal of Aging and Human Development, 10,* 177-185.
Compared geriatric patients participating in either group intervention therapy (IT) or nonintervention therapy (nonIT) designed to "resocialize". The nonIT group demonstrated little change, while the IT group maintained a lively tempo and became more active in problem solving approaches.

1786. Weinstein, W. S., & Khanna, P. (1986). *Depression in the elderly: Conceptual issues and psychotherapeutic intervention.* New York: Philosophical Library.
Surveys and critiques studies on group methods to treat depression in the elderly such as: method used within the institution; the advantages of group therapy in offsetting patients' withdrawal tendencies; the need to shift the focus of group treatment in response to the group members' particular needs and problems; the effectiveness of group methods with senile patients; the effectiveness of a non-

directive, passive therapist style with institutionalized elderly; the effectiveness of short- and long-term group therapy for the elderly; comparative studies of different methods for treating depression in the elderly; and, problems and difficulties encountered in working with the elderly.

1787. Weiss, J. C. (1994). A comparison of cognitive group therapy to life review group therapy with older adults. *Dissertation Abstracts International, 54*(11), 3996. (University Microfilms No. AAC94-10232)

1788. Weiss, J. C. (1994). Group therapy with older adults in long-term care settings: Research and clinical cautions and recommendations. *Journal for Specialists in Group Work, 19,* 22-29.
Compared cognitive group therapy against life review therapy, each with two groups of 10 subjects each, and one control group. Scores on the Beck Depression Inventory and the Life Satisfaction in the Elderly Scale administered before, after eight weeks of therapy, and at six week follow-up showed no significant differences between the two types of therapy groups.

1789. Wellman, L. E. (1983). The ability of elderly nursing home residents to benefit from a rational behavioral group counseling program. *Dissertation Abstracts International, 44*(05), 1612. (University Microfilms No. AAC83-21079)
Examined the impact of Rational Behavior Therapy (RBT) on a group of nursing home residents. Found no significant differences between RBT participants and those participating in other types of group therapy.

1790. Williams-Barnard, C. L., & Lindell, A. R. (1992). Therapeutic use of "prizing" and its effect on self-concept of elderly clients in nursing homes and group homes. *Issues in Mental Health Nursing, 13,* 1-17.
Describes the effects of nurses' high and low prizing during group therapy of 73 elderly persons in nursing or group homes. Self-concept improved in 68.4% of the residents exposed to a high level of prizing, but in only 29.4% of those residents exposed to low prizing.

1791. Yalom, I. D. (1977). The impact of a weekend group experience on individual therapy. *Archives of General Psychiatry, 34,* 399-415.
Compared the use of affect-arousing groups and Gestalt therapy groups in a weekend group experience with thirty-three 20- to 63-year-olds. At six week follow-up, both groups showed greater improvement in individual therapy than did the controls. However, at 12 weeks, there were no demonstrable differences.

1792. Zimpfer, D. G. (1987). Groups for the aging: Do they work? *Journal for Specialists in Group Work, 12,* 85-92.

1793. Zimpfer, D. G. (1991). Groups for grief and survivorship after bereavement: A review. *Journal for Specialists in Group Work, 16,* 46-55.
Reviews research on bereavement groups for a variety of loss targets and a variety of modes of death.

Index

All references are to citation entries and not to page numbers.

abortion, 970, 1023

abstinence: alcohol, 620, 732, 896, 968, 1501, 1712; cessation strategies, 1564; cocaine, 1176; marijuana, 1398; narcotic addict, 736, 1428; sobriety, 968. *See also* drug

abuse: abused women, 867, 1427; battered wives, 821, 1616; battered women, 1590; child, 25, 704, 784; incest, 214, 461, 672, 885, 887, 948, 957, 1021, 1513, 1608, 1644; sexual, 70, 81, 90, 164, 289, 346, 629, 630, 722, 784, 945, 999, 1057, 1080, 1283, 1573, 1699; spouse, 924, 933

academic achievement: behavioral group counseling, 317, 380, 555; group counseling/psychotherapy, 55, 316, 442, 486, 491, 512, 520, 595; high risk students 106, 518; individual versus group counseling, 587; low academic achievement, 60, 512; personal growth group counseling, 533; progressive relaxation and biofeedback, 51;

self-acceptance training, 223; systematic desensitization, 486; transactional analysis, 207

activity group counseling, 135, 196, 400, 473, 843, 1337

addict. *See* narcotic addict

Adlerian approach: 9, 20, 83, 100, 113, 122, 265, 296, 315, 432, 1269, 1415, 1487

adopted children, 15

aerobic exercise, 238, 754; anxiety and depression, 1461. *See also* exercise therapy

affect. *See* emotion

African American/Black, 385, 528, 575, 1715; academic achievement, 60, 512, 595; classroom behavior, 352; delinquency, 391, 395, 474; drama and interpersonal problem solving, 328; group education, 212; individual versus group counseling, 587; informational processing group, 319; mental retardation, 624; role play, 179; self-concept, 77, 474, 506, 548, 588, 590, 595, 774; veterans, 668; vocational

1596, 1607, 1618, 1755, 1793. *See also* grief
Berkeley Group, 811
bibliotherapy, 28, 31, 162, 560, 991, 1110, 1421, 1674 versus group therapy, 1054
bicultural, 397, 519; bicultural assertion training, 519; bilingual 397
biofeedback, 51, 336, 525, 1391, 1585. *See also* relaxation
bipolar affective disorder, 783, 1464. *See also* lithium maintenance, manic
bisexual, 577
blindness. *See* impairment
Body Cathexis Scale, 1648. *See also* cathexis
body image, 389, 715, 1033, 1217, 1235, 1319, 1459, 1680
Bonney Scale, 1493
borderline personality disorder, 469, 1153
boundaries: psychological, 1039
brain, 113, 912, 1368, 1727, 1732, 1733, 1748; chronic brain syndrome, 1732, 1733; organic brain syndrome, 1727, 1748
brief therapy: bereaved, 1240; parents of troubled children, 139. *See also* short-term treatment, time-limited treatment
bulimia, 807, 820, 823, 838, 870, 871, 974, 1002, 1022, 1158, 1192, 1250, 1359, 1405, 1440, 1505, 1536, 1653, 1671, 1680, 1691; meta-analysis, 935

caffeine administration, 689
California Personality Inventory, 1109, 1659
California Psychological Inventory (CPI), 513, 835
Cambodian, 1598
cancer, 715, 788, 799, 825, 826, 927, 937, 1017, 1077, 1087, 1389, 1563, 1618, 1639, 1692; breast cancer, 1017, 1217, 1515; chemotherapy, 606, 1017; gynaecological cancer, 715; death anxiety, 161; malignant melanoma,

928; mastectomy, 643, 791, 981, 1217, 1677. *See also* pain
career, 558, 569; counseling, 142, 306, 539, 1364; life-career management skills, 1657; maturity, 409, 507, 1364, 1645. *See also* employment, vocation
caregiver, 153, 1041, 1773
CARE project, 648-650
Carkhuff model, 85
catharsis, 938, 984; cathartic release 1597
cathexis: body, 906; Body Cathexis Scale, 1648; self, 906. *See also* yoga
cerebral palsy. *See* impairment
change: change mechanism, 865, 1432; change-oriented groups, 705
chemical, 1675; chemical dependency treatment program, 1182
Chicana/Chicano, 313, 381, 397
cholesterol. *See* heart disease and fitness
chronic fatigue. *See* fatigue
chronic medical illness, 803
circumplex, 1508
client centered counseling, 95, 234, 329, 352, 479; long term effects of, 468; techniques, 78; versus psychoanalytic treatment. *See also* congruence, humanistic counseling, nondirective approach, positive regard, prizing, Rogerian encounter group
client/patient perception, 675, 1145, 1210, 1225, 1432
closed versus open groups, 298
co-dependency, 899, 1474
cocaine, 1176; crack, 1204. *See also* drug
cognition, 700, 1707, 1708, 1723
cognitive/behavioral treatment: cognitive, 386, 541, 691, 693, 1058, 1067, 1252, 1360, 1393, 1443, 1625, 1651, 1697, 1720; cognitive-behavioral, 98, 99, 125, 248, 272, 656, 878, 974, 1085, 1086, 1192, 1393, 1463, 1471, 1717; individual versus group, 98, 99, 1466; literature review of graded exposure, 110. *See also*

American/Black, 505; assertive training, 1266; children of divorce, 464; interpersonal communication, 518; irritable bowel syndrome, 1666; marital difficulties, 1597; mental retardation, 408; multicultural, 459; obesity, 646; personal development, 505; psychodidactic, 1552; social skills, 494; vocational development, 505; wives of alcoholics, 946
direct approach: direct decision therapy, 397; versus indirect approach, 86, 182, 421; versus vicarious experience, 1489. *See also* nondirective approach
disabled, 711, 1343; attitude, 1231; cognitive behavior treatment, 173; counselors, 1231; experiential training, 1399; learning disabled adolescents, 204, 446, 471; learning disabled children, 8, 24, 62, 103, 115, 121, 126, 168, 173, 188, 377; mental retardation, 24; parents of, 423, 855, 1438; physically disabled college students, 542, 574; psychiatrically disabled adults, 1193; reading 107, 108, 113; relaxation, 8, 121; telephone treatment, 915, 1735. *See also* handicapped, impairment, mental retardation
disaster. *See* stress/management
disclosure. *See* self-disclosure
disulfiram, 640, 828, 881, 896
divorce, 657, 675, 759, 922, 1092, 1191, 1570; biofeedback, 1391; children of divorce/separation, 10, 26, 28, 32, 45, 54, 56, 59, 61, 63, 64, 67, 80, 89, 92, 96, 123, 129, 130, 133, 150, 198, 334, 349, 425, 464; families of divorce, 66, 1698; group versus individual treatment, 922; separation, 425, 1640
dogmatism, 458, 1617; measure of dogmatism, 514
dopamine-b-hydroxylase, 1486
doubling, 1431, 1561
drama: treatment, 260, 328, 346, 901, 1514. *See also* psychodrama, sociodrama

dream: drama 901, group, 1179
dropout: day program, 1011; group treatment, 716, 806, 1157, 1211, 1247, 1255, 1286, 1544; school, 242, 250, 354, 355, 460, 587. *See also* termination
drug: abuse, 325, 579, 1204, 1533; drug abuse prevention, 579; drug-free, 846; siblings of drug-addicted adolescents, 249. *See also* abstinence, aftercare, cocaine, heroin, LSD therapy, marijuana, methadone, narcotic addict, substance abuse
dual diagnosis/disorder, 710, 874, 1061
dynamic group psychotherapy, 858, 1220, 1292
dysfunction. *See* sex
dysphoric: gender, 1248

ego, 895; deficits, 1584; development, 140, 430, 550, 1044; ego-analytic counseling, 59; strength, 239, 532
ejaculation, 1177, 1696; ejaculatory dysfunction 916; premature ejaculation, 1177, 1696
elaboration likelihood model, 911
elective mute children, 27
emotion, 954, 1174, 1213, 1264; affect, 243, 878, 1175, 1249; affect-arousing group, 1687, 1791; affective status, 1706; mood, 334, 826, 827, 909, 1227, 1389, 1422, 1484, 1585, 1767, 1776, 1778; positive affect, 1217, 1272
emotionally disturbed, 11, 225, 246, 260, 297, 347, 429
empathy, 35, 394, 484, 604, 1040, 1228, 1242, 1387, 1415, 1431, 1624; empathic understanding, 1426, 1619
employment, 1360, 1645, 1667; history/status, 819, 923; interview skills, 446; job performance, 699. *See also* career, vocation
empowerment, 420, 1068, 1590
encounter group, 508, 512, 679, 1109, 1273, 1315, 1319, 1452, 1467, 1526, 1627; alcoholics, 1578; encounter versus psychodrama,

self-esteem: adolescents, 204, 223,
226, 230, 256, 309, 318, 334, 337,
359, 395, 414, 419, 425, 461, 470;
adults, 619, 649, 655, 715, 807,
920, 922, 974, 999, 1002, 1032,
1064, 1098, 1235, 1239, 1240,
1266, 1303, 1306, 1318, 1350,
1397, 1416, 1471, 1491, 1606,
1690; children, 5-7, 17, 21, 30, 54,
63, 79, 86, 115, 119, 159, 163,
197; college students, 499, 502,
524, 560, 569; elderly, 1710, 1713,
1728, 1738
self-help, 25; adult children of
alcoholics group, 1220;
agoraphobia group, 1237; AIDS
group, 938; alcoholism group, 986;
bereaved parents group, 1607;
cancer group, 788, 1692; eating
group, 1158; elderly group, 1754;
epilepsy group, 879; group, 1027,
1084, 1224; herpes group, 878;
immigrant group, 1068; panic
disorder group, 1237; parents of
mentally ill group, 1068;
postpartum depression group, 1468;
professional attitude/use of groups,
1575, 1581; skills, 645; widow
group, 1596
self-image, adolescents, 404, 479;
post-mastectomy, 1217. See also
body image, self-perception
self-perception, 574, 843, 1217, 1319,
1547
semantic cohesion analysis, 977
sensitivity group, 1627
sensory stimulation, 1733
separation. See divorce
sequential analysis, 676
sex, 590, 1229, 1619, 1771; bias,
600; education 219, 681;
mastectomy, 1217;
offenders/molesters, 228, 304, 811,
835, 905, 929, 1629, 1657; role,
119, 539, 1075; role conflicts, 582;
role expectancy, 1062; role
stereotyping, 596; same-sex
friendships, 158; sexual
dysfunction, 916, 1230, 1245,
1512; therapy, 651, 1660. See also
abuse, ejaculation, gender, group

leader, hypoactive sexual desire,
marital, orgasm, paraphiliac sexual
disorders, rape, satisfaction
sexual abuse. See abuse
shame, 96, 243, 999
sheltered workshop, 1650, 1760
short-term treatment, 206, 400, 567,
655, 690, 746, 749, 813, 865, 952,
1099, 1280, 1392, 1599; abusive
husbands, 1336; adult children of
alcoholics, 812; alcohol, 611, 638,
880, 1599; anorgasmia, 1221;
behavioral treatment, 380, 1221,
1301; bulimia, 807, 1002, 1505;
cardiac/stroke patients, 745, 1222;
change, 917; children, 58, 140,
148; children of divorce, 32;
cigarette smokers, 1384;
depression, 276; divorce, 675,
1698; dropping out, 1271;
experiential, 557; family, 311;
family of divorce, 66; gambling,
1567; Gestalt, 484; gifted students,
203; growth groups, 1319;
hospitalization, 1408; imipramine,
1301; interactional, 611; loss,
1272, 1357; LSD, 1270; marital,
1503; men who batter, 893, 1427;
occupational, 1630; offenders, 485,
895; parents of handicapped, 76;
perceptions of, 245, 1210, 1630;
personal construct, 1783;
pretraining, 1157; prison
adjustment, 209; psychoanalytic
orientation, 1272; rational emotive
therapy, 529; Rogerian encounter,
484; self-directed encounter, 484;
self-esteem, 230; sexual, 882;
short-term versus long-term
outcome, 1491, 1786; telephone,
1147; visually impaired, 326, 1147.
See also brief therapy, time-limited
treatment
shy, 571
sibling group therapy, 249
Simontons' method, 1077
skills training, 105, 284, 491, 571,
775, 1178, 1198, 1261, 1397,
1665, 1698, 1781; behavioral-social
skills training model, 727;
constructive thinking, 626; coping,

About the Authors

BERNARD LUBIN is a Diplomate in Clinical Psychology, a Fellow of the American Group Psychotherapy Association, a Fellow of the Division of Group Psychology and Group Psychotherapy of the American Psychological Association, and a Fellow of the American Psychological Society and the American Association for the Advancement of Science. He consults and writes on the use of the small group in treatment.

C. DWAYNE WILSON is Associate Professor in the Graduate School of Social Work at the University of Utah. He is a member of the American Society for Training and Development, and the National Training Laboratories Institute, and has served as a consultant to various organizations. He is co-author of a book and has published articles in several professional journals.

SUZANNE PETREN is a doctoral student in Counseling Psychology at the University of Missouri at Kansas City.

ALICIA POLK is a graduate student in the Department of Psychology at the University of Missouri at Kansas City.

ISBN 0-313-28339-7

90000>

EAN

9 780313 283390

HARDCOVER BAR CODE